ANTHOLOGY OF CZECH PROSE

Auto sie pisse kroniki ma

CZECH
PROSE
WITHDRAWN
AN ANTHOLOGY

Translated and Edited
by
WILLIAM E. HARKINS

Ann Arbor

ISBN 0-930042-51-4

Library of Congress Catalog Card Number 83-50054

MICHIGAN SLAVIC TRANSLATIONS 6

Michigan Slavic Publications
Department of Slavic Languages and Literatures
The University of Michigan
Ann Arbor, Michigan

Ladislav Matejka, *Managing Editor*

The translation and editing of this volume were subsidized by a generous grant from the Progam for Translation of the National Endowment for the Humanities, an independent Federal agency. Typesetting and printing costs were met in part by loans from the Czechoslovak Society of Arts and Sciences in America and Dr. Edward Kupka. All of these sources of assistance are gratefully acknowledged.

CONTENTS

LIST OF ILLUSTRATIONS

PREFACE

The present volume, the first of a projected two-volume work, covers and illustrates the development of Czech prose, fiction and non-fiction, from the beginnings in the fourteenth century down to the foundation of the First Czechoslovak Republic in 1918. In certain respects it is a companion work to the volume of *Czech Poetry* published in 1973 in the Michigan Slavic Translation Series by Michigan Slavic Publications. Unlike the earlier volume, however, considerations of size and cost have prevented the editor and publisher from producing a bilingual anthology, desirable as this would have been, and the present volume contains translations only.

Principles of selection in such a work are not simple ones to decide upon. For the older period, excerpts were frequently used and are the rule and not the exception. For the modern period, however, where leading writers of fiction generally produced stories of merit as well as novels, preference has been given to the translation of complete works. Works translated into Czech have been excluded, as have works written on Czech soil in Latin or German. All texts given are original works of Czech literature, with the exception of the excerpt from the *Autobiography* of Emperor Charles IV and the excerpt from the *Chronicle* of Přibík Pulkava z Radenína, both of which were translated from Latin into Czech at a very early date, the second presumably by its author.

Selection of texts for translation in such an anthology are necessarily more or less subjective, and no apologies are offered; at the same time the selection is no doubt a fair target for critics. No doubt there are important and even outstanding Czech prose authors who are not represented here, some of whom had to be excluded because of considerations of length. Still, it is hoped that the present selection does contain examples of the leading trends, styles and themes of Czech prose literature, if not of all the leading authors, and that it will serve to illustrate the main trends in the development of Czech prose over the centuries.

Gratitude is expressed for a translation grant received from the National Endowment for the Humanities, without which the present volume would hardly have been completed, certainly not in its present form and scope.

The Editor

CZECH SOUNDS AND THEIR ENGLISH EQUIVALENTS

Czech vowels (a, e, i, o, u) have approximately the quality of Italian or Spanish vowels (English "ah," "eh," "e ," "o" (as in or), "oo") but shorter in all cases, and without the quality of diphthongization typical of English vowels. Czech *y* is a variant spelling of Czech i (English "ee"). Czech vowels are long under the diacritic sign ´ (á, é, í, ó, ú, ý) but the sound remains essentially the same. Czech ů is also long. Czech *l* and *r* are vocalic when written between consonants, e.g., V*r*ba ("vurbah"). The Czech diphthong *ou* is pronounced like English *owe*, considerably prolonged. Czech ě indicates the palatal character of preceding *d, t, n* (compare the sound of English *d, t, n* in "duty," "tune," "new"). Before other consonants ě denotes the insertion of a consonantal *y* sound before the *e*, e.g., *dě*dina ("dyedeenah"). Czech ď, ť, ň are palatal (compare English *d, t, n* in "duty," "tune," "new"). The first two palatal sounds are often written with a kind of apostrophe: *d', t'*. But before the vowel letter *i* ("ee") palatal *d, t, n* are written without any distinguishing mark. Czech č corresponds to English *ch*, š to *sh*, and ž to the *z* of English "azure." Czech ř is a sound peculiar to Czech; it combines a trilled *r* and a *sh* or *zh* sound. Compare the Czech name Dvořák ("dvorzhák). Czech *r* is trilled, with a vibrating motion of the tip of the tongue behind the upper teeth. The digraph *ch* is pronounced as in German (*Bach*). Czech c corresponds to English *ts* in ca*ts*. Other Czech consonants are generally similar to English. Stress in Czech, which is light, always falls on the first syllable of a word. Stress on a vowel does not lengthen it; contrariwise, long vowels may be unstressed. Czech unstressed short vowels do not change in quality, unlike English (contrast English sof*a* – "sofuh" – and Czech Sov*a* ("sovah").

x

INTRODUCTION

The history of Czech prose as such has never been written. For Czechs the concept of "literature" has meant first and foremost poetry, and there are periods in the development of Czech literature, such as the early fourteenth century or the late eighteenth and early nineteenth centuries, when artistic prose as such scarcely existed, and almost the entire corpus of belles-lettres consisted of poetry. Only perhaps in our own time is it possible for a Czech reader, as an Englishman, Frenchman or American might do, to conceive the category of "literature" as largely restricted to prose writings, or even to prose fiction.

From this one might argue that it is wrong to look at the development of Czech prose independently as such, and that prose, or what in English is known as "fiction" (Czech lacks such a term, though the Czech word *proza* is frequently used in a not dissimilar sense) should not be considered in a vacuum apart from the rest of literature. Snobbish criticism may in fact regard fiction as inferior to poetry, or even to drama. No doubt fiction is compromised by certain associations, such as its origins in the popular tale, or by its suitability for all kinds of sensationalism and lurid subject matter. But poetry frequently lapses into sentimentality, while drama tolerates melodrama, farce and pure spectacle.

If the origins of prose literature in the Renaissance *novella* and the Baroque picaresque tale are suspect, it may be argued nonetheless that the later development of prose, particularly in the late nineteenth and twentieth centuries, has made prose fiction, and not verse, the most expressive and mature form of literary utterance in a modern spirit. This is not only because prose is more flexible than verse and tolerates, perhaps, a greater variety of levels as well as more frequent and more subtle transitions from one level to another. The irony which frequently results from this interplay is in certain respects the most characteristic literary expression of our times, and prose is its customary, if not its essential form. Noteworthy exceptions, such as T. S. Eliot's *The Wasteland*, themselves share certain characteristics of prose and may well be the exceptions that prove the rule. Whatever the reasons, our time has apparently lost its taste for poetry, especially narrative and dramatic poetry.

To a very considerable extent, the development of literature since the late Middle Ages may be viewed as a largely continuous attempt, not to reduce literature to the level of mere reality, but to incorporate reality into literature, to come to grips with it in the forms of imaginative creation, to employ reality as one of the levels of the literary work which interact to create irony. The whole idea of *fiction*, not excluded from verse but more characteristically associated with prose, suggests an enterprise in which artistic imagination and invention are contained in forms given by reality itself as we perceive it. True, twentieth-century fiction, in contrast to that of the nineteenth century, does depart from reality and objectivity both in its preference for irony as well as its seeking for abstraction, its failure, deliberate or no, to capture the reality of individual personality. This direction might well have led to the creation of a new poetry (again Eliot comes to mind), but it hardly has done this. Recent directions in art working against traditionalism (aleatory art, anti-art, mixtures of art and life in such new forms as the "happening") may well restore poetry, as irony gives way to ritual or even, should this be possible, to religious faith.

*   *   *

In the medieval period Czech literature is inconceivable without verse, and prose writing of a literary type appears only towards the end of the fourteenth century—a good three-quarters of a century after the appearance of a rich vernacular poetry. Even such customarily prose genres as chronicles or lives of saints first appear in the vernacular in verse form. And while Latin prose, which had never quite lost its contact with the stylistic models and standards of classical antiquity, could serve literary functions, vernacular prose apparently could not: for the time being it apparently remained too "vulgar," too debased in level.

Quite suddenly, during the last two decades of the fourteenth century, prose writing comes into its own in Czech literature and actually gains a partial ascendancy over verse. For the first time Czech prose competes with Latin prose in popularity:

xii

chronicles and lives of saints now appear in Czech as well as Latin, and there is a considerable body of prose tales (though most of these are translated from other languages). Tomáš ze Štítného and Jan Hus even write theological works in Czech. Finally, what is almost unquestionably the greatest and most original work of the vernacular literature, the novel *Tkadleček* ("The Weaver") is written in Czech some time after 1407. In its rhetorical brilliance *Tkadleček* can well compete with the Latin prose of its day, or with the older Czech verse which culminated with the beautiful *Legend of St. Catherine* of the mid-fourteenth century, or with the contemporary vernacular literatures of Europe. True, the work derives in part from the German dialogue, the *Ackermann aus Böhmen,* but chronologically it follows that work very closely and shows an enormous expansion of rhetorical means and imagery (*Tkadleček* is approximately four times as long as the *Ackermann*).

What brought this sudden development? No doubt in part the fact that Emperor Charles IV had made Prague the capital of the Holy Roman Empire, and the city and the land of Bohemia had become a center for intellectual and cultural trends coming from all parts of Europe. The foundation of the University of Prague in 1348, the oldest university in Central Europe, served to attract educated foreigners to the city. The earlier existence in Bohemia of a Latin literature, as well as the influence of other literatures in the vernacular—French, Provencal and German—also assisted in this development. Finally, the internal evolution of Czech verse itself played a part: the decline of the verse epic after the appearance of the *Legend of St. Catherine* and the appearance of a highly cultivated colloquial, satirical verse, often rooted in the reality of daily life, apparently laid the foundation for a transition from verse to prose. The satires of the celebrated *Hradec Manuscript* had appeared in the 1340's; they were followed in the next several decades by other verse satires, among which *The Groom and the Student,* a verse disputation between two drinkers in a tavern as to which has the better life, is perhaps the single most original, if not the most elegant, work in all Czech literature of the fourteenth century. True, the prose writing that appears toward the end of the century does not include satire as such; this had to await the Hussite Wars and the eloquence of Petr Chelčický. But though dominated by a religious, even polemical view of life, Chelčický's satire is still firmly rooted in reality. And in this preference for reality as a literary foundation we come upon one of the principal hallmarks of Czech literary prose.

With the early fifteenth-century religious leader and reformer, Chelčický's greater predecessor, Jan Hus, we already find a conscious and manifest concern for the development of literature and its prose. Hus wrote several didactic and homiletic works in Czech. He was concerned for the development and purity of the language, and excluded Germanisms from it; he also standardized and revised Czech orthography. His final letters to his adherents represent a high point in all the older literature in the expression of intimate feeling. But unfortunately, as with the philosopher Comenius' later prose writings in Czech, these letters of Hus did not lead to any permanent development: the uncertainties of a time of harsh religious, social and political strife militated against a normal literary evolution. Except for Hus's follower Chelčický, the literature of the Hussite Time tended to be restricted to new chronicle compilations and religious polemics. The literary genre *par excellence* of the period was actually the religious hymn, sometimes military in character, which accompanied the heroic military campaigns of the Hussite soldiers, who repelled the Crusaders sent to invade their land and suppress their newly reformed religious faith.

Peace was finally achieved and confirmed by the Compacts of Basel, which the Czechs accepted in 1436. The new current of Humanism, effectively kept out by the Hussite Wars, now entered the land. Among Czech Catholics Humanism was most influential in the cultivation of learning and a higher poetry and scholarly prose. Utraquist (Hussite) and later Protestant Humanism was largely concerned for the needs of the reformed Church and of a society in which it would play the dominant role, and cultivated such revived classical disciplines as law, politics, rhetoric, grammar and poetics. All faiths joined in placing an emphasis on education, learning and the classical disciplines.

In such an atmosphere prose, and especially prose fiction, was relegated to a low place. At first sight the prose works of the late fifteenth and early sixteenth centuries may strike us as extensions of the Middle Ages. Essentially they represent a kind of "sunken" higher culture of the Middle Ages which was now popularized and, as such, evaded the prescriptive rules and formulas of the higher humanist literature. Thus, the Czech prose *exempla* (sermon illustrations) of the fifteenth century continued the Latin genre of the fourteenth, while the *Visions of Jiřík*, a picturesque account of a visit to Purgatory, belonged to an older Latin medieval genre, one which influenced the poet Dante. The Czech example of this genre, unlike the work of the great Italian writer, remains on a popular level and in prose form. Finally, *The Tales of Brother Paleček* are purely popular in their cult of common-sense simplicity and folk wisdom. This preference for popular currents, though contradicted to an extent by the higher humanist literature, is a basic trend of Czech tradition, one which, together with realism, constitutes a second of the fundamental hallmarks of Czech prose which was to re-emerge in the modern era. Brother Paleček is a worthy forerunner of Hašek's Good Soldier Švejk, as a man of the people whose apparent idiocy is rooted in common sense.

The borderline of humanist and Baroque periods, coming at the end of the sixteenth and the beginning of the seventeenth century, brought a uniquely great work by a uniquely great Czech writer, Comenius' *Labyrinth of the World and Paradise of the Heart.* Comenius, or, in Czech, Komenský, was also a major poet in the vernacular, though his educational writings, intended for an all-European public, were written in Latin. But he was a great stylist as well as a writer of considerable imagination and inventive power. Around Komenský, however, there were hardly even any second-rate writers one can speak of. The loss of religious independence at the Battle of White Hill in 1620 and the subsequent loss of national independence may conveniently be blamed for this, but there is much reason to suppose that Czech Humanism and Czech reform spirit had already undergone a considerable decline in the sixteenth century, and that Komenský's work is little more than a notable exception.

The Baroque period, which introduced the novel and drama to Spain, France and England, failed to accomplish the same result in Central Europe. The drama was still restricted to the domains of folk art or the didactic school play. Good literary prose was almost confined to the minor genre of the travel diary or sketch, inherited from the older humanist period, and to Baroque religious writings, especially sermons, in which the priests and monks of the Counter-Reformation described Hell and the Last Judgment with an eloquent rhetoric never before sounded in Czech preaching.

No doubt this Baroque literature, with its beautiful devotional poetry, was underrated by the Czech nineteenth-century nationalists, who—even those who were Catholic—often regarded the older literature and culture through Protestant eyes. Still, the process of Austrianization of Bohemian political institutions and Germanization of the society living in the Czech towns tended to work against the further development of national literature and culture. If the last three-quarters of the seventeenth century is not quite the "dark time" the nineteenth-century nationalists supposed, then the succeeding period was: the first half of the eighteenth century is a real time of national darkness, when it is hard to find new books published—or even manuscripts written—in the Czech tongue.

About three-quarters of the way through the eighteenth century, however, the process of decline began slowly to reverse itself, gaining a momentum for the Czech nationalist cause which began in the 1770's and continued its steady growth until the first culmination of the nationalist movement in the revolutionary uprisings of 1848. It is not possible here to consider in any detail the reasons for this reversal, but a few things can be stated briefly. The process of gradual Germanization of Czech society, already well advanced in the Czech towns, began to reverse, and first members of the intelligentsia, and later members of the broader middle classes, the aristocracy and the peasantry began to take pride in being Czech. This was a part of a growing wave of nationalism which took hold of Central, and later of Eastern Europe. This wave affected Germany as well, but the Czech product, though influenced by the parallel German movement, was not to be German but Czech in its nationalist outlook. The work of the scholars of the Enlightenment, including historians who laid bare the roots of national tradition, showed Czech readers that their land had once been Czech, independent of both Germany and Austria, and that it had possessed a great national culture and tradition. The Napoleonic Wars and the spread of nationalist sentiment which accompanied them may have suggested to the Czech people that their interests did not necessarily coincide with those of the Germans or Austrians. Finally, economic distinctions came to reinforce nationalist ones: if the dominant economic classes were largely made up either of Germans or Germanized Czechs, this could serve as an inducement for further Germanization (as it had during the eighteenth century), but it could also have a backlash effect, producing resentment and hatred of the German "exploiters," and this seems to have been its dominant effect during the nineteenth century, when the industrial revolution accelerated economic growth.

The new literature of the Enlightenment period and the so-called "Czech Revival" or "Rebirth" *(obrození)* was to replicate the development of the fourteenth century in that, again, verse appeared first and artistic prose lagged behind. This phenomenon can frequently be observed in newly born or reborn literatures, perhaps because verse, which is opposed more sharply to everyday speech, has a much more pronounced and therefore more perceptible artistic effect. Artistic prose must wait till later, since it occupies a mediate position between poetry and colloquial speech. Another reason for the lag in the late eighteenth and early nineteenth centuries was the fact that the neo-classical predilection of the Enlightenment age was for poetry, which had a tie (or seemed to have one) with the revered classics of antiquity, rather than prose fiction, which in the eighteenth century still had many of its roots in popular culture. Romanticism, which succeeded Neo-Classicism in Bohemia as elsewhere, did not greatly change matters: the Romantic preference for strong passions, absolute values, and a natural world filled with sharp contrasts possessing a symbolic purport, found a more striking expression in verse than in prose. Only when Romanticism began its gradual evolution into Realism, a development that commenced in Bohemia around the middle of the nineteenth century, did literary prose and the genres of the novel and tale come into their own. It was the wish—or need—to deal with reality that seemed to motivate this switch, one that was strikingly parallel with a turn from an escapist Romanticism to a pragmatic attitude toward national traditions and national culture.

Already under Romanticism, isolated attempts had been made to create a new prose. The most successful of these are the stories of Karel Hynek Mácha (1810-1836) and the fairy tales of Karel Jaromír Erben (1811-1870). In one tale, "Marinka," Mácha even attempts to deal with the sordidness of the contemporary urban setting, but most of his prose efforts were violently romantic and even escapist in the sense that they shunned the life and society around him. The prose of both Mácha and Erben was a "poet's prose," rich in rhythmic and euphonic effects and in images, though Mácha's love for ornate epithets and Gothic images was far removed from the pithiness and expressiveness of Erben's folk tales. Neither man's style could serve as a basis for further development of prose, and Erben's tales were not even published until much later. Yet, curiously, it was Erben's example (conveyed, presumably, in his folktale poetry) in turning to native folklore and peasant speech that was to be more influential in the style of the Czech village tale and village novel—the predominant genres of Czech fiction, in both verse and prose—throughout the second half of the nineteenth century. These had their roots and models in popular life and popular speech, observed directly, though initially the model of George Sand's peasant tales provided a considerable stimulus.

Through the medium of ethnography and folklore, popular culture was again to pour into the stream of Czech literature of the mid-nineteenth century. The older prose literature of the Middle Ages and the Renaissance was too little known and too far away to provide a base for the new developing literature; ethnography and folklore, along with observation of country life, served as the new base, and the village tale very rapidly achieved a high point in its expression in the fiction of Božena Němcová (1820-1862), the first Czech writer to create a prose fiction capable of further development in a distinct literary tradition. The genres of the village novel and village tale which Němcová created were destined to dominate Czech literature through the remainder of the nineteenth century and, though it is difficult to imagine that any Czech writer would consciously imitate or follow her today, still it cannot be said that her influence—in style, subject matter, or ethnographic point of view—is now entirely dead; it is a part of the spiritual as well as the stylistic legacy of every writer who has read her in childhood.

Czech literature captured the reality of city life much more slowly; this in spite of the fact that the cities, and especially Prague, were new centers for a rising bourgeoisie which spoke Czech and considered itself Czech. Few writers (Karel Hynek Mácha and Karolina Světlá were exceptions) were born in Prague, not to speak of the few other cities of any size. Coming from the country, writers preferred to depict country life (this is true even of the city-born Světlá, a follower of Němcová). Not till the 1870's did Jan Neruda (1834-1891), himself born in Prague, create prose tales which embodied at least generous slices of Prague urban life, though his stories relate most closely to the sleepy, conservative Prague of his boyhood and convey little sense of a bustling, rapidly growing modern commercial city.

Both Němcová and Neruda are transitional figures, late Romanticists who already use certain devices of literary Realism. Neruda, the younger writer by a whole generation, goes farther along the road leading to Realism. But paradoxically, it was Němcová and the village tale which had the greater success under the Czech Realists. Even the naturalist wing of Realism preferred the country setting, as in the work of such writers as Josef Šlejhar (1864-1914) and Josef Holeček (1853-1929).

While Czech rural realism seems to have developed naturally out of the social milieu itself, with its principal stimulus in real life and the forms of country life, the more self-conscious current of realism which dominated literature at the end of the nineteenth century was much weaker. The statesman and philosopher T. G. Masaryk (1850-1937) and his followers fostered a critical realism which stimulated an effective social and political, as well as literary criticism. Masaryk himself turned most of his critical attention to the writers of other countries, particularly Russia, England and America. But in poetry as well as prose it was the neo-romantics and later the Symbolists, rather, who dominated the literary scene at the end of the nineteenth century, and not the realists. Such writers as Jaroslav Vrchlický (1853-1912) and Julius Zeyer (1841-1901) were responsible for introducing to Czech literature the most diverse and exotic literary influences, drawn from all over the world. Thus they greatly broadened and cosmopolitanized the scope of Czech literature, scarcely prepared to absorb such a variety of influences so quickly. Vrchlický raised the technical level of Czech verse to a European level and reshaped it as a superb euphonic vehicle which maintained its excellence and richness for well over half a century until Communist socialist realism virtually destroyed it. Vrchlický and Zeyer did not eschew national subjects, but they both avoided that characteristic Czech directness of manner and folklike ingenuousness that had marked the work of such masters of rural realism as Němcová and Světlá.

Again prose lagged behind; even the poetry of such realists as J. S. Machar (1864-1942) and Petr Bezruč (1867-1958) probably surpassed the realists' fiction, in spite of the talent of such prose writers as Antal Stašek (1843-1931), Holeček, Teréza Nováková (1853-1912), Šlejhar, Karel Klostermann (1848-1923), or Ignát Hermann (1854-1935). And among the neo-romantics, Vrchlický's prose is only a minor aspect of his work; with Zeyer prose is more important, to be sure, but Zeyer failed, in spite of immense aspirations, to create an oeuvre that would endure. And popular as Alois Jirásek (1851-1930) has been with his fellow-countrymen for his fictional recreations of early Czech history, this Czech disciple of Sir Walter Scott largely failed to capture any international audience.

Symbolist prose (though again marginal in comparison with poetry) does reach a world level in its sophistication and psychological subtlety, as well as its originality of imagery and lexicon. True, the greatest Czech symbolist, Otakar Březina (1968-1929), wrote little prose except for some quite personal and mystical essays. Both others, including Antonín Sova (1864-1928), Viktor Dyk (1877-1931) and Fráňa Šrámek (1877-1952), were more energetic in cultivating the forms of prose fiction, both stories and novels, the cosmopolitan character of which far outweighed the creations of the native realists.

Only with the 1910's and 1920's did the "Czech" national and popular strain, with its folk humor, native realism, and down-to-earth character and (its most sophisticated quality) its all-pervasive irony, come again into its own. Jaroslav Hašek's (1883-1923) great comic masterpiece, *The Good Soldier Švejk,* achieved the status of a world classic with its absurd humor (not infrequently of the "black" variety) and its chronicle of human vanities and follies. Far inferior, unfortunately, were Hašek's many stories, though a very small number of the best share the grotesque absurdity of his *Švejk.* Another writer of the period who succeeded in gaining a world audience was Karel Čapek (1890-1938). Though more subtle and restrained than Hašek, Čapek shares with him his love of irony, his hatred of "Titanism" (an element of Masaryk's philosophical criticism), and his democratic cult of the "little man." Almost alone in Czech prose Čapek was able to create a synthesis and thus heal the schism which had rent Czech literature since the time of Vrchlický, the split between the national realists and the cosmopolitan neo-romantics and symbolists.

Almost as great as his achievements with fiction was Čapek's work in the genre of the feuilleton introduced to Czech literature by Neruda, and he made journalistic prose a completely personal yet flexible form of literary expression. Indeed, it is the feuilletons of Neruda and especially of Čapek which provide the only strong and distinct form of non-fictional prose in modern Czech literature and the closest Czech analogue to the great English essay tradition. The so-called Czech essay, usually a work of literary criticism, appeared only towards the end of the nineteenth century and hardly acquired any distinct national form that was characteristic. The feuilleton, on the other hand, was much less formal and much more intimate, and was eminently suitable as a form for the expression of the democratic ideas of Neruda and Čapek; recently it has been revived as a leading form of expression for protest against the rigidity of the post-1968 Communist regime and its harsh cultural policies.

With the achievement of national independence in 1918, Czech writers apparently acquired that quality of self-assuredness that may well be essential for the production of a great national literature. But this is a new era with new conditions and new problems, on the eve of which the present volume must necessarily end.

AUTOBIOGRAPHY

by

Charles IV

(from Chapter Eight)

Emperor Charles IV, King of Bohemia from 1346 until his death in 1378, left a memoir dealing with his youth and presenting in summary form the chief events he experienced, including his prolonged campaigns in Italy and his eventual return to Bohemia in 1333.

Charles, who was elected King of the Germans in 1347 and Holy Roman Emperor in 1355, made Prague the capital of the Empire and greatly enriched the city with new construction. In 1348 he founded the University which has subsequently borne his name, as such the oldest university in Central Europe. The Czechs have frequently looked back to his reign as a "golden age" of Czech prosperity and cultural flowering, and in many respects the period is the zenith in the development of Old Czech literature.

Charles wrote exclusively in Latin, but his autobiography, the Vita Caroli, *was translated into Czech at an early time. The excerpts given here are from Chapter Eight, and characterize Charles's activities on his first return to Bohemia, when he governed the kingdom in place of his father, King John; the period described is 1333-1335. John's continual absence from Bohemia on various campaigns had resulted in the devastation of his Czech lands, a situation which Charles promptly set to rectifying.*

The text as translated here is taken from the Výbor z české literatury od počátků po dobu Husovu, *published by the* Československá Akademie věd, Prague, 1957.

And from there[1] we came on to the Czech land, where we had not been for eleven years, and we learned that our mother, whose name was Elizabeth, had died some years before our return. And while she was still alive, our younger sister Guta had been sent to France and married to Jean, first-born son of Phillipe, King of France, whose sister Blanche we had married.[2] And then our

1

third sister, named Anna, had gone to stay with her (and our) sister in France. And hence when we came to Bohemia we found neither father nor mother nor brother nor sister nor any acquaintance, and of course we had forgotten how to speak Czech. We learned it again, so that we could speak and understand it as well as any other Czech person. And by God's grace we could speak, write and read not only Czech, but French, Italian, Lombard,[3] German and Latin, so that the writing, reading and speaking of any one of these languages was the same for us as another. . . .

And we found the kingdom so wasted that not a single castle was left free, but all were pledged along with all the royal possessions, so that we had nowhere to reside except in the houses of the towns, like any burgher. And the castle of Prague was so devastated, wasted and destroyed that it had not been repaired since the times of King Přemysl Otakar,[4] but was all fallen in and torn down to the ground. Hence we gave orders that a great and beautiful hall and residence be built, and that it be costly, as those who behold it today can see. So too in time we sent for our wife, for she was then still in Luxemburg.[5] Coming, she bore in a year's time a daughter named Margaret. At that time our father also gave us the Margravate of Moravia,[6] and we took that title, that is, we signed as Margrave of Moravia. And when the community of honest men in Bohemia saw that we came from the old line of Czech kings,[7] they began to love us and gave us assistance in getting back the king's castles and the properties that pertained to them. . . .

And we had many willing servants, and the kingdom prospered more and more each day. And the community of good men loved us, and the evil men, fearing, refrained from doing evil, for justice flourished in the land.

NOTES

1. Charles returned to Bohemia in 1333 from Northern Italy, where he had been involved in his father's campaigns against the Lombard lords.

2. Blanche de Valois (1316-1348), actually the niece of King Phillipe IV of France, was Karel's first wife. These intermarriages were intended to make firm the alliance of the Valois and Luxemburg dynasties.

3. Lombard, a north Italian dialect retaining elements of the speech of the German Lombards.

4. Přemysl Otakar II, reigned 1253-1278.

5. Luxemburg was the hereditary home of the Luxemburg dynasty, to which Charles belonged.

6. Moravia, originally independent, had with time become a hereditary possession of the Bohemian Crown.

7. Charles's mother Elizabeth was the daughter of King Václav II and hence a princess of the native Přemysl dynasty.

CHRONICLE OF THE CZECH KINGS

by

Přibík Pulkava z Radenína

Přibík Pulkava z Radenína, principal of the school attached to the Church of St. Elijah in Prague, compiled a chronicle of Czech history entitled Chronicle of the Czech Kings, *in or soon after the year 1374. The work was written at the initiative of Emperor Charles IV, King of Bohemia. Drawing extensively from older Latin chronicles as well as the so-called Dalimil Chronicle (in Czech verse), Přibík Pulkava's chronicle represents an attempt to give a coherent account of the origin and rise of the Kingdom of Bohemia. Like many medieval chronicles, it begins with the Biblical flood and settlement of the world by the descendants of Noah, and with the Biblical Tower of Babel (presumably the origin of diverse national languages), and then attempts to connect national history with these biblical events.*

Přibík Pulkava wrote his chronicle in Latin, but it was early translated into Czech, perhaps also at the Emperor's initiative, and perhaps by Přibík himself.

The excerpts published here give the opening of the chronicle and the first chapter, on the settlement of Bohemia by the legendary ancestor of the Czech people, Czech. The text is taken from the Výbor z české literatury od počátků po dobu Husovu, 1957.

This chronicle extends from the beginning of the Czech land and concerns all the princes and kings who governed it in their times. And now at the command of the glorious Charles IV, Roman Emperor, this chronicle, derived from all the chronicles of all the monasteries which could be found and consulted, has been translated into Czech speech from Latin, as well as could be done, by Přibík, son of Dluhojov z Radenína, called Pulkava, principal of the school of the Church of St. Elijah.[1] And it should be noted that all matters that are fantastic or untrue have been omitted, and whatever is true and certain has been retained, for all these matters the aforesaid emperor has commanded to be collected and set down with great diligence in an elegant Latin speech.[2]

You should know the events of your land's own history and not be curious concerning strange news of certain wonders from other lands, whatever they may be. After you have done this, you may go hither and yon in search of new things.

> But the wise who maintain,
> Whoever good health would retain,
> Should look for new things at home,
> Not running for fine food to Rome. . . .

When the sons of men on the Plain of Shinar,[3] called thus after the Flood, did not remember or comprehend God's promise which had been made to Noah their father, "I will not destroy the world or any of its creatures with floods, but I will set my bow in the clouds of Heaven, and there shall be a covenant between me and the earth."[4] But they had no trust in God, for they feared that again there would be floods, and out of fear they sought to build cities and towers of a great height. But the Almighty God, chastising their folly and vanity, commanded from his divine power that on that spot their languages be divided into seventy-two different tongues. And hence that tower is known as the Tower of Babel, which means the confounding of tongues. And one of the languages spoken on this spot was the Slavic language, the name of which was corrupted from *slovo,* "word," and from that language the Slavs in turn have their own name. For in their language *slovo* is the same as *verbum* in Latin. And from the word *slovo* the Slavic peoples are also named.[5]

Chapter I

On the Spread of Those People and the Conquest of Different Lands

And certain Slavs left that Plain of Shinar and went through the Land of Babylon and came to the land where the Greeks now live. Then passing over a gulf of the sea along the sea itself,[6] they came to Byzantium, now called Constantinople, and from there to Bulgaria, Raška, Serbia, Dalmatia, Croatia, Bosnia, Carinthia, Istria and Carniola, in which lands they dwell until today.[7] And there was one man in Croatia, by name Czech, who became known for having killed a lord, and he and his brothers and their comrades left that land and set to looking for a new land where they might dwell in security.[8] And so, going from place to place, they came to the Danube. From there they made their way to the land which in Czech is now called Čechy, and in German, Böhmen. And in Latin that land is known as Bohemia, which name derives from the name of God in the Slavic language, and in the Czech as well.[9] And so the Czechs, or Bohemi, are named from the name of God. Bohemia is the name of the land in Latin, and Čechy in Czech, and so from the first settler Czech the land of Čechy is named. And this Czech with his brothers and comrades found the land without any inhabitant, all grown up with forests and full of wild animals in the forests. Then he settled with his servants on a high hill which, according to common report, is called Říp. From this hill a great plain can be seen on all sides, and this hill is placed between the Vltava, the Elbe and the Ohře Rivers.[10] Here first men settled and began to till the soil in Bohemia. These people first ate wild apples and other wild forest fruits, game and fish. They had neither grain nor seeds nor wine nor any other beverage with which they could become drunk, but they drank cold water. All was held in common by them, even women. We do not know what sort of linen or woolen clothing they wore, but in winter they wore furs or sheepskins instead of fur coats. They were ignorant of any law or rule, and lived only according to natural custom. A brother of Czech's or his comrade, named Lech, crossed the Sněžné Mountains, which divide Bohemia from Poland, and beheld a great and deep land, flat all the way to the sea. And he settled there and peopled it with his progeny. It should be pointed out that in the Slavic languages the word *pole* means "field" or "plain," and that from this word the name of Poland comes (Latin *campi plani*).[11] And thus the land of Poland is named from its great level plain, for in it the land lies as a great plain. And from his progeny men took themselves to Russia, to Pomerania, to Kashubia, to Dacia, and southward to the ends of the sea.[12] And so the whole land was filled with people, and they worked and cultivated there. Others went from Bohemia toward the river called Morava, and thus they acquired Moravia. And they also spread out to Meissen, to Budyšín, to Brandenburg, to Lusatia, and in all these lands they dwelt.[13] All these lands were grown up

7

with forests and had no inhabitants previously. And they began to cultivate the land and to dwell there, as they dwell there today.

NOTES

1. St. Elijah (Sv. Ilja), a Gothic church in Prague from the fourteenth century, still extant today.

2. The Czech Chronicle of Přibík Pulkava was actually a translation of his Latin Chronicle (see Introduction).

3. The Plain of Shinar is mentioned in Genesis 11: there the Tower of Babel was built, where God brought the confusion of tongues among men.

4. A paraphrase of Genesis 9:11-16.

5. The etymology for "Slavic" from *slovo*, "word," given here is tempting and even plausible, but of uncertain accuracy.

6. Apparently the Hellespont, Sea of Marmora and the Bosphorus are meant here. This theory of the spread of the Slavs from Southern Europe is erroneous (in fact they spread south from the lands north of the Carpathians); such a view may have been circulated in Bohemia by monks coming from the South Slavic lands. In any event, the idea of a southern origin did serve to connect the Slavs with the confusion of tongues at the Tower of Babel.

7. These are the lands of the South Slavs. Raška is the ancient center of medieval Serbia.

8. This account of the coming of Czech to Bohemia is taken from Cosmas' Latin Chronicle of the early twelfth century.

9. The name of Bohemia actually derives from the name of the Boji, a Celtic people who had inhabited Bohemia much earlier and who were known to the Romans.

10. Říp, an isolated hill, rising above the Central Bohemian plain some seven hundred feet, is located approximately thirty miles north of Prague, near Mělník. The Ohře River is a tributary of the Elbe.

11. Lech is the legendary ancestor of the Polish people, once called "Lechs" (cf. Russian *Ljaxi*). The etymology deriving the name of Poland from Slavic *pole*, "field," "plain," is accurate.

12. Here the chronicler seems confused. His "Dacia" is apparently the land along the Baltic Sea, and his "southward" here is an error for "northward" (as the Latin version of this Chronicle in fact has it). Perhaps the area of Russian settlement to the northeast of Pomerania and Kashubia is meant.

13. These regions, lying north of Bohemia, were in fact peopled by Slavs before the Germans came there. Budyšin (German Bautzen) is the capital of Upper Lusatia.

ANONYMOUS: THE LIFE OF ST. PROKOP

Old Czech literature contained several versions of a life of St. Prokop, including early ones in Church Slavonic and its translation in Latin (both of the eleventh century), as well as a versified Czech version from the mid-fourteenth century. The Latin version served as a basis for a Czech version in prose, freely adapted at some time during the second half of the fourteenth century and included in the Pasionál, *a compilation of lives of saints and other religious writings based in part on the medieval* Legenda aurea *of the Italian Jacobus de Voragine, but including some added Czech material. The* Pasionál *was one of the earliest works of a growing Czech literary prose. One of the older manuscripts of the* Pasionál *(on which the present translation is based) is dated 1379.*

St. Prokop was, together with the martyred ruler of Bohemia, St. Václav, one of the most popular Czech national saints. He founded the Sázava Monastery in Central Bohemia in the second quarter of the eleventh century. Many miraculous legends were associated with his ascetic life, but in general the chief qualities stressed in his Life *are simplicity, piety, modesty, helpfulness and devotion. Stylistically the life is narrated in a relatively simple, straight-forward style with little artifice or adornment.*

The Sázava Monastery which Prokop founded served as a center of the Czech nationalist Church movement and of the use of the Church Slavonic liturgy and Slavonic writing. Introduced in 863 in Moravia by the brother missionaries, Sts. Cyril and Methodius, who came from Constantinople, the Slavonic tradition soon spread to Bohemia, where it competed with the use of Latin introduced by German missionaries. A feeling of resentment at German encroachment in the land, and in the Sázava Monastery as well, are reflected in the Life, *and St. Prokop's anti-German (and hence, presumably, pro-Czech) feelings endeared him to his countrymen.*

There lived in the Czech land a certain abbot whose name was Prokop, who had been instructed in the Slavonic language by St. Cyril.[1] Earlier he had been a parish priest, full of honesty, a most pious example and a most pure life. And he had begun to think what he might do that, parting from the world, he should draw close to his dear lord, Jesus Christ. And he did so. He turned away from all his possessions and from his friends and kinsfolk,

9

went off into the wilderness and dwelt there in a certain cave, there serving God. And in the same cave there lived a thousand devils. That cave is scarce two miles from the town of Kouřim, on the River Sázava.[2] And just as Holy Writ has it: "A light set on a candlestick cannot be hidden,"[3] so the sanctity of this holy father was, by God's marvellous consecration, spread over the whole countryside. And different people began to come to see him in the wasteland, entrusting themselves to the power of his prayer and receiving from him manifold consolations for their souls, for he was a most holy man, full of every charity, excellent in his wisdom, humble in speech and in countenance, most restrained in eating and drinking, and a most diligent teacher of the true faith. His pronouncements the Holy Spirit made sweet for sinners, and so many heard him gladly, sighing with regret for their sins and repenting with tears as they made their way back home. And St. Prokop had the habit of taking whatever he had grown with his own faithful hands, digging, sowing and reaping, and feeding it with charity to the poor, just as if he could see Christ Jesus before him, bidding him on to such charity. From all directions people came to him, desirous of remaining with him in the wilderness and serving God according to his pious example.

Then through the inspiration of the Holy Spirit he undertook to build a church in honor of God and the Queen of Heaven and St. John, Baptizer of Christ. And there he received a number of brethren of an honest way of life and holy action, came to an agreement with them, and together they accepted the rule of St. Benedict.[4] And so he lived with them in all humility, counting himself the least of them. What miracles the Lord showed here the hand of man cannot describe in full, and we will tell only some of them.

We read of his pious goodness that, when according to the custom of the Roman Church, between Easter and the Day of the Lord's Ascension into Heaven, pious people fast for three days and make the procession of the Stations of the Cross, calling on all the saints and beseeching them to intercede for them with God, a certain God-fearing man, whose name was Menno, came to the bank of the Sázava and asked to be ferried across the river, since he wished to join St. Prokop in service to God and in making the procession of the Stations of the Cross. But the boat was on the other side of the river and so he could not cross, which made him very sad. And as he stood on the bank he took thought, seeing the boat on the other side tied to a post, and striking his breast with deep sighs, he prayed to God, saying, "O most mighty Lord, who through your sainted servant Prokop have shown such wonders to the world, and through them brought so many sinners to faith and to religious belief, please hear me, a sinner, and grant that the boat should float across the river to this side to me. Do not turn me away from today's holy service but heed my longing for faith, dear Lord, and let me take part today in St. Prokop's prayers for your holy name, its honor and praise." No sooner had he said these words than with great speed the boat, together with the post to which it was tied, sailed across to him. And on it he crossed the river and took part in the divine service, as he had desired, and made the procession of the Stations of the Cross. Then he started to tell St. Prokop all that had happened to him. And St. Prokop said to him, "Do not suppose, my son, that the Lord has done this for my sake, for I am unworthy, but he, the King of Heaven, has done it for the confirmation of your own faith."

And at this time a certain man in whom an evil spirit dwelt was brought to St. Prokop in the event that St. Prokop might help him. Then the devil cried out and said, "What have I done to you, Prokop? Why do you drive me out from hence?" So said the devil, and he set the body of the possessed man to shaking fearfully. Then St. Prokop commanded that man to fast; entrusting him to one brother, St. Prokop began himself to fast and to pray without ceasing. After a week St. Prokop began to read the prayers of anathema over him, according to the custom. The devil flew out of him and into the body of a black bird, and it sat on the roof of the church. At that very time St. Prokop set to praying and at once the bird collapsed and fell to the ground, broke into four parts and vanished, and the man was wholly free of the devil's possession.

At another time the voices of devils were heard crying, "Woe! Woe! That this false, cruel man lives in this cave we can no longer endure; let us rise up with all our brothers and dwell in the wasteland called Lobek. No one there could harm us more than this Prokop, who does not let us live here."

Various kinds of sick people also came to him, and he healed them. And he commanded them diligently not to betray what had happened, for he sought to avoid the world's praise, though he

11

could not conceal everything. Once some people came to the Bohemian prince, named Břetislav,[5] and told him of the sanctity of the holy father Prokop. The prince and his nobles heard this gladly, and going to him, the prince commended himself to his prayers, and taking counsel with his advisors, he made St. Prokop abbot of his monastery and endowed it with wealth and funds for the poor, to which St. Prokop, not wishing to consider, resisted and said, "He who knows all the secrets of the heart, I call on him to witness on my account that I am not worthy to hold authority over others; my own simplicity will show that." Then the prince and his counsellors entreated him and insisted, and finally against his will he was forced to accept the abbacy.

How he governed there through the teaching of the Holy Spirit has been described thus: he was full of humility, and was never disquieted for any reason, nor was he ever too hasty in speech with those under him, and for this all his brethern in God loved him more than they feared him as their superior. It was his pious habit to reprove the brethern graciously, sometimes publicly, sometimes in private, and to say, "Dear brothers, love God, serve him diligently, for your brief service here will bring you an eternal kingdom in Heaven!" And so carrying on his pious life and teaching people by sacred word and example, he came near to death. Through a revelation of the Holy Spirit he had foreknowledge of his death, and called to himself a God-fearing man, his own nephew, named Vít, and another man, his own dear son in God,[6] named Emeran, and revealed to them, "My dear sons, I have brought you up faithfully in the Church, know this, that on the third day from now I shall take leave of the world. I entrust you to God, but I give your reason warning that you should know and conduct yourselves carefully and in all humility, for you will meet great hatred from evil men. You will be driven out into other lands and there you will remain six years and this your dwelling-place our prince will give to strangers. But you, my dear children, do not lose courage in this contention, but stand firmly in the faith, comfort your brethern in God, ever praise God when things go well, and thank God when they go badly, suffer humbly for the dear Lord's sake, for that hour will come in which the Lord will comfort you. And after six years the Lord will have pity on you and will return you to the same peace you knew and to your former dwelling, and will avenge you upon your adversaries. The

12

time will come when the gracious Prince Břetislav dies and after him Spytihněv will be prince,[7] and he will hate you, and when Spytihněv dies, Vratislav will take his place in Bohemia.[8] Him God will enlighten with his Spirit, in all fear and in goodness, and he will return you again to your dwelling, and coming back here with the help of Jesus Christ you shall have greater peace again."

And when he had told them all this, the next day there came to him a poor orphan whom St. Prokop had fed for a week for God's sake. Taking his leave of the holy father he was about to return home, but St. Prokop said to him, "Dear son, I have nothing to give you now, but wait till tomorrow when my end, now appointed by God, will come, and as soon as I am dead, my garments will be given you." And when the morrow came, though his end was approaching, he completed the appointed prayers for eventide, and he prayed to God and turned away the Devil. Around him stood the brethern. Then he entrusted them to God and passed away. This happened in the year of Our Lord 1,053. Severus, Bishop of Prague, came to his funeral, and buried his holy body with honor in the church of Our Lady which the holy father had founded. And in the hour when they were burying his holy body, a blind man cried out, saying, "O holy father, O gracious Prokop, your sanctity has manifested your grace to many, through your holy prayers to the dear Lord. Have pity also on me, if only that I might see until the end of the service of your holy burial." And as soon as he had said this, he saw and went on seeing until St. Prokop's body was buried. After St. Prokop's burial the brethern, taking counsel in strict piety, chose Vít, St. Prokop's nephew, as their abbot. And he began, according to St. Prokop's example, to raise the level of piety, and carefully and wisely to instill veneration and discipline.

Then the pious Czech prince Břetislav died, and after him Spytihněv was prince in Bohemia. And under him the prophecy of St. Prokop came to fulfillment in this fashion: the enemy of all believing souls, the Devil, carried the envious slanders of evil tongues against Abbot Vít to Prince Spytihněv's ears. When he heard the accusation, Spytihněv began to hate Abbot Vít. Remarking this, Abbot Vít and God-fearing brethern arose and went off to another land. Observe, you kings and princes, how much evil envy works in brotherhoods. The sin of envy does not suffer truth, and whatever it cannot have for itself, it seeks through evil words to

13

obtain from all. If an abbot or a superior wishes to instill veneration and piety into his brotherhood, he must suffer many lying
speeches against him from his inferiors. Hence it is not always
proper to believe all speeches. When Spytihněv learned that Abbot
Vít had gone away with the brotherhood, he made a German, an
ugly man, abbot in Vít's place.[9] And when that German was in-
stalled in the monastery, he, arising the first night for the matins,
saw that St. Prokop was standing in the doorway. The saint stood
firm and said to the German abbot, "From whom, German, do
you have the right to rule here? What are you doing here?" To
this the German abbot replied, "The mighty hand of the prince
has given me the power to govern this monastery, so long as I am
alive." St. Prokop said to him, "Compose yourself, and take yourself off, lest shame fall upon you. If you do not go, then know
that God's vengeance will come on you." Saying this he disappeared. Taking this vision for a delusion, the German paid no
attention to it. On the fourth night the German abbot was going
to matins when St. Prokop again appeared to him and said,
"German, why did you not heed my speech, which I intended as a
friendly warning? Know that I have been granted this monastery
as a dwelling for my spiritual sons in the Lord, but not for you,
German. If the prince gave you power to rule, then I take it away
from you and forbid you here from this day forth." And saying
this St. Prokop took his staff and started to beat the abbot with
it severely. The abbot did not tarry, but hastened to the prince
and began to tell him what had happened to him. The prince heard
this with great astonishment and was terrified, but since malice
had been in his heart, he would not yield, and remained so until
his death. And when his time was come Prince Spytihněv died, and
after him Vratislav was prince, and he was God-fearing, just, and
full of all veneration. And when he rewarded, early in his reign,
those who served him, he recalled St. Prokop's monastery over all
other monasteries. Learning that Abbot Vít was in Hungary, he
sent messengers for him and the other brethern to bring them
back to their monastery. And returning they were honorably in-
stalled in the monastery, and whatever want they had suffered
before, now they had enough of everything through St. Prokop's
prayers, and for long they served God and received his grace, and
they dwell with him forever and ever. Amen.

NOTES

1. St. Cyril, leader with his brother St. Methodius, of a mission to Moravia in 863 which brought from Byzantium Christianity together with the Slavonic liturgy and other Church writings. Prokop, who lived in the first half of the eleventh century, could not have learned Slavonic directly from Cyril, but it is important to note that he was an adherent of the Slavonic rather than the Latin party in the Czech Church.

2. The River Sázava, on which the cloister was located, flows west through East Central Bohemia and enters the Vltava a few miles south of Prague.

3. A paraphrase of St. Matthew 5:15.

4. The Benedictines go back to St. Benedict (sixth century). Their order is relatively moderate, and views the monastery as a community bound together in harmony by family-like relations.

5. Prince Břetislav ruled in Bohemia from 1037 to 1055. He greatly enlarged the Bohemian domains, and brought peace to the country.

6. While Vít seems to have been St. Prokop's actual nephew, Emeran was presumably not his son, but only his "son in God" as a monk.

7. Prince Spytihněv ruled from 1055 to 1061.

8. Prince Vratislav ruled from 1061 to 1092.

9. The German clergy in Bohemia were opposed to the spread of the Slavonic liturgy and Church writings, so that the appointment of a German abbot would have meant an end to the Slavonic rite in the monastery.

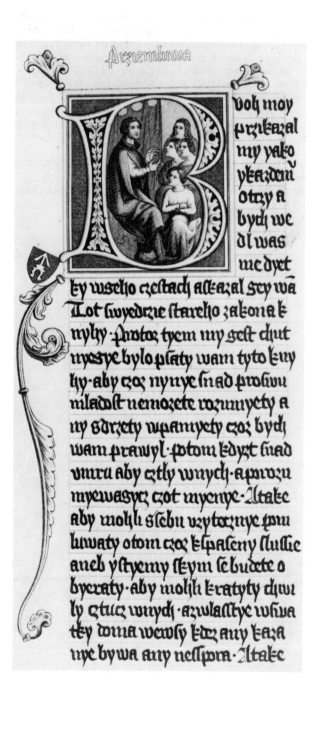

voh moy
prikazal
my yako
ykazdeŭ
otrzy a
bydz we
dl was
me dyet

ky wselio czestach aszazal szy wā
Tot swyedzie starelio zakona k
mylly · phozor tyem my gest chut
mossye bylo platy wam tyto kny
lly · aby czoz nynye snad proswu
mladost nemozete rozumyety a
ny gdrzety wpamyety czoz bydz
wam prawyl · potom kdyzt snad
vmru aby cztly wnych · aprozu
myewasycz czot myenye · Altake
aby mohli slebu vzytoznye pou
luwaty otom czoz kspaseny slussie
aneb ystyemy skym se budete o
byczaty · aby mohli kratyty chwi
ly cztuc wnych · azwlasstye wswa
tey doma wewsly kdz auy taza
nye bywa auy nesspoza · Altake

TOMÁŠ ZE ŠTÍTNÉHO

With Tomáš ze Štítného, or Štítný, medieval Czech prose style reached its zenith. A nobleman whose seat of Štítné is located near Zirnovice in Southern Bohemia, he was born around 1331 and received his education at the newly founded University of Prague. He was keenly interested in spiritual matters, and was a partisan of the movement for the reform of the Czech Church which flourished during the second half of the fourteenth century and preceded the work of Jan Hus. Štítný was chiefly concerned for moral reform; in dogma he took a conservative stance that emphasized adherence to conformism rather than change.

Štítný wrote principally for the spiritual and moral education of his two children, and hence he wrote in Czech rather than Latin. Some of his writings he subsequently revised for a larger circle of acquaintances. The strength of his writing is in his controlled use of Czech, with a strong sense of form and (for his times) of grammatical and lexical standards. He could also write with an enthusiasm and spontaneity that are contagious, so that his didactic works are rarely boring. He died in 1401.

St. Bridget (ca. 1300-1373), the patron saint of Sweden, was a noblewoman celebrated for her account of a series of remarkable spiritual visions, a work that circulated in Latin widely over Europe in the Middle Ages. From these visions Štítný made a selection (some time after 1391) in Czech for the edification of his daughter Anežka. In his introduction, given below, he follows a contemporary Swedish source in asserting the right of woman to an equal place in the eyes of God.

The text as translated here is taken from the Výbor z české literatury od počátků po dobu Husovu, 1957.

THE VISIONS OF ST. BRIDGET

There is a marvellous report in our land. Before now God in the Old Testament was wont to speak to people by showing them his power; now he speaks more softly, seeking to show his mercy. Elijah saw in a vision how a wrathful spirit came toward him, overturning mountains and cliffs; then he beheld fine, calm weather, and the Lord was there.[1] For the Lord watches over his chosen ones in all their deeds, so that on the Day of Judgment evil men

17

should have no excuse, since to no one, neither to the good nor to the evil, did they permit them to bestir themselves so that they might seek the Lord. But now in these times he has showed us his mercy, and has reminded his Church through a woman, through St. Bridget, revealing to her in her faith many visions, and he wished them to be written down, and he proclaimed her sainthood, that she is elevated in the Roman Church and numbered among the saints from the year of Our Lord 1391. And her feast day is fixed on the day after the day of St. Mary Magdalene,[2] on which day the Church should serve her as a holy widow. And she lived during my own lifetime; I did not know her, but I have heard of her sanctity and some of my friends have seen her.[3]

And I said, there is a marvellous report in our land. Often have I heard people say, "There is nothing good to be heard." If you could only hear them say, "Such and such a man has become a saint." And now we hear that she has become a saint, that she loved God, she loved well her neighbors, she hated sinfulness in men and wrote books against it, and in all this was the will of God. And her writings have been carefully investigated by learned masters, and in none of them has any error or heresy been found, though they are written by a woman. But cannot God do anything he wishes? Why, the Scriptures are full of that sort of thing: God often selects weak or base people to shame the strong. And have not women been prophets through whom God has worked wonderfully and done great things: Judith, Esther, the widow Anna, the Sibyls? Hence, though one should not believe any spirit, still not all simple folk, uneducated, or women should be excluded when they speak so, but it is proper to put it to the test to see if it is from God. Had Pharaoh believed Joseph, he would have taken measures to prevent the years of want. And another pharaoh: had he believed Moses' vision, he would have saved Egypt many blows. And then too, if God did not wish women to be believed in their visions, he would not have me do it so gloriously plain in the Gospels that they are women at God's tomb who behold the angels, and who go with the news to the apostles and to Peter. To rid yourself of your fear of deception in the writings of this holy woman, note well how they are guarded against such deception!

She was a noblewoman, of the family of Swedish kings, but she did not seek favors because of that, but ever lived fearing God, and after the death of her husband she gave herself in great love to

18

God's service. And when she began to have her visions, she became more and more humble, fearing a heavier judgment, and the more God manifested to her the gifts of his grace; but she opined that she was not worthy of anything and would prefer to keep all secret which God had revealed to her in her humility. But God wished that she should write it down. He knows for what purpose and for whom. . . .

NOTES

1. Compare I Kings 19:11-13, though Štítný has ornamented the account and added details such as "fine weather."

2. St. Mary Magdalene's day is July 22; St. Bridget's day was originally July 23.

3. St. Bridget settled in Rome before her death in 1373.

THE BOOK OF CHESS

An adaptation of a medieval Latin work by Jacobus de Cessolis, De
ludo scaccorum sive de moribus hominum et de officiis nobilium *(On the
Game of Chess, or On Morals and the Duties of Noblemen), the* Book of
Chess *represents a typical medieval attempt to treat the game allegorically as
a mirror of human social and moral relations. This is done with considerable
ingenuity and wit, and in his version Štítný has expanded the social and moral
applications of the original and their ethical implications. He made his Czech
adaptation some time after 1394.*

*The reader familiar with chess will note a number of differences from
the game as now played (it underwent a major revision in the Renaissance
which gave us the game essentially as we know it today). Thus, the queen was
much less powerful: she moved in a diagonal direction only, and only one
square at a time. The bishops moved two squares diagonally, and could jump
over an intervening piece without displacing it (as the knight still can).*

The text as translated here is taken from the Výbor z české literatury
od počátků po dobu Husovu, *1957.*

Part III

We should speak of why one chessman moves this way and
another moves a different way, as you see happen when people
play at chess. This is explained by the fact that, while we all tend
toward one intent, the common good, we do so according to our
different states and professions, each of which has its own actions.
And that each chessman moves on a four-cornered board reminds
us that, though one of us has his actions and another different
ones, none of us should step outside of the following four virtues,
in which you turn, checked by cautious restraint, a proper moderation, strength of heroic thought, and justice. Hence let each hold
to his own class and profession! For if anyone wishes to be greater
than he is, he will be less than he has been.

It frequently happens in playing chess that someone will
speak, seeking to arouse his side and give it good hope and cheer.
That means it is proper for kings, princes and lords to stir up their

servants and entertain them with good words, with pipers, trumpeteers, drummers and players on stringed instruments. We read that
when God's children of Israel and the pagan people lay next to
one another in armed camps, and when the pagans heard that the
others were rejoicing, they grew frightened and said: "What is this?
They were not so merry yesterday or the day before!" And in
terror they turned around and fled, and the others gained the
victory. And thus too do we read of King David that he was a man
according to God's own heart, that he had singers and drummers at
his court, and others who aroused the young people of his court,
and though we read that he had his hope in the one God, still he
could enjoy these things as God's gifts. Or when he wished to take
one of his faithful servants to dwell with him at court, seeking to
repay his fidelity with a good dwelling and with honor, that
servant would say to the king: "I am old, and the pipers and
drummers and singers of the king's court no longer arouse me, but
if I have found favor with the king, then let the king take my son
instead of me." And from this speech of the old man we can tell
that even King David kept such pleasures at court for his courtiers.[1]

The pawns begin the game of chess and all have the same
move: on the first move they may go two places forward, but after
that one only; however, if any chessman be at a diagonal from
them, either to the right or to the left, they may take that piece.
And if one come to the end of the board, it has the right to
become a queen, moving over the board just as that piece moves.

The pawns denote the common people; in times of peace
these can go off some distance, as to market, if they keep within
limits, but should some disturbance arise, they must not transgress
those limits, and must keep close and step with caution. The fact
that the pawn always moves forward means that the common man
must heed only his own affairs, and those higher than he can safe-
guard him. For, as I have said, whoever seeks wrongly to do what
is not granted to him, or to be greater than he is, will be less than
what he has been. And that a pawn cannot take with his ordinary
move, straight forward, but only when the enemy is on the
diagonal from him, this shows that an ordinary man when a foe is
at an angle from him, to the right or the left, and that foe seeks to
take his life or his goods, then he may act according to that Latin
rule that says, "Vim vi repellere licet,"[2] repel the foe and take
him captive as a proof. For so say those Latin words which tell us

22

to drive off violence with violence, and the rule is completed by adding, "cum moderamine inculpate tutele"[3]—so force is to be repelled with force, but with this limitation, that there should be no more effect than is necessary for one's own defense. For when someone gives a slap and the other replies with a mortal blow, he has done more than is required for his own defense, and so he is guilty. The fact that, when the pawn traverses the whole board, it becomes a queen, means that heroic persons may come to be noble, even if they come from the common people. Yes, David was a common man, and yet the king was to give him his daughter, and he then came to be king himself. So the pawn, when it reaches the end of the board, is like the king's son-in-law and from the princess will receive her right.

The king may move in chess on his first move like any other chessman, but only if there be no check on him; but if he moves like the rook [i.e., perpendicularly] he may go no farther than two squares. For kings and great lords it is not proper to ride far in a single day, for they travel with a great crowd and some of them have a retinue, and they cannot endure a long ride. If a king or a lord suddenly desired to travel far, many horses would be exhausted. We read of Jacob the patriarch that when he was making his way to his land with many servants and flocks, and his wife and brother rode out to meet him and give him welcome, he said to his brother, "Go on first! I must go slowly, I have children and many servants and cattle; otherwise the weaker of them would perish."[4] And so the king, though he may move in any direction, may move but one square and no more. And he may not move any piece from its place so that he should sit there. And so kings must not take the property of their own subjects. And when a king first stirs from his place and takes his queen with him, this shows that wherever the husband goes, if he wishes, the wife must go with him. So it is in chess, a piece may attack the king and move him from his place and do shame to him, and sometimes he will lose one of his own pieces in running away if he is not well defended by his own men. And if mate is scored against the king, the game is lost. If he loses all his pieces, the game is also lost. Therefore, O king, preserve your men so that you may rule with them, and demand that they guard you well, and you people too, preserve and guard your king! For even bees will perish if they do not have a king.[5]

23

The queen moves only on the diagonal, and never moves as the knight does, but like the bishop she can sometimes move first. For sometimes a queen or a noblewoman can give useful advice, but still she should not walk as a knight does, wearing a dagger; she should conduct herself more quietly, for modesty and quiet are better ornaments for women than a man's behavior. The fact that one queen always moves on the white squares and the other on the black shows that both of them are ladies and both good and virtuous: one of them so values the virtue of chastity that she wears it with high spirits;[6] the other, though to her chastity is not a virtue that is dear, still she fears to be thought unchaste, and so from shame keeps herself chaste. Both are good and noble, but watch out for all those, be they men or women, who have an evil tongue, lest you be mocked by them! Be ashamed to associate with the shameless, and guard yourselves against all who are impure!

The bishop[7] moves on the diagonal two squares, and so always moves on squares of the same color, without change. The diagonal move means caution. And that he moves to the third square means that those counsellors who belong to town councils and to courts must hold to three things: first, that when they can assist the right, they must do so; second, when they give advice to anyone, they must give proper advice; third, when they must come to a decision, they must decide as the evidence proves. And a judge must not alter his verdict, as if the same proof could decide first for one party and then for the other, and just so the bishop in chess must not change colored squares, but always move along the same ones.

The knight moves two squares, from black to white or from white to black, so that half his move is diagonal and half straight on. For the three squares of the move are connected so that he touches a corner only on the second square, the same color as the original square, whereas he touches the third one, which has a different color, on its whole length [i.e., to settle down there]. The fact that the knight moves on the diagonal signifies caution against craftiness, and that he moves straight on signifies courage and strength. And the knight must have both these qualities, courage and caution; cautious and ingenious intentions must be kept in check by courage and might. Courage without wisdom brings fools to their destruction; and ingenuity without the power

24

of might and strength—what will it bring? But what can resist the man who is both wise and courageous? Ah, the bear is strong, the fox cunning, the hare swift, fish have their pond, the bird its flight in the air, but all these yield to the will of man if he exert himself with energy.

The move of the knight is such that, so long as he sits on his original square, he can choose to go out onto three squares only, but if he take a position in front of the rook, he can move onto four squares, and if his position is in front of the king, he can move onto six squares, and if he is in the middle of the board, he can move onto eight squares. This shows how the knight can gain courage: so long as he sits in peace he, like any man, must think of death and not take pride in his courage, but if he should come out to the aid of an official of the king, then he should rouse himself and he will be the more courageous; if he comes before the king, he will be still more courageous; and when he is in the field and engaged in knightly encounters, then he must venture all, remembering that this is his estate and his duty, and either alive or dead he must do that which is proper for them. Others in time of peace are very boastful and brave in speech; they may appear to themselves to be a kind of octoped, not considering that they will die, and when that meets them of which better not think, they, not realizing that it has met them, take fright and neglect matters, seeing themselves near to death.[8] For whoever considers something well in advance can meet it more courageously, and whatever collides with someone suddenly will stir him all the more.

The rook moves perpendicularly, any number of squares, straight forward or sideways, if the way is clear, but he cannot move another piece, and so long as the chess pieces are still in place the rook or the king or the queen may not move.[9] For the king or his officials would not be needed if the people all remained in their ranks according to the original rule that is natural for man. And the fact that the rook may not go over his own men means that the king's official has no right to destroy one of his own, even though he wishes to harm the king's enemy. And of the enemy he has no right to spare any, pardoning them, but must destroy all that is contrary to the truth of his office. And the fact that he moves perpendicularly, and not on the diagonal, means that the king's officials must not employ deceit in their offices, but open and evident truth, and openly they must be chosen to fill their offices.

And we should be amazed and wonder that players, having finished their game, return the pieces to a bag. For this reminds us of what will happen to all of us. Here in the world there are kings, princes, lords, young people, old people, short and tall people and, just like chessmen, they are distributed over the board: one in this function and another in that one, but all are claimed in the end by death and put back in the bag. The king who ruled here with honor with a queen, or a queen with her king—where is their place now that they are back in the bag? . . . So each of you look well to your state! We see God's goodness and justice and might; we see how, as if taking chessmen out of a bag, he places one chessman here and another there, one this way and another that way, and then suddenly takes them up again into his bag. Let us serve him now while we have time, each in his own estate, for we do not know how soon we will go into the bag, thus parting with what is here in the world, and taking with ourselves whatever we have deserved here.

And so our book of chess is finished, with its moral exegesis.

Grant, O King, Jesus Christ our Lord,
We may play chess here in this world,
Then receive eternal life as our reward. Amen.

NOTES

1. The speeches improvized here resemble Biblical quotations, but do not have an exact source in the Bible.

2. "It is permissable to repell force with force" (Cicero).

3. "With a restriction to necessary self-defense."

4. A paraphrase of Genesis 33:13.

5. The queen bee is obviously meant here, not the king.

6. White symbolized the virtue of chastity.

7. The Old Czech name for this piece was *pop* (priest), but Štítný refrains from drawing inferences or punning on the term.

8. The sense of this sentence is not very clear in the Czech text, and in particular the reference to an "octoped" *(osmonoh)* is unclear. Perhaps Štítný has an octopus in mind, but if so for what qualities does he refer to it?

9. The bishop (in medieval chess) and the knight (still today) could, of course, move over other pieces.

ANONYMOUS: THE WEAVER

An allegorical dialogue disputation in prose, The Weaver *(Tkadleček) is perhaps the supreme achievement of Czech literary prose of the medieval period. A textual cipher gives the name of the author-hero as Ludvík, and his love, who has deceived him, as Adlička. Internal evidence suggests (if it is not merely fiction) that he is a nobleman, a courtier in the East Bohemian town of Hradec Králové ("Queen's Court"). The lover disputes with an allegorical figure, Misfortune (Neštěstí), concerning the justice of a fate which has deprived him of his now faithless love. The work is strongly influenced by the similar disputation of a farmer with Death, embodied in the Bohemian German writer Johann von Tepl's Ackermann aus Böhmen. The two works are very close in time of origin (on the basis of internal evidence the Czech work is usually dated soon after 1407), but apparently the German dialogue was slightly earlier, and the model for the Czech work.*

The reader today is apt to read The Weaver *as the legitimate if seemingly endless complaint of an individual who maintains his own right to happiness. Something of this there no doubt is in the work, and in certain respects, such as its use of classical mythological sources,* The Weaver, *like its German model, looks ahead to the period of early Renaissance humanism and greater individualism; as such it is unique in medieval Czech literature. On the other hand, the ultimate victory of Misfortune in the debate (the lover finally fails to reply) suggests the victory of the medieval point of view, that individual and worldly happiness does not matter. Misfortune in effect represents the principle of authority of the moral law and its supremacy over individual will; in certain respects Misfortune may further be identified with classic reason or the principle of moderation in all things.*

Stylistically the work is a tour de force *of colorful rhetorical language, rich in imagery, proverbs and witty phrases. No doubt it is somewhat long-winded and repetitive for modern taste, but in spite of the monotony of the subject and plan, there is in fact a surprising diversity of treatment in style and imagery as the dialogue moves forward. The writer stylizes himself as a "weaver," i.e., a weaver of words, and the opening of Chapter Three, given below, draws a great deal of imagery from the trade of weaving in an elaborate literary conceit.*

The text as translated here is taken from Jan Vilikovský, Próza z doby Karla IV, *Prague, 1938, but with reference to the version given in the* Výbor z české literatury od počátku po dobu Husovu, *Prague, 1957, including the notes to the latter text.*

27

THE WEAVER

Chapter Three

Here the Plaintiff Who Accuses Misfortune Is Named in a Cipher and Presented Figuratively. He Tells His Profession and State. Then He Tells Him Why He Abuses Him and What Is the Cause of His Secret Complaint.

I am the Weaver, skilled of profession; I can weave without wood, a frame or without iron.[1] The shuttle with which I cross the weave is of bird's down; my yarn is the fur of different beasts. The dew which sprinkles my roll is no ordinary water, and with it I sprinkle a drop or two, now above, now below. And head and feet I am from all parts of the Czech land. My true name is compounded and embroidered from eight letters of the alphabet. The first letter of my name is the eleventh in the alphabet, the next the twentieth, the next the fourth, and after those again the twentieth and right after it the ninth, and the last letter is the tenth.[2] I am he, O Misfortune, who is called so, know me as you hear me now. Hear what I say: I, the Weaver, must ever hate you, Misfortune, I must defy you, and must ever be set against you. I understand and recollect: once you seduced me with her who is my delight, and at that time I overlooked our differences. But then you took her from me. Do you not know that it is natural for a person, even though it breaks God's commandment, when a man is saddened by a wrong he, wherever he can, will avenge himself gladly, if not at once, then even after some time has passed? And not only man does this and it is natural for him, but it is natural for vermin and for many beasts, dumb creatures. Is that not like vengeance? You, Misfortune, have deprived me of all that was good for me and you do not let me speak of it. I will not be silent, I do not wish to conceal my feelings forever, you cannot threaten me, and I will reveal it. If you were audacious and did such wrong to me, now be audacious again and hear my speech of shame to you, and bear it! Do you not know that the Creator himself speaks in Scripture thus: "The measure with which you measure, with that it will be measured unto you."[3] If you have been brazen enough, vile Misfortune, to make me sad, then kindly do not shrink from that which I have to say. I understand this

28

thing according to your speech, for you have made many orphans in the world by just such separation as you have made for me. Many are those whom you have made to grieve with your hardships and your false guile, and though others have not fully understood from where such trouble came upon them, I now understand it, though unwillingly, and I understand that it is you, vile Misfortune, who not only have separated me and cut me off from all my joy, but that it is you, Misfortune, who have first bound together Medea, the princess, and Jason, the hero, in love, and then have shamefully and unpityingly parted them, and many other such notable people as is known to you and is written, and today even in my own time it still happens so, and for that reason today I, the Weaver, cry out and intend to shout without ceasing with a voice that croaks, ah, alas, against you, evil, shameful, repulsive Misfortune!

Chapter Fourteen

Here Misfortune Recounts a Parable to the Plaintiff, Explaining What He Is and From Where He Comes and What His Form Is and What His Power Is and Where He Comes From, and How the Romans Spoke of Him and What Form They Gave to Him.

Know that we are much surprised at what you speak of, and that earlier at the outset of our debate you called us Misfortune, since we are he, and you abused us a great deal, as if you indeed did know us, and now you ask us who we are, and what we are, and from where we come, and what is our power. You act like poor, untaught physicians do when, without sufficient knowledge of a man's ailment or sickness, they give him medicine, potions, syrups and the like, and when they have treated him for a long time, only then do they ask where he aches and what is wrong with him, where he is sorest. Having abused us quite enough with whatever occurred to you, you now seek to have us say who we are, what we are, from where we come, and of what shape we are, and what is our power. You do great injustice to us and abuse us greatly in that, shamelessly you do us injustice and ever say that we are evil and very injurious. And yet we have often given you to understand that all that we have done to you we have done more

29

for your good than for your harm. Truly you should hold us more in honor than do us injustice, and above all thank us rather than abuse us. But since you have not yet questioned us so diligently what we are or who we are or from where we come, we now wish to tell you, not at your request, to which we give no heed, nor for your threats, which are as empty wind to us, nor for your shouts, at which people laugh, nor for your state in life, about which you yourself are uncertain, but from our own obligation which has been given to us, under which we are bound to give every living thing to know. And so we give you to know and we shall proclaim it to you. Now listen!

We are the emissary of God's hand, his swift agent in all hard matters. We are the silken whip, the cane and staff of the creator of all creation. We are the reaper who wields a dull, hacked scythe in all the fields and all the meadows, both withered and green. Our mission, which we fulfill, is never in vain. We are a whip whose lash cracks hard and which leaves a welt which never heals with time. We are the cane which never breaks on anyone and never bends or parts, though none may count on that: to any man who relies on it, we promise nothing at all. We are that reaper whose scythe is here and there grown dull, but which will never grow duller, neither by the rock of hard thought, nor the soft bosom of fine speech, nor the sand of much feeling, nor the spice of much cleverness. We are the plowman and gardener of orchards and the master of all men's trades; we turn some of them into others, and transplant some as others. We act as you do, Weaver. The tools of our trade are prepared for all men, and with our power we apply them to all men and weave. We need no one's help, we do not inquire about the fineness of the yarn, we do not ask as to the color: white is the same for us as black, black is the same as blue, green the same as grey, yellow the same as flaxen, and we regard people of one color the same as another. For what can their color mean? When we cut at them with the force of our adversity we miss nothing on them at which we aim. The violet will not hide from us even with its luxuriant color which denotes permanence.[4] The lily with its beauty and whiteness will not fell us even in bright hope. The red rose with its scarlet color will not be veiled from us in burning love. The clover, the ivy, the juniper, the periwinkle, which is the leader in all conceived favor, cannot hide from us. The field rose with its russet color, sign of all mystery, cannot escape us. Even the invented, stolen color of grey, ingeniously composed from many colors, will not escape us. The blue cornflower of evil hope or perfection will not resist us. The dandelion with its vigor and its yellow color, a flower much abused, will not profit against us.

Ask how the Romans, who were renowned for wisdom, depicted us. They depicted us as they comprehended and knew us, though not perfectly, as we are in our own person, but in the fashion in which they described us. Listen: in the years of Romulus, who first settled Rome when he founded the city, he built a temple as large in size as he was able, and ordered various gods, that is idols, to be made there. Among his other gods he ordered us to be drawn and described, and then his many successors who came after him ordered us to be carved from stone and ornamented finely and with understanding, so that we were depicted and ornamented thus: a great male figure, or one fashioned as a male,[5] and that man was seated upon a stag, and the stag was depicted as if on the run, about to leap. The man seated upon the stag had his eyes bound, so that he saw nothing. Fiery sparks rained from the man's mouth, and these sparks flew hither and yon; some of them set fire to whatever they touched and flew far; other sparks were extinguished, and vanished. The man also held in each of his hands a sheet of paper covered with writing. On the sheet held in his right hand was written: "With me there is hardship." On the other sheet in his left hand was written: "With me there is grief and sorrow." Over the man's head, as if suspended in the air, was another paper on which was written: "I am power and adverse strength." At the base of the figure was a paper on which was written: "I am the haste and fleetingness of the moment." Behind him this man led a flat ox with ten horns. On this ox, instead of a pouch, was tied a meshwork trap. In front of the man were many people with different kinds of arms. Here were emperors, here were kings, here were princes, here were counts, here were knights and squires, here were different men of arms of different classes, with different weapons, from the loftiest class down to the basest. Here too was a nun, with her Psalter and her veil, here was a monk with his antiphonary and with his short hood. Here was the townswoman with her starched veil, here was the court lady, proud and of spirited gait, with her amulet and her braided trimmings. Here too was the toothless old hag, hunched over her distaff. All these people were against that man, cutting at him and hacking at him and hurling weapons at him, each according to his station, but in no way could they injure him. And if you, Weaver, wish to read the account of our person not as we but as the Romans have spoken of us, then read Fulgentius,[6] the scholar, on images and figures and personages with various virtues and vices; perhaps there you will find something about our appearance as we have described it just now and of that which he who knows us and is in our power and subservient to hardship with us, knows without any explanation, though against his will, and knows us ever: who we are and what we are.

Further you question us, from where we come. Then hear: we are from everywhere, though we are from nowhere. From everywhere in that there is no place or corner in any land of the whole world where we would not be, where we have not dwelt through our power and domination. We need no envoys, for we ourselves are power. A pagan wiseman spoke well of us when he said, "Misfortune has but one leg, but is so swift that he ever catches up with Fortune, who runs on both feet." And we are from nowhere in that we did not come from anywhere or from anything. Our first power and our first hardship were demonstrated on the first man Adam, driven out for the temptation of the apple and given over eternally by our power to Death. Through our action Adam is given and handed over to Death, and until today, we Misfortune are comrades with Death. For to us and Death are given power and full right over all his descendants till the end of the world, so that none should escape our hard dominion. And this power we have from the Almighty Creator of Heaven and Earth.

NOTES

1. The Plaintiff here allegorizes himself as a weaver, i.e., a "weaver of words."
2. The cipher gives the name Ludvík; further on another cipher yields the name of his love, Adlička.
3. Cf. St. Luke 6:38.
4. For each flower the writer gives its symbolic meaning, in accordance with a medieval symbolic system.
5. The Czech name Neštěstí (Misfortune) is neuter in gender, and the pronouns and other gender forms used are consistently neuter, though the present translation gives

them as masculine. Hence there is more surprise for the Czech reader to learn that Misfortune bears the shape of a man.

6. Fabius Planciades Fulgentius, a mythologist of the fifth century, whose Latin treatise, the Mytologiae, was both popular and influential during the Middle Ages. Many anonymous works on classical mythology circulated during the Middle Ages under his name, and it would seem likely that such a work is meant here.

JAN HUS

Jan Hus was the great Czech religious reformer and probably the out-standing writer and thinker of the Czech medieval period. He was born in Southern Bohemia, of humble birth, in 1371 or soon after. He studied at the University of Prague in the Faculty of Theology, and was made a magister (master of arts) in 1396. Renowned for brilliance of intellect and speech, his rise was almost meteoric, and in 1401 he was made Dean of the Theological Faculty, and in 1402 Rector of the University. His brilliant career and his adherence to the party of reform in the Czech Church brought him enemies, as did his insistence that the Czech Church should be independent of German domination and free of German-speaking clergy. Queen Sophia of Bohemia, a partisan of reform, made Hus her confessor and in 1402 had him appointed to preach in the newly founded Bethlehem Chapel, a center of the reform movement, in Prague.

Hus left many writings and treatises on theology and morals, mostly in Latin. A partisan of the reform ideas of the Englishman John Wyclif, Hus sought not only to purify the Church of the many abuses that had crept in, but also to return the Church to adherence to the Scriptures rather than ecclesiastical authority. This stand brought him in conflict with the Arch-bishop of Prague, and ultimately with Rome. In an attempt to heal the dispute, Hus finally agreed, at the behest of King Václav's brother, the Ger-man King Sigismund, to attend the Church Council held at Constance and there defend the orthodoxy of his views. Sigismund gave him a safe-conduct to go to Constance, a guarantee which he subsequently withdrew.

Arriving in Constance in the autumn of 1414, Hus was almost immedi-ately imprisoned, and placed on trial in June of the following year. A long list of charges of heresy was brought against him, many of them absurd, but the charge that he rejected papal authority—one that he wished to debate on the basis of Scripture—was certainly justified. His attempts to speak in his own defense were denied, and on July 6, 1415 he was burned at the stake.

Hus left a few dogmatic and didactic works in Czech, and indeed demonstrated great concern for the development of that language. Thus, he purified it of many Germanisms that had crept in, and normalized its orthography after the great vacillations in spelling the medieval scribes had perpetrated. His most appealing works written in Czech are several letters he sent to his followers in Bohemia at the very end of his life. They testify both to his sincerity and ardor, as well as to his considerable command of the language in stylistic expression.

35

The text of the two letters translated below is taken from the Výbor z
české *literatury husitské* doby, *Vol. I, published by the* Československá
Akademie věd *in 1963.*

TWO LETTERS

[To his friends before leaving for Constance.]
[From an unknown place; probably October, 1414]

Master[1] Jan Hus, in good hope a priest and servant of the
Lord Jesus Christ, to all dear and faithful brethern and sisters in
the Lord Jesus, you have heard and received the word of God
through me, to you be grace and peace from God our Father and
from the Holy Ghost, that you may dwell in His truth without sin.

Dear and faithful friends! You know that I have labored with
you long and faithfully, preaching to you the word of God without heresy or error, as you know well, and that my one desire has
been, is and shall be as long as I live, your salvation. And I had
thought to preach to you before my departure, before going to
answer the summons that I come to Constance, and in particular to
answer to you that false witness and the witnesses who have testi-
fied against me and whose testimonies I have noted down. And
this should be made public now so that, should they later slander
me or condemn me to death, you should not take fright at that or
at any heresy of which I may be condemned there; and also because you should stand in the truth without fear and without
wavering, and that truth is given to you by the Lord God through
his faithful preachers and through me as well, though I am not in
myself sufficient to achieve it alone; and third because you should
know how to beware of deceitful and hypocritical preachers. And
now that I have set out on my journey without safe-conduct,[2] and
am going among very powerful and numerous enemies, among
whom are our worst enemies at home as you shall learn from the
testimony after the end of the council: of them there are more
than stood out against our dear Savior, and among them are
bishops and masters and parish priests and monks.

But we shall have faith in our gracious, wise and mighty
Savior, that through his promise and through your confident
prayers he will give me wisdom and the courage of the Holy Spirit,

that I may persist and that they shall not incline me to the side of evil, even if he permits me to suffer temptation, humiliation, imprisonment or death, as he and his dearest servants suffered and thus gave us an example that we should suffer for him and for our salvation. He is God and we are his creatures; he is the Lord and we his servants; he is the King of all the world, and we are but men and are insufficient; he is without sin, and we are sinners, so why should we not suffer too? Our zeal in grace is our purification from sins and our salvation from eternal torment, and our death is our victory. Surely no faithful servant of his can ever be lost, when we persevere with his help.

Therefore, dear brothers and sisters, pray diligently that he should please to give you perseverance and preserve you against corruption. And if my death is for his praise and for your welfare, let him grant that I should undergo it without pernicious fear; and if it is better for us that he should let me come back again, having taken me there without harm to me, then I should come back to keep his law, and together we should work some damage on the net of Antichrist[3] and so leave a good example for future brethren.

You perhaps shall see me no more in Prague. But if Almighty God pleases to return me there, then we shall take more pleasure in seeing each other again, and even more when we shall see each other in heavenly joy. Our gracious Lord, who gives his own pure peace here and after death, and who has raised from the dead a great shepherd after shedding his blood, which shepherd is the eternal witness to our salvation; may it please you to do good in all things that you should fulfill his will in concord and without division, that having your peace in virtue you should achieve eternal peace through our Lord Jesus Christ, who is eternal God and true man born of the Virgin Mary; may he be praised and may he stand for all ages with the elect, with whom we, standing in the truth, will dwell in joy. Amen.

NOTES

1. Master—Latin *magister,* or "master," an academic title denoting one who had completed advanced university study; the title was generally used as one of great respect, implying "teacher" and "scholar."

2. The German King Sigismund, brother of King Václav of Bohemia, had promised Hus a safe-conduct, which was delivered to him only in Constance, and in any event proved to be no protection.

3. "The net of Antichrist"—here Hus is implying that he and his followers will oppose the corrupt order that has crept into the Church, as well as the papacy and the Church hierarchy.

[To the Czech Faithful]

Constance, June 26, 1415

Master Jan Hus, in good hope a servant of God, to all the Czech faithful who love God and will love him, sends you his wish and his insufficient prayer that you should dwell in God's grace, grow perfect in it and dwell with God forever more.

Faithful and dear to me in God! I have thought to let you know how proud, overeager and full of all kinds of abomination this council is which has defamed my Czech writings without having heard what they contained or having seen them, for in the council were Italians, French, English, Spaniards, Germans, and other peoples; only Bishop Jan of Litomyšl,[1] who was also here, would have understood them, along with other Czechs who are inciters, with the Prague and Vyšehrad Chapter—from them came shame for God's truth and for our Czech land which I hold in God's hope for a land of finest faith, considering its zeal for the word of God and for good behavior. Oh, had you seen that council, which is called a most holy council and which is held to be incapable of error, you would surely have remarked the degree of its infamy, as to which I have heard publicly from the Saxons that Constance, their city, will not rid itself in the span of thirty years' time of the sins which that council has committed there. And they say further that they all are scandalized by the council, and that others have spat, beholding such abominable things. And I tell you that when I stood for the first day before that council, seeing that there was no order, I said loudly when they had all quited down, "I supposed that there would be greater politeness and gentleness, and a better order in this council than there is." Then the highest cardinal said, "How is that you say? For you spoke more humbly when you were in the fortress."[2] And I answered, "In the fortress no one shouted against me, and here everyone is shouting." And because the council was conducted in such disorder, and did more evil than good, you, true Christians

38

who are dear in the Lord, do not feel threatened by their verdict which, I trust in God, will not prosper them. They will fly apart like a flock of butterflies and their decision will perish like a spider's web. They strove to terrify me, but they could not overcome the power of divine aid in me. They did not care to quote Scripture against me, as the merciful lords who stood valiantly for the truth when they ventured on all sorts of infamy, Czechs, Moravians and Poles, and especially Lord Václav z Dubé and Lord Jan z Chlumu.[3] For they stood there when King Sigismund himself came into the council and they heard me say, "I seek instruction—if I have said anything that was evil, I wish to be instructed." And the highest cardinal said, "Because you wish to be instructed, then take this as your instruction: Recant those errors which fifty masters of Holy Writ have found in your writings." Ah, a fine instruction! So St. Catherine would have had to recant the faith and truth of the Lord Jesus Christ simply because some fifty masters opposed her.[4] But she stood firm, dear maiden, and she brought those masters to the Lord God, a thing which I, sinful man, am not able to do.

I write this to you that you may know that neither with any writing nor with any proof did they vanquish me, but rather sought through deceit and with threats to bring me to retraction and recantation. But the gracious Lord God, whose law I have celebrated, has been with me and is with me and will, I trust, be with me until the end and will preserve me in his grace till death.

Written on Wednesday after the Feast of St. John the Baptist[5] in prison in chains, awaiting death, though because of God's mysteriousness I may not say if this be my final letter, or if the Almighty God can liberate me.

NOTES

1. Bishop Jan of Litomyšl in Bohemia was Hus's principal adversary in the Council.
2. A reference to the period when Hus was turned over by the Council to King Sigismund, who then held him prisoner (in violation of the safe-conduct he had given Hus) in his castle of Gottlieben, and then returned him to the Council for judgment on June 5, 1415. The "highest cardinal" mentioned here is Pierre d'Ailly (1350-1420), Cardinal of Cambrai, and a leading mover in the word of the Council.
3. Czech lords who attended the Council and attempted to defend the truth of Hus's teachings.

4. St. Catherine of Alexandria was a legendary Christian martyr of the fourth century. According to tradition the Roman Emperor Maxentius commanded fifty pagan sages to confute her, but she converted all of them to Christianity. Subsequently he appointed another fifty, with the same result.

5. The Feast of St. John the Baptist is celebrated on June 24. Hus was burned on July 6, 1415.

PETR CHELČICKÝ

After Jan Hus, Petr Chelčický (ca. 1390-ca. 1458) was the most influential teacher and writer the Hussite Reformation in Bohemia produced. Like Hus, Chelčický was influenced by the English theologian John Wyclif, whose writings were well known at the University of Prague. The violent nature of the times apparently prevented Chelčický from completing his theological studies at Prague, and he confesses to an imperfect knowledge of Latin. Hence, probably, he wrote in Czech, and his Czech style, based on the popular spoken language, is unusually vigorous and direct for the time.

Chelčický went much further than Hus in his attempt to reform the Czech Church and reassert the purity of the primitive Christian Church community. In this his thought approached that of the more radical Hussite reformers who gathered at Tábor in Southern Bohemia. But he broke with the militant Taborites over the issue of violence: the true Christian, he maintains fervently, never commits violent acts. And he abstains from the pursuit of riches and secular power, both of which Chelčický sees as incompatible with the pursuit of a truly Christian life.

The excerpt quoted here is the celebrated chapter on City-Dwellers, taken from Chelčický's best-known work, The Net of Faith *(Síť víry, written around 1440). The book contains a caustic portrayal of the human social and political order, which the author condemns almost totally for its bloodthirstiness, greed and lust for power. Not only does the work achieve eloquence by virtue of its vigorous, often popular style, but at times it presents the reader with sharp, colorful, sardonic portraits and tableaux.*

In a modified form Chelčický's teachings served as a basis for the foundation of the later Unity of Czech Brethren. Founded in 1457, it is the progenitor of the so-called Moravian Church in America.

The text as translated here is taken from Výbor z české literatury husitské doby, *1964, Vol. II.*

THE NET OF FAITH: ON CITY-DWELLERS

But the Teacher and Adversary,[1] who speaks of the founding of cities, says this: on account of the murder of his brother Cain made a city, the purpose of whose founding was that Cain might accumulate possessions acquired through brigandage and violence.

41

Thus he profited by his crimes and, through the invention of boundaries for the land and of weights and measures he turned simplicity of human life into craft or deceit, and so brought disorder. He first set boundaries for the land and enclosed towns with walls and, fearing those whom he and his men had injured and robbed, he gathered all into his cities. So Scripture and the theologians speak of the first founding of cities.

Therefore it is to Cain that the origin of cities and castles is attributed, and this because of murder, brigandage and violence, for Cain killed his brother Abel from hatred and thus became a fugitive and vagabond roaming over the earth, fearing for his life. Hence he built the first city and then plundered others and did them violence. And from his plundering he collected possessions. And for his villainous deeds he gathered evil men together and then built other cities, so that, settling these with criminals, he could defend himself against those whom he had robbed. Thus his deed of murder led to the founding of cities and his cities led to lawless plundering, for so many men could be kept shut up in cities, ready for war, only by plundering others and feeding on the plunder while warding off the victims of their violent deeds.

Thus cities and castles have their foundation with Cain, and they go on in the same track in which they were founded, for others could not dwell there, but only murderers and violent men, usurers, merchants, market people and swindlers, all of whom support themselves for the most part through dishonesty and avarice. And thus, having founded cities and castles and having settled them with a multitude of persons engaged in such wrong-doing, they must guard against the violence and dishonesty of others, and must ever be ready to murder, for they are ever in danger of acts of enmity and dishonesty and treachery on the part of others, for these are always prepared to reward their enmity with bloodletting, doing evil in exchange for evil. If their city is firm in its defense, they rob and do violence to others to gain wealth, and with these lawless acts they incite many against themselves, and thus bring on war. And they will end up so entangled in their deeds that they can do nothing but shed blood and rob, fighting and making their ramparts ready for warfare. And if they do not have the strength and courage to rob others or go to war, still they are ready to resist violence on the part of others. Thus the great multitudes of city-dwellers are prepared to resist these lawless acts

42

by giving their own lives: desiring to kill others, they are themselves ready to be killed.

Thus, founding cities for the preservation of their lives and possessions, they must shed blood, and, seeking to shed that of others, they must yield their own to the same end. Thus the estate of burghers and nobility which preserve their lives in castles, fortresses and cities, ever thirsts for their brothers' blood and crushes them with violence. Therefore their estate is the estate of Cain, the first murderer. And with this manner of life their killing cannot be excused, for placing their trust in the life of the flesh and the success of worldly goods, they must build cities for this and people them with a multitude of citizens, and they must impart to the city those qualities which will enable it to achieve its original purpose, and hence they take care to surround it with walls and ever watch over it by night and by day, lest anyone capture it by storm and deprive them of their lives and take away their possessions. And if anyone shows his hostility to them, seeking to take something or harm them in some way, straightway without delay a bell calls them all together, the multitude of city-dwellers, to the killing. And if they catch thieves or traitors they will not forgive them and will not rest till they have spilled their blood.

Hence from the time of their founding a multitude of cities has come into being, so that men can preserve their lives and property in peace. But these cities can exist only at the price of the blood of each man who ventures to make assault against them, and thus the city's concern is increased that the populace must ward off all sorts of calamities in order to have a refuge in which to hide. And affirming their intention to protect their lives and property in peace, the city populace thus forgets God's commandment, which speaks of love for our neighbor; for the sake of his peace, which the well-fed man wishes to preserve behind his walls, men will plunder some by force, others they will deceive in different ways and do violence to their enemies, taking their lives. For since they wall themselves in and dig moats to prevent any assault on their lives and possessions, they must ever do evil for evil, warding off assault. Hence all those commandments must be transgressed which ordain sufferance for Christians and which forbid defense of life or revenge. "Dearly beloved, avenge not yourselves, . . . 'Vengeance is mine; I will repay,' saith the Lord.

43

Therefore, if thine enemy hunger, feed him; if he thirst, give him drink. . . ."[2] All these commandments of God must be transgressed when the populace seeks to protect its lives behind walls in peace. And how many injustices they do among themselves, going to law in contention and judging according to pagan laws, often turning justice into injustice and thus transgressing Christ's commandment that we add our coat to our cloak and that we leave off contention and suits at law. Thus none of Christ's commandments concerning our neighbor or concerning God is kept by the city populace: evil hides behind walls and good is bogged down in knavery. For the dear Jesus says, "This is God's love, that you should walk in his commandment."[3] And elsewhere we cannot have his grace, except by preserving his commandments. And when this one thing is lacking in the city crowd, then of course that crowd does not have God's grace nor can it have it, since it dwells in such numerous transgressions and in such confusion that God's commandment cannot come to it from any side. Thus the prophet says a terrible thing of them, "I have seen evil and adversity in the city. By day and by night on its walls there is evil, and toil is in its midst, and injustice and violence; usury and deceit have not vanished from its streets."[4] A rather hard characterization and an ugly thing to tell for those who wish to carry out everything with honor. Let those fat, wise cities expunge it themselves from their records! If anyone equal to them were to send them such a document on official business, they would take offense; those hearts so swelled up with pride would have said: "They're abusing us who are good; they're abusing the town officials!" . . .

And since in these cities there is nothing of God's commandments, so there is transgression on the part of all. Hence there must be all sorts of sin in them, fruitfully multiplied. Vengeance and blood, which has been infused into them from the very time of founding moats and walls, then pride in rank and family crest walks at their heels as they go to find covetousness—this is what the city stands on—gluttony, drunkenness, sensual passion (fornication, adultery, lewd lovemaking, illicit affairs), with which each harms the other in their wicked intercourse, with their base speeches to one another; thus they dig pits for one another to break each other's heads. Pride trapped them in all things like a net, for they are the race which is adorned with coats-of-arms.[5]

44

They wish to carry out all things with the honor and praise of this world, vying with rulers in their appearance, clothes, food, drink, houses, rooms, bedrooms and beds. And whatever they do, they always say, "Let it be done with honor." Only that their toilets smell less honorable than country privies, even if they wish to have everything else with honor. But their greed is inborn, that each of them should seek to acquire property wherever he can. For a multitude of walls surrounds their small properties and a great number of these, and they are determined to have fat tables like rich men, high and costly houses and many other things. Hence they must acquire wealth by whatever means they can, with shops, markets, trading, taverns, crafts, usury, deceit. . . . Hence usury is frequent and open here,[6] and is resorted to in the pawning of estates and fields for a definite term, that the borrower should have use for the money he has borrowed. But should he be unable to pay at the end of the term, he loses a valuable thing for a small loan. And of these usurers' tricks there are many known to those who enrich themselves at the expense of others through usury, and the rich devour the poor with these artifices; it may not be open usury, but is disguised as some supposed favor or some act of justice.

In many ways the true father of the city folk is Cain, for he transformed crude existence into a subtle art through the invention of weights and measures; hitherto the simple folk bartered things for one another without weighing or measuring, until Cain determined, for the profit of the wicked, that things should be sold according to weight and measure. Thus the city folk have great cunning, and possess weights and measures which show more for their own benefit and less for the other's. And even if weights and measures must go to the town authorities for inspection, they still set prices that are too dear. Whatever they weigh or measure can all be falsified: spices can be stored in the damp or mixed with powdered stone so that they weigh more; so too grain can be mixed with weeds. . . .

So a great blow has been dealt the faith when such vile knavery has been intermixed, through the action of Antichrist,[7] into the true faith. . . .

1. Teacher and Adversary (Mistr Protiva), a reference to the English theologian John Wyclif (d. 1384) and his treatise on the political order, *De civili dominio.* Chelčický here supports Wyclif's position as a critic and adversary of the papacy.

2. A paraphrase of Romans 12:19-20.

3. A very loose paraphrase of I John 2:5.

4. This Biblical "quotation" cannot be identified, though in style and subject matter it would seem to derive from the Prophets, e.g., cf. Ezekiel 7:23.

5. I.e., the nobility.

6. Usury was officially forbidden in the Middle Ages, since Church teaching opposed it.

7. Hussite reform thought regarded Antichrist as already ruling in the world, and associated his rule with the secular power of the Church, to which Chelčický adds the State as well.

ANONYMOUS: THE VISIONS OF JIŘÍK

This colorful work is known in both Latin and Old Czech versions; the oldest Czech manuscript extant dates from the late fifteenth century. The work belongs to the popular genre of visits to purgatory or hell, a genre which found its culmination in Dante's great Divine Comedy. *The prototype and a principal source for the present work is the Old Irish* Purgatorium Patricii *(St. Patrick's Purgatory): in the present narrative the hero Jiřík is said to visit "the Purgatory of St. Patrick," i.e., he follows the same route discovered by St. Patrick when the saint supposedly entered purgatory from the world.*

A number of spurious details have been added to the original treatment: the hero Jiřík, a nobleman, serves the King of Hungary as governor of the city of "Troy" in the land of "Apuleia." Jiřík, who is characterized as cruel and severe by nature, runs the danger of being eternally damned, but his visions bring him to repentance and finally to salvation.

The First Vision of Jiřík

. . . When Jiřík had passed through the door, he stepped out onto a plain, fair to behold but without a single tree; on it he saw nothing but the earth itself and the path along which he was to make his way. Going along this path, he came to a chapel, very white, and he was greatly pleased, supposing that some pious man must dwell there. And when he saw no one in the chapel, at once he prostrated himself in the doorway in the form of a cross, praying to God and saying, "Lord Jesus Christ, I beseech thy great mercy, help me a sinner and give me counsel how I am to act according to thy will."

And when he had finished praying, three men appeared to him, very like one another in countenance. And they were clad in robes white as snow. At this Jiřík was greatly amazed, for he saw three men, but it was as if there was only one, so like one another were they. And he tried to decide whether in fact there were three men or only one, and he could not decide. And one of them stepped forward and said to him, "What do you seek?" Jiřík

47

replied, "I seek the mercy of Our Lord Jesus Christ and the Holy Trinity, and of the Holy Virgin Mary and all the saints."

And the man answered him in anger, saying, "You cannot have it, for you must suffer much more than the light punishments you have already received."

Jiřík replied to this very humbly, saying, "I care not for earthly things, for through the power of Our Lord Jesus Christ's crucifixion I will receive his mercy."

Hearing this the elder, seeing his piety, took him by the hand and led him into the chapel and blessed him with the sign of the Holy Cross while he recited in his ear all those future events which were to occur to him in that wilderness, good as well as evil, such as visions and the temptations and seductions of the Devil intended to lead him astray from the true faith, and he said, "When the devils appear to you in any form whatsoever, make the sign of the Holy Cross and say these words, 'Lord Jesus Christ, Son of the Living God, be merciful to me a sinner,' and at once the devils will vanish. And when you come to an iron bridge which belongs to the realm of Hell and which ever shakes, an angel will appear to you. And conjure the angel, saying, 'I conjure you by the power of the Living Son and the power of the crucified Jesus Christ to tell me whether you come from Heaven or from Hell.' . . . And the angel will show you the torments of Purgatory as well as the joys of Heaven."

It seemed to Jiřík, as that old and honorable man was speaking, that he was being nourished with heavenly food. Then the three men began to sing very sweetly, and they sang for a long time of the passion of Our Lord Jesus Christ. And when they had finished their singing the three men gave Jiřík their blessing and disappeared, and he was left there alone. . . .

The Ninth Vision of Jiřík

And when Jiřík went a little farther along the plain, a devil appeared to him in the person of his father Kryzafan with three other devils in the persons of his brothers, and of these Jiřík had loved most of all his youngest brother Štěpán. Then the devil in the form of his father greeted him joyfully and said, "Welcome, dearest son, to these unknown lands! For it has been a long time since we have seen one another. And so I must tell you that we have died and our souls have been taken from the misery of that other world and set here, in this path and this dwelling place, and all for a single cause. For Jesus Christ was a great tempter and seducer from the true faith when he said he was God's son, which he most certainly was not, for after the crucifixion he did not rise from the dead, and he is a great deceiver. Know this for certain. And I lived for a long time and for a long time was deceived thus. But then being assured of the falseness of that faith by the Holy Spirit, I abjured that false faith. Therefore you too, dear son, for I wish to redeem you as I have myself from eternal damnation, I ask you to abjure Christ and his faith, for he cannot help you. If you do not do this, and do not deny his faith and him, I promise the God of Heaven I will at once cut off the head of my son Štěpán, your brother."

Hearing this speech, Jiřík was frightened, but he did not abjure his faith. Whatever other strong temptations he had undergone, this was the heaviest. And Jiřík said, trembling, "I believe that Our Lord Jesus Christ is the son of the Living God and has risen from the dead and rules forever."

Hearing this the devil in the form of his father Kryzafan fell into a great rage and seized the devil in the form of Štěpán and, taking out a sword, cut off his head. Jiřík, seeing that these temptations were from the Devil, sighed to the Son of God and said, "Lord Jesus Christ, son of the Living God, be merciful to me a sinner."

And at once those four devils vanished before him. . . .

The Seventeenth Vision of Jiřík

Then St. Michael the Archangel took Jiřík by the hand, saying, "Do you wish to see the torments of Purgatory?"

Jiřík answered him, "I have already seen terrifying and wondrous things in Purgatory."

St. Michael replied to him, "Whatever things you have seen, great and wondrous though they be, are far less than those things I will show you."

And taking Jiřík by the hand, St. Michael said, "Follow in my path."

49

Then he led him up to the side of that hellish abyss. And Jiřík saw there men and women, in the body as they are in the other world, and one soul had belonged to a king, and there were people of other classes there as well. And the devils greatly tormented these souls. And Jiřík saw some souls hanging by the neck from fiery ropes and cords, and serpents crawled over the face and on all sides of the body of these and stung them fearfully, and in whatever member or part these souls had enjoyed pleasure against the law of God and against righteousness, that part suffered torments in Purgatory, inasmuch as those persons had come from that other world here without doing sufficient pennance for their sins. Jiřík saw countless souls tortured on iron wheels turned without cease by devils, and this was the torture of the proud, for the sin of pride. And again he saw countless kettles and pots full of molten gold and silver, burning hot, and in them saw souls chained with fiery chains, and devils held their mouths open and poured molten gold and silver into their mouths, and this was the torment of the greedy, of merchants and others who had turned away from God for uncertain gain, and of those fornicating women who had sinned for the sake of money, selling their bodies for gain. And he saw the souls of men and women wearing fiery spikes over their navels, and the chains of these reached to their loins, and the devils rolled these about like millwheels, and this torment is for lechery, for whatever member sins in particular, that member must suffer in particular. And Jiřík saw them hacking at countless souls and cutting away all the limbs on all sides of the body, and this torment is for anger and vengeance. And there are many who in this world do not wish to forgive their enemies, but seek vengeance on them with all their heart. And Jiřík saw souls sitting at a table, and they were given to eat as food poisonous beasts such as snakes, scorpions and frogs and whatever else is poisonous. And alongside that table there flowed a stream full of all substances which can melt in great heat and burn such as pitch, grease and oil, and from the repulsive liquid of this stream devils gave the souls to drink, and this was the torment of the sin of gluttony, that is to say of those who violate the fast of Lent and the vigils of the saints, which fasts are fixed in the Holy Church's canon law. And Jiřík saw souls the breasts of which the devils pierced with sharp swords, and this is the torment of those who envy their neighbors or anyone else in some honor or profit, and who are therefore cast down in their hearts. And Jiřík saw some souls in a house in which there were all sorts of serpents of different kinds, and these serpents had sharp stings in their foreheads with which they stung the souls, and this torment was for the sin of complaining in God's service, and this is set in particular for monks and priests who complain or who are lazy in this world, for they must hold to their vows. . . .

The Thirtieth Vision of Jiřík

St. Michael left Jiřík and ascended into Heaven. And Jiřík beheld how St. Michael and all the saints and Mary, the Mother of God, besought the Lord for the soul of Jiřík's mother. And God at once heeded them. And Jiřík saw that his mother was absolved of all torment, and he gave ardent thanks for this to the dear God.

* * *

Then St. Michael came to Jiřík and took him by the right hand, and in his left hand he held a golden cross. And at that moment all that Jiřík had seen vanished. And St. Michael led Jiřík to the door through which he had entered here. And this was the final hour, the sixth of the day, so that in all he had spent twenty-four hours there. . . .

51

ANONYMOUS: THE TALES OF OLOMOUC

Didactic narratives, often provided with a specific moral explication, were popular in the late Middle Ages and early Renaissance. The prototype collection is the so-called Gesta Romanorum *(Tales of the Romans), which originated in Latin in Switzerland around 1300 and circulated all over Europe, sometimes in vernacular translations. The sources of these tales are largely unknown, but many derive from the oral traditions of various peoples. The purpose of compiling this and similar collections was to provide priests with a body of didactic tales and anecdotes for use as illustrative material in sermons; as such they were known as* exempla *("examples" or "illustrations").*

Exempla were compiled in Bohemia during the fourteenth century, but most of these are in Latin. A Czech collection, the Tales of Olomouc, *so called from the Moravian town in which the manuscript has been preserved, dates from 1482. The compilation as such may be original, but the tales apparently are not, and most of them have parallels in other literatures of Europe in the late Middle Ages.*

As time went on, such tales often lost their original didactic character and assimilated more elements of eroticism, popular satire and humor. At times their exemplary character seems to have served as a pretext for masking or making acceptable secular narratives that otherwise might not have been tolerated. It should be noted that such exempla *later served as a source for the writing of Chaucer and Boccaccio.*

The translation of two of these Olomouc tales is based on the text as published by Eduard Petrů in Olomoucké povídky, *1957.*

No. 21. *A Very Fine Tale About a Roman Emperor*

There was a certain emperor in Rome to whom the Lord pleased to give, in his grace, an empress blessed with good manners and habits, and fair in countenance. Between them there was no improper loving or anything physical in nature, but they dwelt in grace, living virtuously and justly, fearing God.

Then it occurred to the emperor that he wanted very much to go over the world to visit the tombs of the holy fathers. He asked the consent of his empress, to whom he entrusted the realm, and of his brother, a youth, and took his leave.

Then the youth, the emperor's brother, for the sake of the empress' beauty, fell in love with her and began to speak improperly to her. And when often he would give her no peace and she could not rid herself of him in any other way, she promised to give in to him. And she commanded a tower to be built, and in that tower she placed two young men and two young women to serve that youth, the emperor's brother, and pull all things needful for him up by rope. Then the empress appointed a date when she would meet him in that tower to be there in secret with him, and so they agreed. And the youth was very pleased with this. Then the youth went into the tower and the virtuous empress, locking the tower door after him, returned to her own apartments.

The empire remained in peace until the coming of the emperor. When she heard that the emperor was coming home, she was most glad and ordered all the princes and nobles and friends she had with her to go out to meet the emperor and prepare the place of meeting. And she commanded that the emperor's brother be released from the tower without questioning, that he too might go to meet his brother. But he ran to meet the emperor before her and slandered her to the emperor most shamefully. When the emperor asked him why he looked so pale and so ill of countenance, his brother answered him, saying, "My beloved brother, your base empress had her will with one man, then with another, and she wished that I too do so with her, for everyone has had his will of her who desired her, after your departure. And I could not prevent this nor could I even bear to behold it. So I went off to a tower and stayed there until you came."

Hearing him speak things he so little expected to hear said of his empress, the emperor took leave of his senses with great grief and sorrow, and fell from his horse to the ground. After a long time he arose, as though bewitched, and again mounted his horse. The next day the empress met her emperor with a great multitude of people. And when she tried, as was proper, to embrace the emperor, he gave her a mighty blow, so that she almost fell down. And calling two retainers, he said: "No speech is required with an evil daughter. Take her into the forest and cut off her head."

And when they had brought her to the place where they intended to cut off her head, they saw how fair her face was, and they said to one another, "Before we cut off her head, let us have our will with her, for there is none fairer in all the world." And she gazing up to Heaven with tears began to beseech God that he please to acquit her, and Mary as well, the Mother of God. And at that time the dear Lord God caused to pass by there a certain wealthy nobleman who had been to Rome to pray at the tomb of St. Peter and the other saints. As they rode past they heard how her voice sounded through the forest, and they first supposed it was some wild beast caught in a trap. They urged on their horses and saw her, with her fair face, and the two base men clutching at her; at once they cut them to pieces on the spot and asked her what the cause of this event might be. And she, hiding her rank, humbly begged the nobleman to take her and make her his servant, according to his honor and the order of his house. He was very glad to fulfill her request. And he brought her to his estate, where his lady welcomed her very affably. And taking her in, they entrusted her with the care of their only son. And she treated him with greater care than if he were her own, and she served the Lord God, not heeding the needs of the flesh, that is, despising lewdness.

But even here the Devil did not cease to tempt her, though he could not overcome her. There was at that lord's court a knight, and he was the lord's brother. He wished that she would love him, and tempted her with many speeches and promises that she would marry him. But she answered that she did love him for the sake of the duty she owed to her lord, but that she could not marry him. Hence this wretched, evil and dishonorable man took thought as to what he could do to that noble lady that she might lose her life or be driven away, since she had spurned him. So he came to her, instructed by the Devil, early in the night while she was already asleep. And the child, the son of the lord, lay beside her. Then he took his knife out of its sheath and cut off the child's head and, bloodying her hands, left the knife there. And she slept through it all. And when the blood had flowed over the bed, it reached her side. Then waking up, she was greatly frightened. And when she cried out, the mother and father, concerned for the child, started up in haste and came to their son's room with a light. And seeing him slaughtered and the bloodstained knife lying by the woman, they were seized with great grief, along with all their servants, so that no one could describe their grief. Then that sinful murderer came and, as if purifying himself and weeping, he sought to destroy her, the poor innocent, and he said to his brother, "You have brought a base woman here, one condemned in another land.

At the least have her burned to death; she has earned that because of your son."

Nor wishing to destroy her, the noble lord and his lady ordered some seamen who were close by to take her to another land. She, the poor woman, came with the lord's retainers to the shore, weeping and tearing her hair. And when they were sailing over the high seas, seeing that she was fair of face, they tried to persuade her to let them have their will. And when she, loving virtue, did not wish to yield, they said: "Choose one of these two things: either yield to our will, or be drowned in the sea." And she replied that she would rather be drowned than that their will should be fulfilled. Then they altered their first intent, and set her on an island which lay before them, and this according to God's will.

She was awake all night, and only towards dawn, from great grief and faintness because she had been fasting for three days, did she fall asleep for a little while. And in her sleep the sweet Virgin Mary appeared to her in marvellous beauty, and said, "Now you have endured enough hardship for the sake of your intention to preserve your chastity in marriage until this very day. You shall be freed of all temptation, and it shall be made manifest what wrongs you have endured. When you arise tomorrow, dig under your head for a certain root. And when you give it to lepers to drink, they will be healed in God's name." The woman awoke, greatly consoled by the vision, and singing hymns she began to dig for the root. Then at the third hour sailors sent by God came toward the island. And when she called to them, they sailed toward her. And when they saw an honest woman, they took pity on her and sailed to the shore to get her. And she seeing that one man who got off the ship was a leper, made a powder of some of the root and gave it to him to drink. And drinking, he was at once made well.

Then her fame spread to all parts. And she happened to come to the city where that vile murderer was, the one who had killed his brother's son when the child was sleeping beside her in the bed. And he fell ill with leprosy. The people, begging her and employing great inducements, brought her to him, but no one recognized her. Then the brother of the leper besought her to help him, and to take for her help whatever she wished. And she promised him help on condition that he confess all his sins before his brother. Then he confessed many things, but concealed that sinful deed which he had done to her. Then the woman again said

56

that it would not avail him if he did not reveal all his sins, or if he concealed any kind of mortal sin. And his brother, whose son he had killed, told him, "Open your heart and confess everything you have done to me of which you are guilty, and God will forgive you." Then bursting into tears, he confessed all that he had done. Hearing it his brother was seized with violent terror, and grieved more for the loss of that most noble lady than for the death of his son. Then she spoke to him and said, "Dear Lord, it is I; I do not reward evil for evil, but I give back good for evil." And in a second she returned him to health. And they started to beg her to stay there and to marry the man she had healed. But she refused and, going away, came to Rome, healing lepers on her way. And in Rome no one recognized her. And there too she healed many lepers.

At that time the emperor's brother, by God's will, fell ill with leprosy. She was brought to him, and again no one recognized her. And to him too she commanded that he confess his sin against her and against the emperor and the All-Highest. When he heard the confession the emperor burst into tears and began to beat his breast and to bewail his sins. And everyone who was there began to weep, sorry for the virtuous and noble empress. Then she could endure their tears no longer and, having first healed the youth, she told them who she was. It is no easy task to tell what joy the Romans felt. And the emperor wished to take her again as his empress, as raised again by God from the dead, and all the Romans wished this as well. But she, having another intention, said to the Pope, "In my sorrow I promised the Lord not to live with any man again, but to enter a convent and there live in chastity till my end comes. Hence, O man of God, unless you clothe me in sacred garb, you will answer for me on the Day of Judgment."

Then the Pope dressed her in the garb of a nun. And so she ended her holy life and then went to her dear Lord.

No. 35. *A Very Fine Tale Concerning a Witch Who Was Worse Than the Devil, and How She Brought Good Husbands to Hate Their Wives*

A certain husband and his wife lived in harmony together. And the Devil was moved to envy, and labored for three years,

57

seeking to bring disharmony between them, and could not. And he observed to himself that there is no one more clever than an evil woman. And he went to see one wicked woman and asked her to accomplish their temptation and if so, he would pay her for it. And she told the Devil, "If you give me five shillings, I will keep them at odds for the rest of their lives." The Devil said, "Truly, if you do it, I will give you even more than that."

And she, gladdened, went to see the good woman. And greeting her, she asked, "How do you and your husband get along together?" She answered, "Very well, and with love." The evil woman replied, "You are deceived, for your husband loves another woman more than you. And if you wish things to be well again, heed my word: on Thursday at midnight, when your husband is asleep, take a scissors, cut off six of his hairs, and place them on the threshold. And if you do this seven times, he will soon come to love you again." And she promised to do all this.

Then the evil woman went to her husband, greeted him and said, "How do you and your wife get along together?" He replied, well. She said, "You are deceived, for your wife loves another man more. I must warn you that this Thursday, at midnight, she will try to kill you. But if you should wake up then, she will make some explanation."

Hearing this, he refused to believe her. That base woman then answered, "Try it, you will see if I am deceiving you." The husband answered her, "I will do what you say."

And when it was Thursday at midnight, the good woman's husband pretended to be asleep, and the wife then began to look for scissors to cut off the six hairs. And her husband, seeing this, was seized with rage and killed his own wife. And when he had killed her he came back to his senses, regretful that he had killed her. Then taking out his own sword, he killed himself.

Then that wicked and base woman, seeing that both of them had perished, came to the Devil to receive her fee. But the Devil, standing off from her, said to her, "O you wicked whore, you have done more than I asked of you. Get away from me!" And flinging the money toward her, he said, "Go, accursed, base woman, for even the devils in Hell fear you in your evil." And at once he took her to Hell. And our dear Lord Jesus Christ and the good Lord God preserve us. Amen.

ANONYMOUS: THE TALES OF BROTHER JAN PALEČEK

These tales, lively examples of popular Renaissance wit and humor, probably had their origin in oral tradition; they were finally collected into a single cycle, probably in the first half of the sixteenth century. Their hero was a real person, a courtier of knightly rank named Jan Paleček who served as jester, advisor and confidant to the Hussite King of Bohemia Jiří z Poděbrad (reigned 1458-1471).

It is difficult to tell to what extent these anecdotes are based on a real historical personality and on real events, but without doubt popular migrant motifs entered into the formulation of the final cycle. One can discern a number of diverse popular literary traditions which were strong in Central Europe in the early Renaissance period: the tradition of the wise fool who gives his master good advice; the tradition of the rogue who is disrespectful of authority and wealth and who protects the oppressed common people; the tradition of the saint who lives a life of purity—the last tradition conflicts considerably with the first two, and its appearance here may well have been motivated by the fact that the original Paleček was a member of the Protestant Unity of Czech Brethren, and his fame was very likely celebrated among members of that sect, as the anti-Catholic tone of the work also suggests. On the other hand, the slight hagiographic coloration of several of the narratives may also have resulted from a need to mask elements of burlesque humor and criticism of authority.

The entire cycle consists of twelve "paragraphs" or anecdotes, of which six are given below. The text of the original as translated here is taken from the version prepared by Rudolf Urbánek and published in the Czechoslovak Academy of Science's Příspěvky k dějinám starší české literatury, Prague, 1958.

The paragraphs which tell the deeds of Brother Jan Paleček, a gentleman of the rank of knight, a very noble man and very dear to the king and precious to each good man, though held by the world and those who esteem it to be a fool, since he could not but speak the truth to everyone. . . .

Paragraph Two. Once when Brother Paleček was out riding with the king near Prague, Paleček asked, "Brother King! Whose is this fine village with fish ponds and fine meadows?" The king replied, "Brother Paleček! It belongs to those poor people of the Hospice of the Holy Ghost by the bridge." Then on Friday Paleček, without tarrying, went to that hospice to visit those poor people and to dine with them. At his table he had only soup, groats and small fish in jelly. And on a second Friday he went to the steward of the hospice, though he had not been invited, and dined with him, and at his table there was more than enough, and two kinds of wine, and young women. Not expecting this last dish, Brother Paleček rose from the table and ran off to the king and lamented to him: "O Brother King! It's bad there, it's bad, it cannot be worse!" And the king said to him, "What's happening dear Paleček?" "How can it happen, Brother King, that poor lords who own a fine estate must die of hunger, and their servants and stewards have more than enough?" The king said, "Where does that occur? It would not be good if the servants were to be better off than their masters." "Do you remember, Brother King, when we were riding outside Prague, I asked you whose was that fine village with fishponds and large meadows, and you told me that it belonged to the poor people of the Hospice of the Holy Ghost. And so I had to find out how they were enjoying their estate at their table. A week ago today I went to have dinner with them and ate: those poor lords have only soup and groats without fat, and small fish with many bones, in jelly. And today I was dining with their servant, the steward of the hospice, and we had more than enough of everything: there were several kinds of fish: with spice, fried, in jelly, baked, two kinds of wine, and young women as well. And so, Brother King, send for that servant and command him to give his masters fish with spice too, and to take better care of them from the provision of their estate, so that they should suffer no more from hunger and want, lest the King of Heaven punish you for injustice and for failing to take care of those poor lords!" And so King Jiří at once sent his chamberlain to the hospice and commanded that two kinds of fish, with spice and with jelly, be served, as is still done today.

Paragraph Four. In the Prague Castle the canons came from the church to stand before the king in their ash-colored hooded cloaks, and they spoke very respectfully and seriously of their wants. And Brother Paleček, going past those canons on his way to the king, grabbed at the tie-strings of one of the canons who was speaking for the rest of them to the king, and pulling the strings, he said, "How, how! Our people have turned their coats inside out, and it is not yet Carnival time." Then the speaker grew ashamed and said, "King, I beg you, tell this good man not to interrupt us!" Then King Jiří reluctantly came forward and said, "Brother Paleček! Why don't you let these good priests alone?" Paleček said, "Brother King! Those are priests? I beg you, do not wonder at me! I thought that they were fools at Carnival time, for at Carnival people like to wear their coats inside out."

Then the king ordered a letter to be written to Rome, to be sent along with those canons. The chancellor came up to the king and asked what title he should use to address the Pope. And the king said, "Write to him as is the custom, 'To the Holy and Most Holy Father!' " Paleček said, "Brother King! Never employ such a title! You will be sorry for it." The king said, "Because that is the custom to write so to him." Paleček said, "Brother King! Follow truth and justice, as is proper for a Christian king, and not an unjust custom! I beg you, Brother King, if you should have to write to Heaven to the Lord God, what title would you give to his divine grace, when you employ such a title for the Pope?" And the king said, "Well, Brother Paleček, by what title am I to address him then?" Paleček replied, "Order them to write what is true and cannot be questioned: 'To the proud and most wealthy bishop and lord in Rome, this letter is to be delivered.' "[1]

Paragraph Five. It happened that a certain Lady Ričanská, a widow, became greatly angered with her village steward, and laid a fine upon him. He besought Paleček to intercede for him to obtain a return of the fine. And Paleček said, "I will do my best. Come on Sunday to the lady's; I will be dining there." The steward followed Paleček's command and came there and, entering the door, said, "God grant you a good day, lady, Your Grace, most gracious lady." Then Paleček said to him, "Oh, you base liar! Get out of my sight!" And the lady said, "Dear Paleček! Why do you speak so rudely to him?" And he said, "Because he is not speaking the truth. He is telling you that you are a gracious lady, but for him you are a cruel tyrant. But if he were to say, 'God grant you a good day, ungracious lady,' he would not be a liar. And hence, if you do not wish to have a liar, but a truth-speaking steward, return him his money and punish him not in his purse, but with words or with imprisonment, and so you will in truth be a gracious lady!" And so Paleček helped him recover his money from his lady.

Paragraph Six. Brother Paleček had the custom of going in summertime to help the poor in the villages build and repair their huts, but he would go to dine at the great houses of either the squires or the bailiffs. Some of them said to him, "Dear Brother Paleček! You haven't worked here! Why then are you eating here?" and Paleček would say, "Ah, do you know what, Brother? When you will be as poor and as needy as they are, then I will help you. And when they will be as rich as you, then I will go to their house to eat." And so everyone welcomed Paleček to his house.

Paragraph Nine. On Good Friday Brother Paleček was always merry and sang as if it were Easter, and on the days of Shrovetide he wept greatly and prayed to God, keeping them more sacred than other days and often regretting that excess and gluttony that prevail among people at that time.

Paragraph Twelve. Brother Paleček had many garments throughout the year, for whenever he saw a man who had no garment and had many children and was in want, he would take off his own garment and give it to him at once and then going to the king, he would say, "Brother King! Give me a garment; I have given mine to the Lord God." And the king would say to him, "Where have you seen the Lord God, that you have given him a garment?" "Brother King! Have you not seen it in Holy Writ: 'If you have done it unto one of the least of these, you did it unto me.' "[2]

Many other remarkable things and many deeds of charity were done by Brother Paleček which are not described here. . . . Ane he reminded King Jiří that at every turn he should fear the King of Heaven and rule, govern and care for his people in peace and in justice. And so during the reign of that king he came to the end of a life that was pious and Christian, he took leave of the king and entrusted his soul to the Lord God. After his death King Jiří greatly grieved for him and did not live long. Amen.

62

1. King Jiří, as a Utraquist, was attempting to conciliate Rome, while Paleček, as a member of the Protestant Unity of Czech Brethren, had no reason to venerate the Pope.

2. St. Matthew, 25:40.

J.A.Comenii
DIDACTICA OPERA
OMNIA.
Ab Anno 1627 ad 1657.
continuata.

JAN AMOS KOMENSKÝ

Together with Jan Hus and Thomas Masaryk, Jan Amos Komenský, better known under his Latin name of Comenius, belongs to the truly great representatives of his nation, all three of them philosophers and writers. Komenský represents, both for his people and in some respects for European thought in general, the culmination of the humanist philosophy which grew out of the Protestant Reformation.

Born in 1592 in a small town close to the border between Moravia and Slovakia (then part of Hungary), Komenský grew up in Moravia. His father was a miller, a member of the Protestant Unity of Czech Brethren, the Church the son was to serve all his lifetime.

In 1608 Komenský was sent to the school of the Brethren in Přerov, and in 1611 he went to Germany to continue his education, finally entering the Protestant University of Heidelberg. He returned to Moravia in 1614, was consecrated a priest of the Brethren, and began a career as a teacher in the schools of the Unity. The coming of the Thirty Years War to the Czech lands and the persecution of the Czech Protestants forced Komenský to flee to Bohemia, where he took refuge in 1623 in the castle of a wealthy Czech Protestant Lord, Charles the Elder of Žerotín. The end of religious toleration in the Czech lands forced Komenský to emigrate in 1628, going with other members of the Unity to settle in the town of Lešno in Poland. There Komenský was elevated to the rank of Bishop of his Church, the last Bishop of the Unity, in 1632, and there the Labyrinth was written and published in 1633. Komenský played an active role in encouraging the Protestant powers, in particular Sweden, to resist the Hapsburgs, but the Peace of Westphalia, concluded in 1648 among the warring powers, confirmed the Hapsburgs in their rule of Bohemia and brought an end to his hopes for a Czech Protestant restoration. In 1650 he went to Hungary to engage in educational projects for the Prince of Transylvania. He returned to Lešno, but in 1656 the Polish-Swedish War put an end to his residence in Poland, for a second time destroying his library. He settled in Amsterdam, where he died in 1670.

Komenský was a theologian and philosopher who had one foot in the Middle Ages, the other in the Renaissance. He used the classical disciplines revived by Renaissance humanism, including logic, rhetoric and philosophy, to construct a grandiose synthetic philosophy in which all human knowledge and science were to be brought together under an apex of spiritual faith and God's rule of the Universe. The plan for such a philosophy and synthesis of

65

the sciences was projected by him in the outline for his Pansophia, *but the individual parts were never completed.*

Komenský *was able in his lifetime, however, to reform thoroughly educational theory and practice in a progressive spirit of toleration which looked forward to modern times. His numerous treatises on education and his textbooks were published and republished in his own times, and have had an enormous influence on pedagogical theory and practice ever since. He viewed the human mind as a* tabula rasa, *a "blank slate" on which the teacher could write what he would, so that education could be employed as a vehicle of human progress toward perfection. He argued for reward rather than punishment as an inducement to learn, and insisted that the beginning stages of education should be carried out in the pupil's own language, though higher stages should continue in Latin. He was especially concerned with language education, and produced several textbooks and multi-lingual glossaries. One, called* Orbis pictus *(The World in Pictures; 1653-1654), introduced and popularized the principle of visual education by incorporating illustrations of objects next to their names in a number of languages.*

Komenský's Labyrinth of the World and Paradise of the Heart *is perhaps the outstanding example of the genre of religious allegory so popular all over Europe in the early Baroque period (John Bunyan's* Pilgrim's Progress *is a later example of the genre known to English-speaking readers). The world is depicted by Komenský as pure vanity; all pursuits and professions, even religious ones, are found empty and frivolous. Horrified, the pilgrim flees from the world he is being conducted through and, taking refuge in a small chamber and looking within himself, he finally finds salvation within, in the inner "Paradise of the Heart." The first, satirical part, the "Labyrinth of the World," is longer, more vivid and graphic than the second, though Komenský was also able to endow the less rhetorical and more spiritualized second part with considerable conviction and expressive power. The first part shows a strong link with the satire of Petr Chelčický, whom the members of the Unity of Czech Brethren regarded as their spiritual leader. Komenský's satire is constructed on the almost uniform use of neutral or derogatory language, so that activities we normally accept as purposeful are stripped, through linguistic distortion and the use of metaphoric imagery, of their proper significance and made to seem purposeless and even frivolous, e.g., books are called "boxes," while a library is described as something like an apothecary's shop; learning is depicted as ingesting food which can easily upset our stomachs, etc. Komenský describes the world as a walled city of six main thoroughfares surrounding a central open market place; each is overshadowed by the Castle of Fortune at one end and the Palace of Queen Wisdom at the other, but both these figures of authority are fraudulent.*

66

Chapter Ten, "The Pilgrim Examines the Estate of the Scholars," is translated here complete according to the second edition of 1663, published in Amsterdam.

THE LABYRINTH OF THE WORLD AND THE PARADISE OF THE HEART

Chapter Ten: the Pilgrim Examines the Estate of the Scholars: First a General View

And my guide said to me: "Now I understand your state of mind and where you are drawn: among the scholars with you, among the scholars, that life is attractive for you, the easiest, most peaceful, the most useful life for cultivating the mind." "Yes, it is so," said my interpreter. "For what can be more pleasant than that a man, abandoning and not heeding the labor and toil of the physical body, should deal with the very study of all sorts of exalted matters? This is in truth that which makes mortal men resemble immortal God and makes them more nearly equal to him, so that they become omniscient, following all that goes on or has gone on in the sky, on earth, in the abyss, and knowing all; though it is true that not everyone attains an equal perfection in such knowledge." "Take me there, why delay?" I said.

And we came to a gate which they told me was called that of the Disciplines: it was long, narrow and dark, full of armed guards to whom everyone who wished to enter the Street of the Scholars had to present himself and request an escort. And I saw that crowds of people, in particular the young, came up and were at once subjected to various painful tests. The first examination in every case was of what sort of purse, what seat, what head and what brains (which they judged from the nose's snot), and what sort of skin each had brought. If his head was of steel and his brain of quicksilver, his seat of lead, his skin of iron and his purse of gold, they approved him and at once gladly let him go on. But if anyone did not possess these five things, they either ordered him to turn back or, predicting a bad outcome, reluctantly let him pass. And I said in astonishment, "What is so important in those five metals that they look for them so diligently?" "Much," said

The severe entrance examination

67

my interpreter. "If one's head is not made of steel, it will burst; if he does not have quicksilver brains, he will not have a mirror there; if he does not have an iron skin he will not survive the training; if he lacks a leaden seat he will not hatch out anything but will scatter it all; and without a purse of gold, where would he find the time and where the teachers, living and dead? Or do you suppose that such great things can be obtained for nothing?" And I comprehended where his hints pointed: to this estate one must bring good health, wit, persistence, patience and capital, and I said: "Then one can say in truth, 'Non cuivia contingit adire Corinthum.'[1] Not every log can have a solid core."

Difficulty and painfulness of gaining admission. Memory created by artificial means

And we went on through the gate, and I saw how each guard, taking one or more of them as his assignment and going off with him, blew something into his ears, rubbed his eyes, cleaned out his nose and nostrils, pulled out his tongue and trimmed it, folded and unfolded his hands and fingers, and I don't know what all he did. Some even tried to bore a hole in the head and pour something in. At which my interpreter, seeing my fright, said, "Do not be astonished, for scholars must have their hands, tongue, eyes, ears, brain and all other inner and outer senses different from those of the race of stupid men, and hence these are reshaped, and this cannot be done without difficulty and unpleasantness." At that moment I looked and saw how much the poor man had to suffer in that reshaping. Not of their purse nor of their skin which they were forced to present, do I speak. Often, to be sure, a fist, a stick, a cane or a ferrule could be found on their face, their skull, their back or under their seat, until they shed blood, and almost all the time they were covered with stripes, scars, bruises and calluses. Some men who were just looking in at the gate noticed this before they presented themselves, and backed away; others tore themselves from the hands of their reshapers and ran. A smaller number persisted until they were past the gate; I too, since I had a taste for that estate, underwent reshaping, though not without difficulty or pain.

Each scholar assigned a pass

When we came out of the gate I saw that each man who had been shaped and polished was given tokens by which it could be recognized that he belonged to the estate of the scholars: an inkhorn behind his belt, a pen behind his ear, and an empty book for recording knowledge. And I too received these things. Then Inquisitive, my guide, said to me, "Well, now you have four side

68

roads, which lead to philosophy, to medicine, to jurisprudence and to theology—where shall we go first?"[2] "As you judge wise," I said. He said, "Let us first go to the square where all assemble, so that you can look at them together, and then we can walk through the different auditoriums."

And he led me onto a square and behold, here were crowds of students, masters, doctors, priests, young men and gray-hairs! Some of them held together in clusters, speaking together and disputing; others squeezed into the corners to avoid being seen by their fellows. Some (which fact I observed quite well, although I could not tell it to them there) had eyes and no tongue; others had a tongue and no eyes, some had only ears and were without eyes and a tongue, etc., so that I comprehended that here too people were imperfect. Seeing that all of them were emerging from some place, and then entering again, like bees swarming forth from a hive or back into it, I proposed that we too enter there. Even the scholars lack for something

So we went in: and ah! there was a great hall, so large I could not mark its end, and all its sides were filled with shelves, compartments, boxes and cartons, so that a hundred thousand carts could not have hauled them all away, and each of them had its own inscription and title. And I said, "To what sort of apothecary's have we come?" "To an apothecary's," my interpreter said, "where medicines are kept for ailments of the mind: it is called a library. Just look, what infinite pillars of wisdom!" So looking, I saw the spines of scholars approaching and circling in different ways about these medicines. Some, selecting the best-looking and most appealing boxes, pulled bits of them out and swallowed these, gradually chewing and digesting them. Going up to one of these, I asked what he was doing. He answered, "I am making progress." "And what flavor does that have?" I asked. He replied, "Until it is well chewed in the mouth, it tastes bitter or sour, but then it turns quite sweet." "But why eat it?" I asked. "It is easy for me to carry it inside," he answered, "for that way I can count on it more surely. And can you not see the benefit?" I looked hard at him and saw that he was thick and fat, red in color, with eyes which glowed like candles, his speech was well considered and his movements agile. And my interpreter said to me, "But just look at these!" The library described

I looked and oh, some of them were handling the medicines very greedily, ever stuffing into themselves whatever came to their Abuses in study hands. Observing them closely, I could not see that their color or their body or their girth gained anything, save the belly itself which was swelled and stuffed: and I noticed that whatever they stuffed into themselves seeped out again, undigested by them, at both ends. Some of them fell into convulsions and lost their senses; some turned pale and wizened and lay dying. Others who observed this pointed it out to each other and told each other how dangerous it was to deal with these books (for so they called these boxes). Some fled; others begged their fellows to deal more carefully with the boxes. Those so prompted did not stuff the boxes inside themselves, but hanging many pouches and satchels both in front and behind, they crammed the boxes into these (especially those called by such titles as *Vocabulary, Dictionary, Lexicon, Famous Quotations, Oratorical and Poetic Phrase-Book, Fixed Phrases, Commentary, Scriptural Concordance, Herbarium,* etc., each one as he judged this to relate to his subject), and carrying these about they would take them from their pockets and from there into their mouths or onto their pens when there was need for them to say or to write anything. Remarking this, I said, "These, I suppose, are carrying their knowledge in their pockets?" My interpreter replied, "Memoriae subsidia,[3] or have you not heard of such books?" I had heard them praised by some, and that it was said that only with their aid could generally recognized things be learned. Perhaps so, but I remarked other disadvantages and inconveniences. It happened in my presence that some dropped and scattered their boxes, while others, putting them away, lost them to fire.[4] Ah, what running about there was then, what wringing of the hands, what wails, what cries for help! No one wished then to discuss his subject any longer, or to write or preach of it, but hanging their heads they walked about, cowered and flushed; by begging or purchase they acquired new equipment from others who had it. But those who had their "equipment" within their heads did not have need to fear such an accident.

Students who did not study Meanwhile I had observed others who did not stuff their boxes into the pockets, but carried them away somewhere to their rooms: following them there, I saw how they made fine cases for them, coloring them with various colors, and sometimes even encasing them in silver and gold, arranging them on shelves and, pulling them down again, looking at them, then again assembling or disassembling them, coming up or drawing back as they pointed out to one another and to other people how fine it all looked, especially on the outside; some gazed long at one title or another so that they could name it by heart. And I said, "What foolish sport is this?" And my interpreter said, "Dear brother, it is a fine thing to have a good library." "Even when you don't use it?" I asked. And he: "Even those who only revere libraries are counted among the scholars." And I thought to myself: "Just as those who collect hammers and tongs without knowing what to use them for are counted among the smiths." But I did not dare say this, lest I be ridiculed.

Before we returned to the hall, I noticed that there were ever more and more of these apothecary containers on all sides, and I looked to see from where they were bringing them. And I observed that they came from behind a curtain, and when I too went behind, I saw many lathe-turners working: each of them sought to outdo one another in shaping boxes diligently and attractively out of wood, bone, stone and various materials and, filling them with ointment or medicine, delivering them for general use. And my interpreter said, "These men are worthy of all sorts of praise and veneration, for they serve their race by supplying its most useful objects, so that they do not grudge any labor or effort in multiplying wisdom and learning and thus they share their glorious gifts with others." And I conceived a desire to see from what and how they (that which he called wisdom and gifts) were made. And I noticed perhaps one or two of them who collected fragrant spices and herbs, cut them, grated them, distilled them and prepared various medicaments, potions, syrups and other remedies useful for human life. On the other hand I noticed others who merely collected from other vessels and transferred the matter into their own, and there were hundreds of these. And I said, "These men are only pouring water back and forth." My interpreter answered me: "So knowledge is multiplied. For cannot one and the same thing be remade differently, again and again? And to the original thing one can always add something or other." "And ruin it, too," I said in anger, seeing that obvious adulteration was going on. One of them, attacking vessels that were plainly not his in order somehow to fill his own, diluted what he took as best he could, with an admixture of slops; another added all sorts of waste, such as dust and sweepings, to thicken the mixture so it would look like a new product. At the same time they affixed labels that were more

Abuses in the making of books

71

magnificent than the original had possessed, and shamelessly, like any other quack, each praised his own wares. It was strange for me, and it angered me that (as I have already pointed out) rare was the man who examined the inner essence, but they kept taking everything, or at least they took indiscriminately, and if any of them were choosy, then it was only insofar as the outer shape and the title were concerned. And then I comprehended how it was that so few of them came to any inner originality of mind: for the more of those medicines anyone gulped down, the more he suffocated, turned pale, faded and wasted away. I observed here a very great part of these fine remedies which were fated never to undergo any use by men, but became the lot of moths and worms, spiders and flies, dust and mould, and finally of trash baskets and back corners. Some feared this and as soon as they had finished preparing their medicines (some even sooner, before they began to prepare them), they would run to beg from their neighbors prefaces, verses and panegyrics; they looked for patrons who would lend their names and purses to these new products; at once they adorned the titles and inscriptions as beautifully as they could; at once they added various illustrations and copperplates to ornament it all as floridly as possible; themselves they delivered it to those they met, handing it to them and even stuffing it into their hands, without their consent, so to speak. But I saw that in the final analysis even that did not help: multiplication had gone too far. And I was sorry for some of them who, though they could have had unblemished peace, devoted themselves to this quackery without any need or profit, thus risking their own good name and bringing harm on their friends and loved ones. But when I gave these my opinion, I earned their hatred as if I had interfered with the public good. I do not mention how some prepared their syrups from poisonous substances; so many of such poisons were sold as medicines that I bore this disorder unwillingly, but there was no one to set things right.

Quarrels and disputes   Then we came out again to the Square of the Scholars, and ah! the quarrels, disputes, brawls and clamor! Rare was the man who had no scrap with anyone: not only the youths (which could be put down to their immature age) but the old men too were squabbling. For whoever considered himself more scholarly, or was held to be so by others, he began the more disputes and fenced, hacked, threw and shot at others around him till it was

72

terrible to look, though he considered that all this should bring praise and fame upon himself. And I said, "But what is this, for God's sake? I thought, and indeed you promised me that this would be the most peaceful estate, and I find so many disputes among them here." My interpreter replied, "Son, you don't understand: they are only polishing themselves." "What do you mean—polish?" I said. "I see wounds, and blood, and wrath, and murderous hatred for one another. Why, I did not see anything similar among any of the tradesmens' estates." "No doubt," he said, "Their arts are those of trade, slave-like, while these are free and liberal. Therefore, what those men could not permit themselves—indeed it would not be endured from them—these have license to carry out." "But how this can be called order," I said, "I do not know." It was true that their weapons did not, at first glance, seem so terrible. For the spears, swords, daggers with which they hacked and stabbed at one another were made of leather: they were held not in the hands but in the mouth. Their fire employed reeds and sand which took up dust dissolved in water;[5] their shot was made of paper. Nothing, I say, looked so terrible, at least on the surface, But I saw how, when anyone was hit lightly, he would jerk, cry out, writhe, run away, and thus it was easy for me to understand that this was no joke, but a real battle. Many of them would attack one fighter and press him hard, so that nothing could be heard but the sound of swords clanking around his ears, while a hail of paper shot fell on him; some, fighting bravely, defended themselves and scattered all their opponents; others, overcome by the blows, fell. And I saw here a cruelty unusual elsewhere: even those already defeated or dead were not forgiven, but all the more and all the more pitilessly did the others hack and lash at them, each at whoever could defend himself no longer, thus preferring to show his heroism. Some got along more peacefully, but even they were not entirely free from quarrels and misunderstandings. For hardly had anyone said anything, than someone else would arise to confute him; there were disputes, even, as to whether snow was white or black, or fire hot or cold.

At that point some interfered in this dissension and began to counsel peace, which gladdened me greatly. Word spread that all disputes would be submitted for settlement, and then arose the question of who would do this? It was answered that, by consent of Queen Wisdom, the most judicious members of each estate

Complete confusion in their ranks

73

should be chosen and power should be given them to hear the disputing sides. They should decide each matter according to their own judgment and should find for the side that is more in the right. And there gathered no small number of those who were to be or wished to be judges: first and foremost a great multitude of those who had differences between themselves. Among such I saw Aristotle and Plato, Cicero and Sallust, Scotus and Aquinas, Bartolus and Baldus, Erasmus with the men of the Sorbonne, Ramus and Campanella with the Peripatetics, Copernicus and Ptolemy, Theophrastus and Galen, Hus, Luther and others with the pope and the Jesuits, Brenz and Beza, Bodin and Weyer, Selidanus with Surius, Schmiedlein with the Calvinists, Gomarus and Arminius, the Rosicrucian Brothers with the advocates of false wisdom, and others without number.[6] These arbiters now charged that all petitions and complaints, proofs and counterproofs be submitted to them couched in as few words as possible, but the contentious disputants piled up such heaps of books that six thousand years would have sufficed to look through all of them. Hence the arbiters requested that these books be summarized briefly and that the summaries be accepted for the time being; in addition to this, should the necessity arise, full freedom would be permitted each one to explain and demonstrate his views at greater length. And the arbiters started to examine those books, and whatever they took up and read, they became a partisan of that work. And thus serious ruptures broke out among the disputants and peacemakers when one stood for one source, another for another. And so, resolving nothing, they all fled, and the scholars returned to their disputes, which brought me to the point of tears.

NOTES

1. "Not everyone can succeed in getting to Corinth" (i.e., not everyone can succeed or win), Horace.

2. These were the disciplines taught by the four faculties of the medieval university.

3. "Aids to memory."

4. Komenský himself twice lost his library and manuscripts to fire, the first time when he was serving the parish of Fulnek in Moravia when the town was burned in 1621 by the imperial forces during the Thirty Years War; the second time in Lešno, Poland, in 1656, during the Polish-Swedish War.

5. Symbolized here are pens, sand for drying ink, and ink.

6. These are all philosophers and theologians, most of whom lived before Komenský. They are arranged in pairs or groups to signify their involvement with one another in disputations, or the fact that one of them criticized the other.

CHRISTOPHORUS HARANT BARO DE POLZICZ ET BEDRUZICZ ET IN PECKA SCM CONSILIARIUS ET CUBICULARIUS ❀

Quo mea me quondam traxit fortuna, sequeh,
fact, Idumææ gentis ab orbe Redux.
Ne murare meum, si fors rimabere factum:
Me Mea delectant, Te Tua, Quemq Sua

J. Sandrart sculps.

KRIŠTOF HARANT Z POLŽIC A BEZDRUŽIC

The Renaissance opened up men's horizons and attracted them to travel; it also popularized the genre of the travel account with readers who perforce remained at home. Perhaps the outstanding Czech example of the genre (though there are a number of fine ones from the nineteenth and twentieth centuries) is the account, by Krištof Harant, of his journey to the Holy Land.

Harant was a lesser nobleman, a soldier who had taken part in the Turkish campaign of 1596 and received recognition from the Emperor Rudolf II for his heroism. Relatively well educated, and ambitious, he rose rapidly in wealth and favor. A convert to Protestantism, he was a supporter of the Protestant "Winter King" of Bohemia, Frederick of the Palatinate, against the Catholic Hapsburgs, and he paid for his choice with his life in the executions of 1620 which followed Frederick's defeat at White Hill near Prague.

Harant made his journey to the Holy Land with a companion, Heřman z Chudenic, in 1598. The trip was a traditional religious pilgrimage, and Harant displays the appropriate piety when he visits the holy places in Palestine; he is obviously excited to see sights known to him already from the Bible. Still, his interest is perhaps more taken by the colorful and exotic life he sees around him. A sense of relativism of values, perhaps derived from his study of the Latin classics, gives him a certain tolerance and respect for Moslem social institutions, which he frequently compares to his own, not always to the advantage of the European ones. He gives accounts of food and other pleasures, including the extensive description of Moslem bathing customs translated below. Strange animals and plants also fascinated him. Like Karel Čapek, he illustrated his own travel record, and the book, first published in 1608, contains some fifty woodcut illustrations based on his own sketches.

The present translation is based on the text published by K. J. Erben in 1854.

JOURNEY FROM THE BOHEMIAN KINGDOM TO VENICE,
FROM THERE BY SEA TO THE HOLY LAND,
AND FROM THERE ON TO EGYPT

Chapter 17

CONCERNING OUR RETURN TO CAIRO

. . . After the long time away we arrived at our lodging toward
dinner time,[1] and after dinner we agreed that, being so weary,
dusty and dirty from the road, we should go to a bath and bathe.
And hence we went with our interpreter to the bath which was
nearest to our inn, and which was only a few streets away. When
we arrived there, our interpreter asked at a distance from the
entrance whether anyone was bathing there, and the answer came
that there were women there. Then we went on to another, and
approaching it, we made interrogation as to which sex was bathing
there? And the answer came again that they too were women.
And we went on to a third, but there too we could not get in because there were women; and so to a fifth, a sixth and even more,
each time asking and seeking in the face of great hardship to find
an opportunity to bathe after our fatiguing journey on foot, and
we were already determined to return to our inn when we came
upon a bath in which, as we learned, men were bathing. We entered there and found, instead of a corridor, a vaulted space,
something like the ambulatory of a cloister, surrounding a court
or small square, which was uncovered and open. The old men
called it by the Latin name of *apodiarium.*[2] There we saw many
heathen Turks, always in pairs with one beside the other, sitting in
specially made niches in the wall which were half vaulted but open
from the front, on knee-high benches of stone spread with mats,
some dressing and others undressing. In the open court there was
a fine fountain, a quadrangular baisin of marble into which clean,
cool water flowed which they carried into the baths and wherever
else they required it and used it.

And while we were looking about to see where we could find
empty niches for ourselves, the bathman came up to us and took
us into one which was empty, and there he threw to us to serve as

a garment to cover our nakedness one blue rough linen cloth apiece, and he brought each of us a small brass washbaisin in which we could take water and rinse ourselves. Coping with all of this as best we could, we were conducted by the bathman into the bath, and our clothing, like that of others, was carefully guarded by a person assigned to this task and called since ancient times *capsarius.*[3] Now we viewed a remarkable bath, quite spacious within, entirely vaulted over and solidly constructed, paved with marble of various colors, and lined with the same material along the walls. In the middle of the vaulted roof there was a large window with fine glass panes through which light entered the bath. The benches and surfaces were of polished marble, and on them many people were sitting or lying on the floor. Around the outside of this bath there were also many recessed spaces, one after another, with doors which were closed, and our bathman led us into one of these, so that we could have peace there without any interference from the Turks, though for this luxury we had to give him something extra. This recess was like a little chapel and was well constructed: its bench and floor were also of marble, and on one side in the wall there were three brass spiggots: from one of these came hot water, from the second warm, and from the third cold water in sufficient quantities, so that we could turn them according to our pleasure. What seemed most strange to us was that neither in this small chamber nor in the great bath did we see any loose stones or holes, although the heat poured in there, and it was as hot as it is at home in a well-heated bath. After we had warmed ourselves and sweated a bit, the same bathman came to attend to us. He scraped and rubbed us hard with a rag which was wrapped around his two hands, as we are accustomed to do with a rough and well-soaped pouch. Then he told us to lie down on the floor and stretch out and he pulled us up and shook us in a strange way by the arms and legs as if he wanted to shake the souls out of us, turned them this way and that, and pressed our arms onto our spine, and then knelt on us with one knee and pushed down hard with it, all of which was no laughing matter, but rather terrified us, for we feared lest he might strain some joint or break some bone, though he dealt with us graciously enough, perhaps realizing that we were not used to such rough pleasures, for with others he would stand with both feet on their back and, clasping the man by the shoulders, would ride and slide his feet up and down his spine, and then do the same in front and on the sides until all his bones would crack. But he did not harm anyone who was accustomed to such treatment. If any of us at home should overexert himself and have a back strain, he will find that stretching and rubbing will ease the pain, and so here too their joints and bones seemed to recover and to feel better and fresher, and we too felt fitter and nimbler. Then he washed us and rinsed us all over except for our heads; they wash their heads along with their upper garments, since they have their faces shaved regularly with a razor and do not need to wash them on other occasions as we do. Thus, if we wanted to rid ourselves of the dirt on our heads, we were forced to wash them ourselves.

Such is the manner of bathing the Turks and other peoples who live in those regions have received from the times of the ancient pagans, who used baths a great deal for pleasure and who would rub their skin with oil and scented ointments and after sweating to wipe dry the skin, rather than employing them for washing away dirt. For it was first with the Asiatic peoples, devoted first and foremost to pleasures, that baths appeared, and then later they came to Europe, especially to Rome, which was at that time the capital of the Roman Caesars. There baths were built at great expense, like towns or castles, and in them were whole forest groves, ponds, arbors, inns, and in them all sorts of games, entertainments and amusements were carried on, to excess even, and whatever pleasures could be conceived for both the male and female sexes, these were all permitted so that the great lords or whoever else cared to spend his money on resplendent living and on vanities, would stay there day and night. . . .

In spite of this it is for other reasons the Turks are so diligent in bathing and washing. For according to their law it is forbidden to go to the mosque, or even to pray at home, without first washing all dirt from the body, and even if the body is already clean, still they must bathe it, because they believe that just as with elemental water and rinsing they wash away the outer dirt from their body, so they also cleanse themselves and rid themselves of their sins. . . . Their women, though they are always shut up in their homes and may not go out anywhere, or even look out, still for the religious purpose of bathing they go often to the baths that on the way they may deceive their husbands by turning off, according to the purpose or caprice, somewhere else, perhaps for lovemaking, or simply so that, strolling a little outside their houses, they can take the air. For their husbands, knowing that no member of the male sex may enter a bath where there are women, and that no one of the male sex may serve in such a bath, are free from concern and do not realize what roguery may go on, and does go on in a great degree, beneath the surface. Such was the reason why we had to roam so far from one bath to another, for strictly and on pain of death it is forbidden to enter a bath in which women are bathing.

They are especially fond of going to the communal baths, and there they often come together in groups, so that one can rub and wash another, and so they encounter many delightful pleasures: at times they ascertain in which bath or in which street a certain pretty person is to be found, be she maid or married woman, and they will go after her like any bitch might, even going far from home to visit a bath to look at her and inquire whether they may serve her, having no other service in mind than that usually performed by the male sex, for such women, inflamed and lecherous for their own sex, are described by Suidas and Martial, who call them *tribades*.[4] When they are to go to the baths, they dress themselves in their finest garments, and one of their maidservants carries a vessel on her head made of tin, or of silver, or of brass, in which they carry their bath costumes, garments and other finery, and all this they cover with a silken cloth trimmed with lace; another maidservant carries a carpet on which the lady will sit; another carries a basket or a coffer in which the lady keeps her jewelry and other things, and so on.

The entire population is permitted to go to the baths, and all are admitted gladly, even those who pay but little, and in some places there are even baths which are endowed with an income, and these provide remarkable comfort, and one bath is built more lavishly and grandly than another, and the one which we visited is one of the shabbiest, and they say there are several hundred of them in all in the city of Cairo. . . .

NOTES

1. Harant and his companion had made an expedition to Mt. Sinai, with its celebrated Monastery of St. Catherine.

2. *Apodiarium,* apparently a mistake for or a corruption of Latin *apodyterium,* the undressing room of a public bath.

3. *Capsarius,* originally, a slave who carried the satchels of a schoolboy; here, one took care of clothes in the baths.

4. *Tribades,* women practising homosexual acts; Lesbians.

Kryſtoffa Haranta z Polžic ꝛc.

177

mage korunu Biſkupſkau na hlawě. A wedlé něho ginj dwa Mniſſi / tosižto *Diaconus* a *ſubDiaconus* kterj *Ewangelium* a *Epiſtolu* zpjwali / tež ſe priſtrogili do *habitu,* ſlowe *Dalmatica,* o němž co wyznamenawá / pjſſe *Guilhel: Durand: lib: 3. cap: 11. lib: 2 c: 9.*

Kontrffekt Koſtela Hrobu Božjho.

A wyſſli ſme z té Kaply / Mniſſi napřed a my za nimi ꞏ a ſſli do Geſtyňky w které Hrob Božj geſt / a tu Gwardyan zpjwal welkau mſſi / wſſak pro vžkoſt mjſta, ſotwa ſme ſe Pautnjcy w Kaplicce před Geſtyňkau ſmeſtknali / a Mniſſi w Koſtele před Kaplickau zůſtali/a *Kyrie, & in terra, Patrem,* a giné wěcy zpjwali, Po wykonanj toho / dal Gwardyán wſſem požehnánj / a napřed wyſſel ſedwěma mnichy, kterjž *Epiſtolu* a *Ewangelium* zpjwali / a my za nim do Koſtela : kdežto po třikrate około Kaply hrobu Božjho/ zpjwagjce *Te Deum laudamus* ſme obeſſli/ a giž na wýchoz z Koſtela ſe ſtrogili.

M   Po dobré

82

BOHUMÍR HYNEK BILOVSKÝ

A celebrated and eloquent preacher, Bilovský was born in 1659 in Silesia. He served in the Jesuit Order for some years in the school attached to the Church of St. Bartholomew in Prague. Leaving the Order, he subsequently served as a parish priest in Písek and later in Moravia near Olomouc. He died in 1725.

Bilovský was greatly renowned in his lifetime for the eloquence of his sermons, many of which were published. In these, typical productions of the Baroque style of the Counter-Reformation in homiletics and other religious literature, he painted vivid pictures of the joys of Heavens and especially of the torments of Hell; his language, in spite of his penchant for Latin quotations, is popular and down to earth, and his style, for all its sustained emotional expression, relatively direct and straight-forward. He published a number of collections of sermons; the present example is taken from his Cygnea cantatio: Hlas duchovní labutě (The Voice of the Spiritual Swan; 1720). He also published devotional poetry and some hagiographical writing.

The text of the sermon as translated below is taken from Zdeněk Kalista, České baroko, Prague, 1940.

SERMON FOR THE SECOND SUNDAY IN ADVENT

Almost never does the merciful Lord punish the world for its sins or hold forth the whip of his just wrath against any land or kingdom unless he, kind Lord and Father, has given a sign by some unusual or at times unnatural means, in warning and admonition. We read the chronicles from the world's beginning, the sacred and profane histories, those of the Church and the State: throughout them we find cruel wars, cities destroyed by sword and by fire, kingdoms ravaged by famine, lands depopulated by plague, and almost always these events are preceded by some sign, if not on earth, then certainly in the heavens or in the air, whether on the sun or on the moon or in the motions of the planets of the comets.

I offer only one such example from Holy Writ, which we read of in the First Book of Moses at the beginning of the account of the Greek Deluge. God saw, Moses writes in Chapter 6, that

83

there was much evil done by men in the world, and he said, "I will destroy man and everything I have created for man's use, I will destroy, ravage and lay waste." So he appointed and gave judgment, and thus it was according to judgment that the just Lord acted. But not without a sign, for earlier as a sign of his impending punishment he had commanded Noah to build his strange ark of planed wood, three hundred cubits in length, fifty cubits in breadth and thirty cubits in height, to set in it a window, to make compartments and, along with other things, to provide for a door below in the side of the ark. According to commentators on the Holy Scriptures this work of construction lasted one hundred years. And this was a sign of God's impending judgment. But people did not grow better. They heard from Noah: "God will punish you for your sins with a world deluge, behold, here is the ark into which I will enter that I should be preserved together with my family." They saw how Noah gathered the beasts and the birds, male and female according to their kind, they saw how he collected all sorts of fodder into the ark, they noticed the clouds in the sky, the rain in the clouds, the water on the earth, and still they did not leave off their wickedness. . . . They did not believe the sign and, as if they were not doing anything wrong, they wallowed in lechery. Only then, after so many signs, did God send the world deluge, through which he buried the whole human race, save for Noah and his kinfolk, in one wet grave.

So God does not send his general punishment until a sign has preceded it. We have an instance of this in our own times. God punished us not long ago with the War with the Turks,[1] but not without a sign, for before that war we saw a comet of unusual size in the heavens. God punished the Austrians twice with plague, once long ago and the other time recently.[2] God punished the Hungarian Kingdom and Silesia and Poland, but not without a sign: we saw a sign in the sun when we experienced an eclipse of that luminary such as our ancestors had not remarked for many years. Thus God does not punish without a customary sign. But what are the signs which will precede the Day of Judgment? What are other signs, I say, compared to that sign of which St. Luke speaks in today's Holy Gospel: "Erunt signa in sole, luna et stellis"—there will be signs in the sun and moon and stars.[3] Nothing similar. Therefore I will expound that sign for you today and God grant that it be for the improvement of your manner of life and then for the eternal salvation of your soul!

A terrible and frightful sign of his wrath and his punishment the just Lord showed when he admonished Pharaoh through Moses and the ten plagues. The first sign and plague were bloody—the water turned into blood. The second sign was ugly and repulsive— frogs crawled over beds, dining tables, plates and into food, they swam in beverages, they peeped into slops. The third sign was the turning of dust into lice. The fourth the great swarm of flies. The fifth the plague on all sorts of cattle. The sixth the boils and blisters on both people and beasts. The seventh was the hail, when hail mixed with fire fell together and struck down every herb of the field and broke every tree in the land. The eighth sign, which came after the hail, was the plague of countless locusts which covered the whole face of the earth. After that came the ninth plague, terrible darkness for three days, so that no one dared stir from his place. The last sign of God's punishment was the death of every firstborn child, from the firstborn of Pharaoh to the first- born of a maidservant. A terrible and frightful sign! . . . But much more terrible than these will be that sign which on the Day of Judgment will foretell God's wrath. And therefore the Holy Church, on the last Sunday of Trinity and the First Sunday in Advent, reminds us that we should fear such signs and, fearing them, better our sinful life.

Thus the Holy Church acts like a cautious mother who ad- monishes her disobedient and unrepentant children, "Be silent, sit quiet, say your prayers, or the goblins will get you; Dad's got a whip, watch out!" In this way she frightens us with such signs of terror as goblins or the approach of an enraged father, but we, like unrepentant children, do not heed. Let us watch out then indeed when we behold such signs in the sun, the moon, or the whole expanse of the world!

On the sun, for as the Prophet Joel says, it will turn into darkness.[4] On the moon, for it will turn into blood; at the stars, for they according to Richard[5] and St. Augustine secundum visionem et apparentiam—according to appearance and to sight— they will fall from the skies! O horror, O terror! O sign as yet unseen! Pulchritudo huius mundi ignium conflagratione peribit— the whole beauty of this world will perish in fire. Glossa[6] says, "The sun was darkened, as if it were ashamed of the whole world when for the 40 days and 40 nights of the Flood the sun did not shine." But that dark sign, even, is nothing compared to those of the Last Day. The sun was darkened in the reign of King Pharaoh when for three days the blind world did not see. But that too was nothing. The sun was darkened during the Crucifixion of Jesus Christ, and the whole earth shook, but that too was nothing. There will be a greater and more repulsive sign in the sun on the Day of Judgment, on which one can say with St. Dionysius the Areopagite, "Mundi machina dissolvetur"—the whole world is inclining to its destruction.[7] . . .

And you, O Christian, will you wallow in sin and not fear the justice of God, and not take fright at that fearful sign? You are fearful of lightning, you are fearful of the thunderstorm, you take shelter from the storm and the weather, and you do not fear that last storm? Ah, can it be that you will run away too late, when not only those signs of which I have spoken till now, but also those which shall follow (some of these were taken from St. Jerome from old Hebrew writings and inserted in the total count of fifteen, which are to last for fifteen days) you will have seen and experienced.

On the first day of the fifteen all the sea and its waters shall rise over the land fifteen ells.

On the second day abysses will turn back and descend into the earth so deep that they will disappear and vanish.

On the third day they will return to their places, but, as if angry at sinners, they will vie with one another in a fearful fashion.

On the fourth day all the fish and whales, indeed all creatures and monsters of the seas will assemble over the waters and, as if they were bewailing their fate, they will all begin with one voice to roar and whistle.

The fifth day: all the birds and feathered creatures will fly down onto the fields, where they will remain without food or drink and give out mournful, hitherto unheard sounds. Do you wish to know the reason for this? Noted writers have remarked that they can foretell their end and that of the world by the talents and inspiration with which the angels have endowed them, and thus they will first thank the Lord God with their voices and then, against you, O sinner, and your ingratitude, will they voice their wrath. Oh, woe is you!

The sixth day: the terrible flame of the sun will rise in the west and move towards the east, from which the sea will take fire and burn like oil, but it will not be consumed.

The seventh day: all the stars and planets will shoot out such great fires that it will seem they have turned into comets.

The eighth day: such a great earthquake will occur over all the earth that it will turn to ruins all castles and palaces, towers and fortresses, houses and strongholds. Ah, where then will your house be, sinner? where your palace, king? where your fortress, commander?

The ninth day: all rocks from the mountains and from buildings will crumble to rubble, all the cliffs fallen in a heap will then be crushed and will burst.

The tenth day: all the trees of the forests and the orchards, plants and herbs will begin to exude blood, though they were preserved by God's divine power from the fire and water which had come before.

The eleventh day: all mountains, hills and knolls will turn to dust and will be levelled to the ground.

The twelfth day: all beasts, animals and other creatures which are still left in the woods, all like the birds before will crawl out of their lairs into the open with a great roaring, bleating, wailing and lamentation against you, O sinner, until your hair and all men's stands on end.

On the thirteenth day all earthly hiding-places and tombs will open from the east to the west, from the south to the north, and dead bodies will be thrust forth from them.

On the fourteenth day whatever is left of mankind will come out of the caves where they have taken refuge in their great fear, into the light but, as if they were intruders, they will run hither and yon, but will not speak or greet one another.

On the last day all will die, rise from the dead with the rest of us and be delivered to God's judgment.

Oh, frightful judgment! Oh, horrible sign! And are you not fearful, O sinner? . . .

NOTES

1. The war between the Turks and Austria of 1716-1718 is referred to.
2. The two plagues mentioned occurred in 1713 and 1679, respectively.

3. St. Luke, 21:25.

4. Compare Joel, 2:10.

5. Richard of St. Victor, a Scottish mystic of the twelfth century.

6. The reference here to "Glossa" is unclear. Perhaps Bilovský is referring to a manuscript gloss, i.e., a marginal note, though he apparently mistakes this term for an actual name.

7. Presumably this is not from the writings of St. Dionysius the Areopagite, but from the so-called "Pseudo-Dionysius," an anoymous writer of the fifth century A.D. who circulated his works as those of Dionysius.

KAREL HYNEK MÁCHA

Karel Hynek Mácha was born in 1810 in Prague, where his father was a miller. He attended a German high school from 1824 to 1830 (his first poetic attempts were written in German), and then the University of Prague, where he enrolled in the Faculty of Philosophy (1830-1832), and subsequently in the Faculty of Law (1832-1836). Though educated as a German, Mácha early came under the influence of Josef Jungmann's Czech nationalist circle, and beginning around 1830 he wrote in Czech. He was enthused by the European revolutionary movement of 1830 (which, however, did not reach Austria) and in particular he sided with the Poles in their uprising against the Russians, though many of his countrymen opposed the Polish liberation movement as a blow to Slavic unity. Mácha acted in Czech-language plays as an amateur. He loved to take long, solitary walks in the country, and these helped to inspire his early, surrealistic Pilgrimage to Krkonoše *(written 1833). He also made a trip on foot across the Alps to Northern Italy.*

On the completion of his law studies at the University, Mácha began a clerkship in law in the North Bohemian town of Litoměřice. Meanwhile he had taken a mistress who bore him a child, and whom he intended to marry. But, playing a heroic role in saving people from a fire, he exhausted himself physically and, developing pleurisy, he died in 1836 in Litoměřice at the age of twenty-six, on the very day his mistress was expecting him to come to Prague for their wedding.

Mácha's major work (and one of the very few published during his lifetime) is a long poem, May *(1936), combining themes of fate and doom, eternal recurrence, and Oedipal guilt in the murder of a father by his son. The poem's narrative is fragmented and the fragments set in a rich matrix of lyric and symbolic imagery; the action is played out against the landscape, first in a time of youth and love which, paradoxically, foreshadows age, torment and death. At the end of the poem the author quite literally identifies his hero's tragic fate with his own—in what may be considered a premonition of his own premature death.*

Besides May, *Mácha wrote a number of lyric poems as well as a short novel,* The Gypsies *(written 1836), which represents an interesting variation on the treatment of the themes of* May. *The tale* Marinka *(written 1834) is a romanticist attempt to cut across genre boundaries: it mixes a Goethe-like romantic figure of a Mignon—Marinka—fated to die and already turned toward death, with snatches of a real urban atmosphere of a poverty known to Mácha from his own existence in Prague. Prose is mixed with songs, and the construction, with its frame of an "Overture," an "Intermezzo" and a "Finale," is musical, whle the narrative itself is divided into two "acts."*

Pilgrimage to Krkonoše is a youthful work, derivative in part from German Romanticism, from which it takes its extravagant love of ecstatic imagery, ghostly scenes, and wild extremes of landscape, scenery and climate. Still, Mácha has achieved considerable originality as well as conviction of feeling, and there is something truly "surreal" in the wild nightmare fantasy he gives us. As in May, youth passes here suddenly and inevitably into age and death.

PILGRIMAGE TO KRKONOŠE

Evening approaches. A lonely wayfarer strode along a narrow path on the broad summit of the Krkonoš Mountains, below the peak of Mt. Sněžka.[1] The wind howled, as if Silesia were trying to speak to her Sister Bohemia across the ramparts which separated them. "How deserted it all is," the youth sighed. "Both bird and beast avoid this land, and not even the tree or the flower takes root here; only man presses ever higher toward the pure azure of heaven, and finds nothing here but the rustling moss of the cold snow." At that moment the wind carried a butterfly past his face; in terror the insect struggled vainly, fluttering its bright-colored wings, seeking to fly back down to the land of blossoms from which the stormy wind had torn it away. "Unhappy insect! You long to return to those many-colored meadows which were your cradle; you do not wish to be here, and against your will that same wind which once rocked you on the cheek of a blossoming flower now carries you off to the cold highlands—I said that man presses higher toward the bright heaven, and so he must," and he covered his forehead with his hand, "he must. Yield me that butterfly, O wind, I will take it back down again to that land from which you have torn it away." Just then he caught the butterfly, but in vain: the insect was cold already, destroyed by the winter that reigned there. Saddened the youth sat down on the edge of an isolated cliff, glancing out at times over an empty white meadow onto the fertile plains of Silesia, while at other times his gaze turned to the dark forests that covered the land of Bohemia. The youth was perhaps twenty; his black clothing clung tightly and revealed the slimness of his tall figure; his dark hair hissed in the wind around his pale cheeks, lined with a black beard, and his blue eye revealed its ineffable longing—so his whole figure seemed to be but an echo reverberating from the deserted cliffs in the evening twilight, an echo of the song, "Kennst du das Land?"[2] This was his first pilgrimage: scarcely four times had the sun visited the graves of the Czech kings in the Prague Cathedral from the time when he had taken leave of empty Vyšehrad.[3] Only twenty times had he seen the cold snow of the stiffened land melt into cool tears, and yet already on this his first journey he had learned that the world he was now entering was not the one his youthful imagination had promised him. With his heart full of longing he had entered the world, hoping that all the dreams his youth had adorned with rosy crowns he would now find turned into reality—if so he would have clasped the whole earth in his embrace—but the curtain dropped too quickly and he awakened from his youthful dreams. He wished to pluck a flower blooming in a moonlit meadow, and like a cold teardrop the night dew had wet his ardent hand. He had bent down toward a full-blooming rose, enchanted by its perfume, and had noticed that the bush that bore it grew forth from a premature grave; at dawn he had admired the snow-white glow of the lily but by nightfall already he had seen its silver-white crown droop to the damp earth. He sought for people such as lived in his dreams, and mere larvae with empty grins gazed into his sensitive eye. In short, he had sought to find the paradise of his dreams in this world, he had opened his arms to it, he had clasped the earth, devoid of love, to his burning breast. Terrified, he had tried to return to the realm of his childhood, but in vain he only wept for his fleeting dreams, and so, a solitary now, he sat in this wilderness, with blossoming nature far below him, unloved and loving nothing he lingered on this lonely cliff above the reddened mountains lit by the now setting sun. The sound of the angelus arose from the Czech lands and from the Silesian plains, meeting here and bringing the recollection of the days past more vividly to his mind—in his spirit flamed up the thought of her, beloved maiden—but a multitude of mountains and five rivers now separated them. "Did I say that I love nothing?" Oh, he still loved her—but too late, too late, she was now lost for him. She had risen for him like a morning star over the dark waves of his present thoughts, and those first rays had fallen back into his dark, dead night. But the thought that the one

91

star which was able to illuminate the paths of his journey with a rosy light was not his star, and that its rays only smiled thus at the darkness surrounding them so that they might soon be extinguished and so that they might kindle, even more powerfully, his longing for light—this thought cast him back down into the night of his earlier thoughts. Arising he gazed down toward the countryside, smiling in its evening gold, and his sobbing sounded loud through the quiet land: "You were my sun, but ah! you are gone forever, and never again will day dawn red over my life. A solitary pilgrim I will walk again through unending night, whose deserted silence only my own sobs will bring to life again. In total darkness I will stretch out my arms to those worthless figures and illusions of my dreams, until the crown of some solitary comprehending tree will welcome me for the night and then awaken me with icy tears from my burning dreams to a terrible reality, until my own hot tears stiffen into ice and my own dreams perish in an eternal sleep free from dreams. And then my final breath will mingle with the glow of twilight in the evening sky, and my last thought will spread, mixed with the light mist, over my land; then the rain will wash out and the wind efface the traces of my steps, as if I had never gone through these mountains—you, O nature, my grave, in self-deception will cover with grass the greener landscape round about, and you will laugh at me again as if I had never been here and as if my lips had never cried Good Night to these mountains!" He fell silent, and around him was silence, only the echo from the mountains towering around repeated his cry of Good Night—Good Night! The sun set behind the dark mountains; like a black cloud their peaks stood out on the horizon of the Czech Land, and behind the mountains on the other side there arose the suns of other worlds; in the fissures in the mountains it was already black night, on the plains there still lingered traces of twilight: like white spots the towns peered out of the shades of dusk. Over them circled light smoke which, lowering, crept over the face of the silent lakes in which were reflected the rising stars; here and there they were colored by the glow of fires burning along dark wiers. The evening was clear and pure, as it is only in the mountains; the moon was almost full, and its glow cast a silvery gleam on the snow-covered foreheads of the bluish mountains which towered forth out of the dark night like the pale heads of dead kings crowned with silver crowns. For a long time the youth stood thus, lost in thought, gazing at the silent land; all the stars were already celebrating the fair night, and he still lingered on his lonely cliff—it was cold, the cold wind howled amid the mountains and down below the forests murmured and the rivers rushed from the deserted mountains to the fertile plains; the moon stood high in its path and the youth had not yet stirred from his place. Just then a clock struck midnight, though he had heard nothing from that direction before; it seemed to be close to him even, and the dark sound of its striking was wafted, hollowly and terribly, along the broad summit, and it was echoed from the foreheads of the mountains until the final echo, dimmer and dimmer, returned, and then again all was silent. Quickly the youth looked about, and the glow of the moon played tricks with his tired vision—or was it a frightful reality that he saw?—it was as if the peak of Mt. Sněžka had spread out and was hanging directly above him: a fine Gothic cloister, now half ruined, with a magnificent church adorned its summit. A high flight of stairs led to the Gothic vaulted entrance, with slender columns, finely chiseled, in places broken statues stood by the tall Gothic vaultings through which the moonlight crept, while the rays of the stars shone through the ruined windows, shedding their silver on the remnants of smaller columns and other Gothic ornaments, or reflected from the images of various saints whose figures were depicted in the many colors of the stained glass, of which a few fragments still clung to the Gothic vaulted windows. On both sides stood tall towers, already half in ruins, adorned, like the whole edifice, with slender columns, human heads and the heads of various animals, with plants and fruit and with the figures of humans, animals, trees and so forth, but carved in the stone on such a fine scale that the highest ones could not be distinguished in the moonlight; all these figures seemed, in the quivering rays of light, to be living and moving about. In the middle of the church, on high between the two towers was the clock; on the face resembling an eclipsed sun the numerals shone like a starry lettering, and the bright golden hand shone like the moon in its last quarter, through the pale night, pointing exactly to midnight. Recollecting himself, the youth started to hasten upwards to the wall of the cemetery, which too was adorned in the Gothic style with the effigies and arms of those who rested there, and to go into the cemetery through its low entrance and thus up the high flight of stairs to enter the open church, in which on the high altar some mysterious light glimmered. But the more he tried to hasten, the more the high wind blew against his clothing, so that, as in a nightmare, it seemed that the more he essayed to come near, the more he remained at the same distance away. Thus morning approached, the wind quieted down a bit and he reached the wall of the cemetery at a time when the whole cloister shone in the rosy light of the rising sun. The doors of the church closed by themselves; coming up the youth entered the ambulatory of the cloister where he met a monk hurrying past. The latter spoke to the youth as if he knew him: "You come just in time, for today our dead brethren shall awake, and you can ask them all those things you have been so eager to learn." And then it dawned on the youth, or rather seemed to him that he had heard of that cloister, and so he already knew what was going to take place. The brethren of that cloister had amid their walls a large hall in which some of their number entered after certain rites; these stiffened and seemed to die, but each year on a certain day they came to life, and at the end of that day they became stiff again and remained so all year long until that day again returned, and so it went on until the end of the world. He followed the monk who was leading him and came into an antechamber that was pointed out to him. Along the walls around there stood a number of dead monks, their arms folded on their breasts, both young and old; their faces, pale in death, still betrayed a kind of terrible uneasiness. And he asked the monk whether they too were to come to life, to which the latter replied, "No, they will not be brought back! For those who enter the hall once a year to be revived are also free to leave it, and if they do not return to the hall, but remain here in the antechamber, they die and can no more be brought to life, and the next year they are buried. Life has become repulsive to those who are here, even life for but one day a year, and they prefer to sleep a sleep that will not be interrupted; when the sun reaches its zenith they will be buried in the cemetery, which you have seen next to the church. But now you must enter the great hall." He stopped speaking, and the doors of the great hall flew open. Through curtained windows the light fell faintly into the high ornamented Gothic hall, one of terrifying size. In the half-darkness there clustered here and there an innumerable multitude of dead monks, each in the position in which death had come upon him. One stood with hand stretched

94

out as if he had been recounting something; beside him another kept his dead eyes fixed on the first as if he had been engaged in listening to that speaker who had just lapsed into silence; a third was bending over to lift something; a fourth was kneeling with clasped hands, seemingly in prayer, and so on. And the monk gave the youth the following instruction and warning: "You must run about among these countless dead and propound various questions for them. Should you happen to stand still, they will die again, and will not come to life again until their dead brethren have been buried forever—nor can you remain amongst them more than three hours, or you will have to remain a whole year alive among those dead." And so the youth ran into the hall and in his course asked various questions of them, and they began to move, like shadows, not touching the earth, as if moved by the course of his running as by stormy weather, and in mysterious whispers they replied to his questions so that his heart trembled in horror. Before three hours had passed, he ran out of the hall, in horror he ran through the antechamber and found himself at the edge of a cliff rising over the countryside far below, but his eyes were unused to the bright light, and, as if wounded by the brilliant gleam of the late morning sun, they shed copious tears; he could not recognize anything around him, and a terrible pain clasped his heart. Noontime approached, his eyes grew dry and he recovered. The cloister bells rang hollow and dark, and the mournful hymns of the monks carrying out the burial ceremony reached his ear. The youth looked around and saw, through the cloister gate, a procession of monks now forever dead making its way toward him. Great grief and ineffable longing seized his heart when he saw how the live monks carried their forever dead brethren to burial, while the monks who were revived crowded out of the cloister gates a bit farther off. Sadly he turned his gaze to the luxuriously blossoming countryside lying below: in the distance it was lined by blue-gray mountains like the waves of the sea at night, while a black cloud sprinkled heavy rain on the blooming meadows encircled by those mountains. The grain, reaped, smelled pleasant and sweet on the fields below and on the summit of the mountains; the joyous clamor and dance of the birds in the groves and forests beneath him mingled with the noise of the waters, falling fast from the mountains into the valley, and into the mournful hymns of the monks. It seemed to him as if the gray mountains were whispering in the distance and a heavy rain were droning: "We raise our bright foreheads eternally, until we perish"; "We sprinkle dew on the faded blossom, so that it will not die, but bloom again and give out its pleasant scent!"; "We shall sleep a sleep without interruption!" resounded, as if the dead monks were mocking. A countless multitude of monks come to life again flocked over the mountain in all directions. The youth hastened back to the cemetery, anxious to behold the burial of those forever dead; he stepped aside, seeking to avoid the crowd which flocked toward him, but the shades come to life rushed after him; he stepped to the other side, and again the shades rushed after him and after him; he stepped back, and there too the shades followed him. And one of them said, "In vain you seek to evade us; the wind blowing behind draws us after you; stand still and the least gust of wind will blow us past you over the summit." The youth stood still and the monks crowded to the edge of the mountain, seeking to go down by the path—many a one hurled himself down from the cliff towering over the countryside; with ineffable longing their inflamed eyes stared beyond the dark mountains, but the cutting wind always drove them into a group along the summit of the mountain. The sun was setting—late evening was at hand—the grain smelled more strongly from down below, and a holy peace spread over the broad countryside. The sadness of the monks, gazing after the setting sun and after the dying twilight, cannot be described. But all in vain: the day of life of the shades was ended, and the wind drove the captive monks into that terrible antechamber.

It was cold night; along a narrow fissure between two mountains the pilgrim made his way with languid step. Across from him stood Sněžka in all its height; on its snow-covered peak there now stood only a solitary cross; the full moon shone through it into the fissure in such a way that the cross seemed to divide it into four equal parts. "Good night, good night!" the weary pilgrim whispered in a weak voice. Like a lost ray of moonlight there seemed to rise in front of him the pale figure of a woman; her dead eye was fixed upward toward the cross; her face was chalk-white, her bluish lips aroused terror, and her stiffened snow-white arm continually pointed with its finger stretched upwards to the ray of moonlight, though whether it was pointing at the cross or at the moon it was not possible to tell. At that moment the pilgrim rounded a cliff and Sněžka disappeared from his sight. The figure changed more and more, until finally a gray old man stood before him; his long gray hair fell around his dead face and mingled with the hair of his beard, white and falling down to his waist. A wreath of white and red roses was plaited in his hair. At his feet foamed a river, tumbling from the high cliff over him, in the white foam a black entrance loomed open and the old man's hand indicated that he should enter it. The pilgrim looked at himself: he was terribly changed, and his gray hair fell past his wrinkled forehead down his puffy cheeks and mingled with his white beard which reached down to his waist. Behind him flamed the early morning sky; he wanted once more to look back to behold its rosy color that gleamed golden on the path he had trod, but the wind moaned loudly and fiercely and spoke to him with mysterious words, and an unknown force pushed him forward, an ineffable longing drew him after it into an unknown land along an unknown path. The pilgrim followed the old man into the dark passage.

The fair morn rose over the deep vale east of the Krkonoš Mountains. Dark firs and pines stood on the mountainsides in dewy dress, from a high cliff fell a river into an etched out baisin, in which it was whipped up into white foam. But where it ran more calmly, its waters were already pure and clear, and its depths shone green with the color of a spring meadow. In these depths the pilgrim slumbered, the noisy fall of the water lulled him into a silent sleep, and the waves of the river swept in succession over him with a noise like the wailing of evening bells spreading through the quiet countryside. But no longer did they bring the sound of bells to the pilgrim's spirit as they had done before.

NOTES

1. Krkonoše, or the Krkonoš (Giant) Mountains, a range located in Northeastern Bohemia, along the Silesian border. Mt. Sněžka, the range's highest peak, stands 5,259 feet above sea level.
2. A famous song sung by the girl Mignon in Goethe's novel *Wilhelm Meister*. The land in question ("Do you know the land?") is Italy.
3. Vyšehrad, a high prominence over the River Vltava, once outside Prague but now inside the city limits. A traditional site of the citadel of the ancient Czech princes, it is now the site of a cemetery where the Czech immortals are buried: Mácha himself was re-interred there in 1939.

KAREL JAROMÍR ERBEN

Mácha's great Romanticist contemporary (though as a writer he matured only long after Mácha's death) was Karel Jaromír Erben. Erben brought to literature qualities almost the opposite of the gloomy, impassioned, self-dramatizing romanticism of Mácha. His faith in Czech nationalism, rooted in the soil and in popular culture, led him to seek for a conservative shared communal spirit and to oppose the restless and revolutionary individualism Mácha had preached.

Erben was born in 1911 in a small town in Northern Bohemia, attended high school in Hradec Králové, and subsequently the Faculties of Philosophy and Law in Prague, where he was a student at the same time as Mácha. He worked as an archivist: first as Secretary of the Bohemian National Museum and, after 1851, as Archivist of the City of Prague. In the revolutionary years of 1848 and 1849 he supported the Czech nationalist struggle and edited the newspaper Pražské noviny *in a liberal, pro-nationalist spirit. He died in 1870.*

Erben's literary activities are in a sense an extension of his life-long career as an archivist. He collected all kinds of folklore, and edited and published an anthology of Old Czech literature. His volume of Czech Folk Songs and Rhymes *(1864) contains some 2,200 songs, and is one of the basic sources for Czech folklore study. He also translated extensively from other Slavic languages, including the Primary Russian (Nestor's) Chronicle, and the great Old Russian prose-poem,* The Lay of the Campaign of Igor.

Using Czech and Central European folk materials as a basis, Erben created a cycle of ballad narratives of great power, Kytice *(The Nosegay; 1853; enlarged in 1861). They excell in their masterly grasp of folk speech with its potential incisiveness and pithiness, as well as popular poetic eloquence and force. A collection of* Czech Folktales, *numbering several dozen and never completed (published posthumously by Vaclav Tille in 1905) was in some respects an attempt to create a prose parallel to* Kytice, *though Erben's adaptations of prose tales were more restrained and closer to the originals than in the case of his ballads. The fairy tales that are finished, including the celebrated "Longman, Broadman, and Sharp-Eyes," and "The Three Golden Hairs of Děd-Vsěvěd," have become favorites not only of Czech children and adults, but have passed in translated form into the international repertoire of classic folk tales.*

THE TWINS

There once lived a king and a queen who had no children, and because of this they were very sad. Once when they were looking out of the window together, an old woman came with seven children, each one tinier than the other, and the smallest she cradled in her arms. She asked them to give her something, for she had nothing to give to her children. The queen burst into tears and wept until her heart almost broke, and when the woman asked her why she wept, she said, "How can I help but weep when I see you with seven children and you have nothing to give them to eat, and I have food to give them and I do not have a single child!" The woman told her, "Do not weep, O queen! You have an easy remedy for children. The king has a fishpond and in it many fish. Have one caught and cook it and eat it: whatever you don't eat, give to the mare, and what the mare won't eat, give to the bitch, and what the bitch won't eat, bury the bones in the garden."

When the time came, the queen gave birth to two fine sons, the mare bore two white-eared foals, the bitch two brown puppies, and in the garden there grew two canes like swords. The two sons of the queen grew, but not slowly like other people: when they were a year old, they were like boys of seven years; when they were two years, they were like boys of fourteen; and when they were three years, they were already as mature as other lads of twenty-one. They were so like one another that even the king their father could not tell one from the other.

Now that they were grown up, they went to their father and said, "Father, we wish to go out into the world!" "Go," said the king, "so you may experience something and learn something." Good then. Each took one sword named White-Ears and one dog named Brown and one sword called Keen,[1] and they mounted their white-eared steeds and rode off, they rode and rode until they

100

came to a thick forest. In the forest stood a great oak and in front of that oak the road branched in two directions: one went to the right, the other to the left. When the brothers came to the oak, they did not know which road to take. The elder said, "Do you know what, Brother, let's part. It isn't good for us to ride together: you go one way and I'll go the other. Let's each strike his knife into this oaktree as a sign we shall return here in a year and a day. If the one of us who comes back first finds the other's knife clean on both sides, he will know that the other is well; but if he find the other's knife rusty on both sides, he will know that the other is dead, and then he shall not wait, but shall go home by himself." So they took leave of one another, and the elder went off on the road to the right and the younger to the left.

First let us follow the elder.

The elder rode for a long, long time through the forest until he finally came out and reached a great city. The city was draped both inside and out with black silk in sign of grief. Near the city gate was an inn. He went in and asked the innkeeper the news and what the cause of mourning was? The innkeeper replied, "Oh, dear lord! You must be far from home if you do not know the misfortune we have here!" "What then?" "Do you see that cliff there in the forest, and below it a small chapel: there in that cliff a gigantic dragon has lived for many years, and each year we must bring to that chapel a maiden chosen by lot, for him to eat; if we did not do this he would crush us all and destroy our city. This year the lot has fallen on the daughter of our king. The king sent envoys to all four corners of the world, but no one was found who would kill the dragon and free his daughter, so that he could give that man his daughter in marriage and half his kingdom, for he loves her very much, because she is a maiden fair and good beyond compare. But till now no one has appeared to do this and tomorrow they are to carry her out to her death." "Then I will do it," said the prince, and at once went to the king and told him he wished to kill the dragon and free his daughter. The king rejoiced greatly at this and promised that he would give the prince his daughter in marriage and half his kingdom.

Next morning early they led the maiden to the chapel; the prince mounted his horse White-Ears, took with him the dog Brown and at his side girded on the sword Keen, and so rode to the cliff and stopped in front of the cave from which the dragon

101

was emerging. Suddenly the dog Brown began to bark, the horse White-Ears to rear up, and the sword Keen to jerk in the prince's hand like a living serpent; from the cave a voice sounded like thunder striking: "Is my food ready?" "It's ready," said the prince, "and there's loads of it!" Then the dragon stuck his head out of the cave. When he saw the prince prepared for battle, he roared until the cliff shook and the trees bent over, and sparks flashed from his eyes, smoke poured forth from his nose like two pillars and flame lashed from his head. But the prince did not delay and attacked him with the sword Keen, the dog Brown tore at him with his teeth, and the horse White-Ears bit him and kicked him with his hooves. For a long time the skirmish went on, till at last it was decided in favor of the prince and against the dragon. The dragon lay dead, two hundred feet in length, and blood poured from him like a river.

The king did not know what to do from joy when the prince brought back his daughter healthy and merry, and at once commanded that they should take the black silk down everywhere and cover the whole city with red silk in sign of joy. Soon afterwards the king fulfilled everything he had promised and gave his daughter to the prince in marriage and received him as his equal as king and his successor after his death. So for a time everyone lived happily and merrily, but it did not last long.

One evening the young king looked out the window and saw to the north a great light deep in the forest. The next evening he saw it again, and a third yet again. And he was greatly astonished and said to his wife, "A strange thing, my dear wife! We've been together almost a year now, and you have not told me yet the meaning of that light there in the forest which I see every evening." The young queen was greatly frightened and begged him, "Do not ask to know that, nor think of that, or it will be to your and to my misfortune!" But he had no peace and determined that the next night he would go to see what it was.

When it had turned dark already, the young king buckled on the sword Keen, saddled his horse White-Ears and took the dog Brown and rode into the forest to that spot where the light was shining. But the deeper he went into the forest and the closer he came to that spot, the more the light disappeared, until for darkness itself he could not go farther in that deserted and unknown forest. He climbed from his horse and, since it was winter, made a fire, added wood and warmed himself. Suddenly an old woman emerged from somewhere: "Oh oh oh, sir, it's cold, it's cold!" and she trembled all over with cold. "Come here, woman, warm yourself." "Oh oh oh, I'd like to, but I'm afraid of that horse and that dog of yours." "Don't be afraid and sit closer to the fire." "But then, good sir, just let me switch the horse and the dog a bit with this branch, to chase them away from the fire." She drew out a branch and switched the horse White-Ears and the dog Brown and at once they both turned to stone, and before the young king could realize it, she came close to him, switched him with the branch and he too at once turned to stone.

But now it is time to see what the younger brother is doing.

He had ridden over many foreign lands and seen many wonderful things. And when the year and the day were coming to an end, he set out towards home and came to that great oaktree in the woods where he and his brother had parted. When he did not find his brother, he pulled his knife out of the oak and was greatly terrified. The knife was all covered with rust on one side, but on the other it sparkled like glass. "Brother is neither alive nor dead," he said to himself, "but things are not right with him! I will go look for him." And at once he turned his horse around and rode off after his brother on the road to the right. He rode a long, long time through the forest until at last he came out and came to that great city, as his brother had done a year before, to the very same inn by the gate. The innkeeper, when he saw him, at once greeted him most politely and said, "Ah, Your Majesty! what anxiety you have been pleased to cause us! For three days we have been searching for you everywhere and Her Majesty, your beautiful queen, cannot be comforted." The innkeeper supposed it was the young king, for the two brothers were so like one another that no one could tell one from the other. From this speech the younger prince knew his brother had been here already and he knew that he had become king, but he did not wish to betray himself. And when word spread that the young king had returned again, the courtiers came for him and led him to the castle. The young queen ran to meet him with great joy, kissed him and said to him, "For three nights I have not shut an eye because of you and because of the fear I had for your sake, since you didn't return for so long, and because of what must have happened to you!" But he was silent and when she asked him where he had been so long, he made an excuse: "I was hunting, I came to the depths of the forest and was lost." So she was satisfied with this.

But when night came and they all went to take their rest, the prince placed the sword Keen on the bed between his sister-in-law and himself. The queen was very astonished at this and asked him what it meant, since he had never done this before. But he answered her, "I have made a vow not to touch you for three days and three nights. Do not ask why, fair lady, God willing you soon shall know!"

That very evening the prince had observed when he looked out the window that there was a great light in the forest to the north. The next evening he saw the light again, and the third yet again. And he asked the queen, "Tell me, fair lady, what that light in the forest, which I see every evening, can mean?" She was astonished at this and said, "But I asked you once already not to seek to know that, or even think of it, or it will be to your and to my misfortune!" The prince said nothing, but at once thought that there in the forest, at that light, was the place where he must look for his brother.

The next day when it had already turned dark, he buckled on his sword Keen, saddled his horse White-Ears, took with him his dog Brown and rode into the forest to the place where the light was shining. But the deeper he went into the forest and the closer he came to that spot, the more the light vanished, until he could not go on longer because of darkness itself. He climbed from his horse and since it was winter, he made a fire, added wood and warmed himself. At that moment an old woman emerged from somewhere: "Oh oh oh, sir, it's cold, it's cold!" and she shivered all over with cold. "Come here, woman, warm yourself." "Oh oh oh, I'd like to, but I'm afraid of that horse and that dog of yours." "Don't be afraid and sit closer to the fire." "But then, good sir, just let me switch the horse and the dog a bit with this branch to chase them away from the fire." Here she drew out a branch and switched the horse White-Ears and it at once turned to stone. But the dog Brown jumped away from her, barked and ran about the woman. The old woman switched at him with her branch, but the dog never came within her reach.

From the start the prince had kept a good watch on the old woman and saw what she was up to, and that she had already turned the horse White-Ears to stone. He jumped towards her when she started to run after the dog and all of a sudden tore the branch from her hand from behind. "Now I've got you, cursed old woman! And woe to you if you do not do what I order you: I'll have Brown tear you to pieces." "Oh oh oh, good sir! oh, oh, oh! I'll do whatever you ask, only give my branch back again." "Give life to these three rocks here and to my horse, and if you don't, old woman. . . !" "I'll do it, sir, I'll do it. Here is a glass with living water: sprinkle the rocks and they will come to life again." "You did the harm—you fix the damage!" The old woman was obliged to heed and when she had sprinkled the four rocks—the young king, the dog Brown and the two horses—they at once came to life again, as if they had awakened from sleep. "And here's your reward for your work!" said the prince and with a single blow cut off her head with the sword Keen. Suddenly it was as if lightning had struck, the earth shook and instead of the old woman a lovely young maiden stood before the prince so that he feared to look at her, and she thanked him that he had liberated her from a long, evil enchantment. "I am queen of this land," the maiden said, "and these are my subjects." And when the prince looked around, he saw in place of the forest a great and fair city, and from all sides people flocked toward him: old, young, noble, common, and all thanked him for liberating them and called him their king.

Then with great joy the two brothers returned to the castle, and the young queen could not believe her eyes when she saw that in place of one husband there were two, until the young king told her everything that had happened, and why he had placed the sword Keen between himself and her in the bed.

Soon afterwards was celebrated the bustling wedding of the younger prince and the queen who had been enchanted in the forest, and the festivities lasted three whole weeks. There was rejoicing and celebration for you, there was food and drink in plenty! He who has told this tale was also at that wedding, he ate tarts and drank wine: too bad he had only hunger and thirst for his trouble![2]

NOTES

1. English is inadequate for the task of translating the first two names given here, formed in Czech with an adjective plus the affective suffix -ouš. Roughly equivalent

105

would be "Whitey" and "Brownie," but these names lack any suggestion of the heroic. The name of the sword in Czech is Samorost, "self-produced," "self-generated," a concept which can hardly be expressed in English with sufficient pithiness to yield a name.

2. This is a common folktale ending in Slavic tales, and supplies a hint that the audience should treat the tale-teller with food and drink.

KAREL HAVLÍČEK BOROVSKÝ

Karel Havlíček, who added the name Borovský to commemorate his place of origin (he came from Německý Brod in southeastern Bohemia, today renamed Havlíčkův Brod in his honor), was born in 1821, the son of a shopkeeper. He attended high school in Německý Brod, and then enrolled in the Faculty of Philosophy of the University of Prague, where he studied from 1838 to 1840. In 1840 he entered a seminary, intending to study for the priesthood in order to use the office as a teacher and leader of the Czech-speaking people, but was soon expelled for his lack of religious belief. The Slavist Šafařík found him a post as tutor to the children of the Russian aristocrat and well-known Slavophile literary historian, Professor Shevyrev, and he spent the years 1843 and 1844 in Russia. His experiences there sobered him, and he realized that Czech hopes for liberation from Austria by Russia were vain, and that the Czechs must achieve freedom and social progress on their own account.

Returning to Bohemia, Havlíček devoted himself to newspaper work, and became editor of Pražské noviny, *as well as of its literary supplement,* Česká včela. *He used his editorship to achieve the political education of his people, since he realized that a well-educated citizenry was a first prerequisite for national political life. As a critic he worked to raise literary standards, and he mercilessly criticized contemporary Czech writing, which he found backward and provincial.*

During the revolutionary movement of 1848, Havlíček played a leading role as a liberal who sought to gain constitutional government and a maximum of individual liberty, but who distrusted the socialism of the more radical left. Forced to give up the editorship of Pražské noviny, *he founded* Národní noviny. *He served in 1848 as a delegate representing the Czech party in the new imperial Diet. But the failure of the Revolution brought back a stricter censorship, and Havlíček was finally arrested and exiled by the military police to Kutná Hora in Eastern Bohemia, where he founded another paper, the weekly* Slovan. *Again arrested, he was freed by a jury. Finally the police exiled him under "protective" arrest to the town of Brixen in the Tyrol. The Alpine climate proved too severe for his health; he developed tuberculosis and died shortly after the police permitted him to return to Prague, in 1856.*

Havlíček is the father of the Czech national press and its journalistic style. Practical, down to earth, straight-forward, he writes with great logic and clarity, and often with caustic wit and irony. Curiously, he had not a drop of romanticism in his make-up, and was strangely out of touch with contemporary literary trends as reflected in the writing of Mácha or of Josef Kajetan Tyl, the latter of whom he criticized savagely. But his hard-headed intelligence and realist sense served his nation well, and he laid the foundation of a journalistic style which matured in the later work of Neruda and Karel Čapek. And his political liberalism was a major source of modern Czech democratic philosophy, as with T. G. Masaryk.

Havlíček also wrote a number of extremely witty satirical poems, in a rich comic earthy language and with a hard-headed, down-to-earth view of life. His masterpiece is the unfinished Baptism of St. Vladimír, *ostensibly concerned with the Christianization of Russia in the ninth century, but actually a comic exposé of Austrian absolutist rule and the hypocrisy of the Church and clergy.*

The present article was published in Slovan *on August 10, 1851, at a time when Havlíček finally realized the complete failure of the revolutionary movement and the need to develop a new, long-term resistance to the re-encroaching Austrian absolute rule. It is characteristic of Havlíček's liberalism that he conceives legal resistance as strictly and literally "legal": for him the legal resistor must be scrupulous in not overstepping the boundaries of law in the slightest.*

ON LEGAL RESISTANCE

The best and most splendid examples of legal resistance are found in English history, and we have several times brought them to our readers' attention in *Slovan,* and specifically as models for our own action: Hampden and O'Connell.[1] Legal resistance is the

108

best means for defense of freedoms against greater force, for arousing a heroic spirit in the nation, and the first and unavoidable step for achieving true liberty. So long as a nation will not go so far as to demand, without flinching, the fulfillment of the laws and to oppose, heroically, with legal means every arbitrary and illegal step: so long is the nation not ripe for freedom or for the respect of the ruling authorities. It is a characteristic, unfortunately, which is almost innate in every power that it seeks to surpass its own limits, and if it find no resistance to that, then every law and every right will surely disappear in its face, and its will then constitutes the only law.

Legal resistance and all the benefits which derive from it are based on the fact that in almost every man there is an innate sense, given by God, for justice and right. Every man who has not been corrupted will be angered and filled with vexation if he sees that violence and injustice are done to anyone, and he is disgusted by anyone whom he sees commit an act of violence or injustice or anything against the bases of the law; anything against truth or right; anything against a given promise; under these conditions a man who is not corrupted will feel compassion toward anyone against whom illegal and unjust action is taken. Whenever, then, any official or organ of the government does anything illegal to anyone, we should not bear that injustice in silence or adhere to such comfortable precepts as "It's hard to swim against the current," but we should always oppose such injustice with every legal means, even if in so doing we undergo greater discomfort and more harmful consequences for ourselves than if we had borne the whole wrong in silence. If everyone bore every such wrong, every evasion or violation of the law silently and in complete passivity, in a very short time there would be no sense of law or legality. But the greater the uproar that each individual violation of law causes, the less often will the organs of the government dare to take such steps. For every government, even if it has not yet proclaimed it publicly, knows secretly and perfectly well that all power actually resides in the nation, and that the government is only a representative, a personification of that power of the nation. Every government knows full well that if the wishes of the entire nation are opposed to it, it will not stand long, and hence it must always guard against and prevent the whole of public opinion, or at least too great a part of it, from opposing it. But with each step, while

109

it violates its own laws, the government unavoidably antagonizes public opinion, and the more of such actions of the government reach public awareness, the more it hurts the government.

On this is based the tremendous effectiveness of legal resistance, especially in countries where constitutional and legal rights are not yet established. Through the use of good, intelligently led legal resistance to the government one can always achieve, if nothing more, at least a state in which the government loses confidence in its power to turn events back so quickly or so openly, so that at least in something it will preserve the laws, if only for the sake of appearances—this is already a great victory for future liberty. Examples and proofs of this we can see everywhere: there are, for instance, governments that treat their individual provinces quite differently, and all the more cautiously and therefore justly, the more enlightened the population of a given province and the more emphatically it demonstrates its desire for liberty. The more the population submits to the government's caprice, the less cautiously it will deal with them. For examples we need not look far.[2]

Legal resistance, if it is to be effective, must also have its own proper characteristics. We must not behave toward the authorities or their officials rudely, frivolously, insultingly or in provocation, we must not permit ourselves any transgression of the law, bad as it may be, but must always behave with the greatest freedom from passion, with the greatest seriousness and respect, but also with the greatest firmness and unyieldingness when the law is on our side. Legal resistance may not extend to violence; that means that, if the government or its organs employ violence against anyone in an illegal matter, legal resistance towards its actions must not itself extend to violence or to defending our rights with physical force, for wherever force and physical power have stepped in, there legal resistance itself comes to an end.

But to neglect our rights, not to denounce injustice done us, to bear in silence every arbitrary action: this is not worthy of the rank-and-file citizen, who must be conscious of himself and of the fact that he is not a slave in some Asiatic sultanate, but a free inhabitant of a country which may be ruled only by laws and not by the caprice of individuals.

So it is not good to think, "What would I achieve if I spoke out; what could I influence; what good would it do me?" and so forth. Even if you achieve nothing in the matter at hand, still you will at least achieve the result that the injustice which has been done to you will create greater clamor and uproar, will come more to public attention; you will achieve the result that nothing similar can be done to you again so easily, or at least that those who use you unjustly cannot proceed again in their unjust ways quite so quickly. And that is achievement enough.

NOTES

1. John Hampden (1594-1643) was an English parliamentary leader, the cousin of Oliver Cromwell. He was imprisoned in 1627 for refusing to pay a forced loan to Charles I. In 1637 he challenged the king's right to impose ship taxes on landlocked parts of Britain; his conviction inflamed popular resentment against the king and helped to bring on the Civil War and the Commonwealth of Oliver Cromwell.
  Daniel O'Connell (1775-1847) was the leader of the fight for the Catholic Emancipation in Ireland. Like Havlíček, O'Connell believed in legal means and was opposed to violent ones: in this he lost the support of the younger generation seeking a solution to the Irish Land Question in the late 1840's. Havlíček had frequently written about the struggle for Irish liberties because of its implicit similarities to the Czech situation in Austria.
  2. Havlíček is writing here, in part, about differences in the treatment of German-speaking and non-German-speaking citizens of the Austrian Empire.

BOŽENA NĚMCOVÁ

Božena Němcová was the first great Czech writer of fiction. Born in 1820 in Vienna, the illegitimate daughter of a coachman and a servant girl, she grew up as the child of a servant on a great feudal estate in Northeastern Bohemia. In 1837 her mother married her to Josef Němec, a tax official, a man some fifteen years her elder. The marriage was hardly a happy one, and the couple were eventually separated. A great beauty, she had a number of love affairs, one with the poet Václav Bolemír Nebeský, who helped to inspire in her an interest in writing. Her husband was frequently transferred from place to place in the service, and she used the opportunity of residence in various places to record folktales and other ethnographic materials, including popular customs and festival rites.

Husband and wife supported the Czech cause in the Revolution of 1848, and in the reaction that followed Němec was dismissed from the service. The subsequent period was extremely difficult for the family, and the mother and children lived in absolute poverty. Němcová was able to publish her writings, but the publishers paid her miserably for them. The illnesses of several of her children and the death of her favorite son Hynek made this a time of tragedy for the mother. She died in 1861, of complete physical and spiritual exhaustion.

Němcová took as her literary model George Sand: like Sand she was interested in peasant life and ethnography, though her life circumstances gave her a far more accurate and vivid knowledge of these than George Sand possessed. Her tales have simple, rather sentimental plots, but they come alive through their vivid comprehension of the peasant way of life, and are frequently influenced by the fairy tales she collected. It is true that, in contradiction to the hard circumstances of her own life both as a child and in marriage, she often portrays village life as idyllic, but her later tales show the real poverty and many of the social and economic contradictions of country existence.

Němcová's masterpiece is The Grandmother *(1855), the shining portrait of an old Czech peasant woman, her life rich in a store of folk wisdom, customs and beliefs. She dominates the family and her grandchildren; she was in fact modelled on Němcová's own grandmother. The grandmother is depicted against a background of the customs of Czech peasant life throughout the year and in particular the holiday festivities. Thus the tale, though idyllic and at times sentimental, is grounded by its richness of ethnographic details.*

Wild Bára (1856) is one of Němcová's finest, if one of her most Sandian stories, and it has the distinction of being perhaps her liveliest and most vivid.

WILD BÁRA

I

Vestec is a large village, and has a church and a school; beside the church is the rectory, and beside it the sexton's cottage. The village elder also lives in the middle of the village, while at its very end stands the tiny hut of the communal herdsman. Beyond this hut there stretches a long valley, walled in on both sides by mountain peaks, grown up for the most part with evergreens. Here and there a clearing in the woods can be seen, or a green meadow on which white, bright-leaved birches are standing, those maidens of the arboreal world, as if nature had let them grow there to entertain the dull firs and spruces, the staid beeches and oaks. In the middle of the valley among the fields and meadows flows a river which goes right past the herdsman's hut; its banks are lined with alders and willows. The village herdsman's name was Jakub and in this cottage he lived with his daughter Bára. Jakub was already in his sixties, and Bára his firstborn and only child. He had wished, of course, for a son who would inherit his name, but when Bára had grown up a bit he ceased to have regrets: she was dearer to him than a son, and often he thought, "Even if she is a girl, still she is my child; I will die like a human being and have a ladder to help me get to Heaven."

Jakub had been born in the village; as an orphan he had had to work from childhood. He had served as a herder for geese, cattle

114

beater, cowherd, as herder of oxen, as groom and plowman, until he reached the highest rank in the hierarchy and became communal herder. That was a fine position, and now he could marry. The hut was given him as a place to live in, the peasants brought wood to his very yard, and he could keep a cow; bread, butter, eggs, milk, groats—he received them all every week. He got enough linen every year for three shirts and two pairs of underdrawers, along with two pairs of shoes, a short coat and a wide-brimmed hat, and every other year a coat and a blanket. Besides this on every festival day and on patron's day white bread and his pay, so that even the priest didn't have it better. In short, it was a good job, and Jakub, though he was ugly, tactiturn and morose, could still have gotten a wife, but he did not look to it. In summer he excused himself on the ground that he had no time to pay attention to the girls, that he must pasture; in winter he carved wooden shoes and in the evenings, when the lads were courting, he preferred to go and sit in the tavern. When it happened that one of the farmers' wives would come to the tavern to get her husband, Jakub was always happy at the thought that there was no one to come for him. He didn't even mind when they made fun of him as a bachelor and said he would have to spend time in purgatory after his death binding sand into sheaves. So he passed forty. Then someone implanted the idea in his mind that if he died without children he could not get to Heaven, that children are ladders for getting into Heaven. This bored into Jakub's brain for a long time and when it had finally settled he went to the elder's and brought back a girl named Bára.

Bára was a pretty girl during her young years. The boys liked to take her dancing, and some of them even courted her, but those who did were not serious in their intentions and none of them would have her. When Jakub inquired whether she would marry him, she reckoned that she had all of thirty years behind her, and though she did not like him very much, she thought to herself, "A bird in the hand's worth two in the bush." They plighted their troth and the elder arranged the wedding celebration.

A year later they had a girl child whom they named Bára after her mother; Jakub scratched behind the ears when he heard it was a girl and not a boy, but the midwife consoled him with the thought that the child was as like him as one egg like another.

A short time after the girl's birth an accident occurred in Jakub's hut. The neighbor woman had looked in to see the young mother just at noontime and had found her lying under the chimney by the fireplace, half dead. She made a clamor, the women came running, the midwife too came and they revived the mother. From her they learned that she had been cooking her husband's dinner; she forgot the precept that, for six weeks after giving birth, a mother must not step outside the sittingroom at high noon or after the angelus, and she had stayed by the chimney and cooked. Then she told how a loud rustling went past her ears like a fierce wind, she saw spots before her eyes, and something began to tug at her hair and hurled her to the floor. "It was the Noon Witch!" they all cried.[1] "Just so it didn't exchange a wild child for little Bára," one of them thought and went over to the cradle. At once they all clustered about her, took the baby from the cradle, unwrapped her, looked her over, and one said, "It's a wild child, it is, it has big eyes!" and another, "It has a big head!"; a third attributed short legs to the baby, and each of them something different. The mother was frightened, but the midwife gave the child a conscientious inspection and pronounced that it was her own child whom she had carried under her heart. Still, more than one of the women kept to the conviction that the baby was a changeling, put there by the Noon Witch.

From this mishap Jakub's wife never recovered, and after an uninterrupted illness of some years she died. Jakub was left alone with his daughter; no matter how much they pressed him to remarry becuase of his little daughter he did not wish to. He took good care of her, as of a young lamb, all by himself, and protected her as she grew up. When she was a bit grown, the schoolteacher sent word that she should come to school, and though Jakub considered reading and writing to be superfluous, still he obeyed. For a whole winter Bára went to school, but with spring and the work in the pastures and fields he could not do without her. From spring to fall the school was locked for the most part, anyway: the teacher worked in the fields and the children too, such as their strength permitted. The next winter Bára was no longer able to go to school; she had to learn to spin and weave.

At the age of fifteen no girl in the village could rival Bára in strength and size. Her body was made of large, coarse bones and strong muscles, though it was well proportioned. She was as lively

116

and nimble as a trout. Her skin was dark brown, partly from nature, partly from the sun and wind, for never, not even in the heat of summer, did she cover her face as the village girls were wont to do. Her head seemed too large, but that was the effect of her thick hair, black as a raven's, and long and coarse as horsehair. She had a low forehead, a short stubby nose, a mouth that was too big and pouting lips, but healthy, red as blood. Wide, strong, clean teeth. Her finest feature was her eyes, and on account of them she had to put up with many scoffers. They jeered at her that she had eyes like an ox's. Her eyes were large, unusually large, and blue as cornflowers, surmounted by long black lashes. Above them arched thick black brows. When Bára frowned, her face looked like the sky covered with dark clouds, in which only a bit of blue sky shone through. But she rarely frowned, only when the boys and girls called her "Ox Eyes," her eyes would flash with anger and often she would break into tears. But Jakub would tell her, "You silly, why make anything of it, I have large eyes too. And even if they do look like an ox's, there's nothing wrong with that—that dumb beast can look much more kindly at a man than those kids can!" (As he said this last he usually pointed in the direction of the village with his cane.) But later, when she grew to be very strong, the young people did not dare harm her, since for each insult she gave a ready payment. Even the stronger boys were no match for her; when her strength was insufficient, she would use all sorts of tricks to employ dexterity. So she had peace.

Bára had so many unusual qualities it was no wonder that the neighbors talked about her: unable to explain such a character any other way, the women again began to maintain that she was only "a wild child" after all, and if not that, still the Noon Witch must have taken power over her. With this pronouncement all the girl's behavior was explained and justified, but there was this consequence, that the villagers either abhorred her or feared her, and only a few good souls really loved her. Whoever wished to get her very angry would call her "Wild Bara!" But all of them were mistaken if they thought that this nickname would anger her more than any other; with this name they did not hurt her, and every other nickname wounded her more. She had heard tales of noon witches, evening witches, of the watergoblin, of the incandescent man of the woods, of will-o'-the-wisps, of the Devil and of ghosts, she had heard of these things while a child from the other children,

117

but she was not afraid of anything. As long as she was little, her father would take her to the pasture and there she would play all day long with the dog Lyšaj who, after her father, was her closest friend. Her father didn't talk much to her; he would sit and carve out wooden shoes, at times he would raise his head toward the herd, and if the animals were not pasturing together, he would send Lyšaj to bring a cow or a heifer back into line, which task the dog would carry out to perfection. If he had to, he would get up himself and walk several times around the herd. When Bára was bigger, she would always accompany Lyšaj on his missions, and if any cow tried to sniff at her, Lyšaj would chase it away at once. When she was bigger and it was required, she would often drive the herd out for her father; the cows knew her voice as well as they knew Jakub's horn, and the fierce bull, which the sturdy boys feared, listened when Bára threatened him.

When Jakub wished to cross a ford with the herd, he would drive the cattle into the river and would place Bára on the neck of one of the cows, "Hold on," and himself then swim after the herd. Once Bára didn't hold on well; she slipped into the water, Lyšaj pulled her out by the skirt and her father gave her a good scolding. She asked her father what you must do when you want to swim, and he showed her how to move her arms and legs, Bára learned it and continued to practice till she had mastered the skill. She grew so fond of swimming that in summer she would go swimming both morning and evening, and would swim not only on top of the water but under it. Of this skill only her father knew, however. From dawn to ten o'clock at night there was no time of day when Bára had not been swimming, and she had never seen a water-goblin; she did not believe in them, and did not fear the water. Both at noon and at midnight Bára had been out of doors, in summer she slept for the most part in the stable by the open dormer window and still she had never seen ghosts, nor had anything unusual shown itself. Once, when she was lying in the pasture under a tree by the edge of the woods, she recalled a story about a wanderer who was also lying under a tree in the forest, and how he wished to be with the beautiful princess in the castle, and was ready to sell himself to the Devil for the fulfillment of his wish. As soon as he had thought of the Devil, the latter was standing beside him.

118

"What would I wish for, if he were to stand here right now in front of me?" she asked herself in her thoughts, scratching Lyšaj on the head. "Hmm," she smiled, "I would ask him for a great big piece of cloth in which I could wrap up and no one could see me, and if I said, go here or there, I'd be there at once. I'd like to go to Elška's." And she thought and thought for a long time, but all was silence, even the tree didn't rustle; at last curiosity forced her and she called quietly:

"Devil!" Nothing. Then louder—and still louder, so that the echo sounded far off, "Devil, Devil!" The black heifer raised its head among the herd and when her voice sounded still louder, it ran off from the herd, running merrily toward the woods. But then Lyšaj leaped out and sought to turn it back, as was his duty; the black heifer stopped short, but Bára burst into laughter: "Let her alone, Lyšaj, let her alone; she's obedient, she thought I was calling her." She jumped up and stroked the "Devil" on its neck, and after that she no longer believed the tales about the Devil.

Near the woods, a few hundred steps across the river was the cemetery—after angelus people walked on that side uneasily, and there were many fantastic tales of risen dead who had their romps there at midnight. But Bára went there at nighttime as well and nothing frightening ever happened to her. So she did not believe that the dead arose and went scaring people, or that they danced on their graves.

When the young people went to the woods to pick strawberries or bilberries and saw a snake anywhere, how they ran; if the snake even raised its head and showed its fangs, they would all run to the water so that they would be there before the snake and it would have no power over them. Bára never ran; she did not even fear a fierce bull, not to speak of a snake or a scorpion. If it lay in her path, she would push it away; if it did not let itself be pushed away, she would kill it. When it did not get in her way, she would let it alone.

In short, Bára knew no fear or apprehension; even when the thunder roared and the storm poured out its rage over the valley, Bára did not tremble. On the contrary, when the villagers closed their windows and doors, lit their consecrated candles and, trembling with fear, prayed that the Lord God should not be angry with them, Bára stood on the threshold in order to have a better look at the horizon spread out before her gaze.

119

Jakub often said to her, "I don't know, girl, what pleasure you can find in looking at the sky when the Lord God is angry."

"The same I have in looking when he is laughing," she replied. "Look, Father, at that fire, what beauty there is in the black clouds!"

"Don't point!" Jakub shouted her down, "God's envoy might knock off your finger! If you aren't afraid of a storm, you aren't afraid of the Lord God—do you know that?"

"The priest's niece Elška read me a book that said we shouldn't be afraid of storms—they aren't God's wrath, and we should admire in them the power of God. The priest always preaches that God is full of good and is all love, so how could it be that he would get angry at us so often? I love the Lord God and so I'm not afraid of his envoy."

Jakub didn't care for so much talk and so he left Bára alone. But the neighbors, seeing the girl's dauntlessness and the fact that no harm ever occurred to her, were all the more convinced in their belief that the child was protected by some supernatural power. Besides her father she was loved only by Elška and Josífek, her contemporaries. Josífek was the sexton's son, Elška the priest's niece. Josífek was a boy of short stature, pale, blond, good-hearted but always timid. Bára was a whole head taller than he, and in fights he would always hide behind her skirts. Then Bára magnanimously took him under her protection against the boys, against whom he would otherwise have achieved nothing. For this Josífek loved her very much, brought her apples and every Saturday small round cookies. Once on Sunday, when Bára was still little, he took her home, wishing to show her his little altar and how he could play at being priest. They walked along holding hands nicely and Lyšaj trailed after them.

In all the village farmhouses the doors were closed on the clasp, at night on the bolt; at the priest's house the oak doors bound with iron were always locked, and whoever came had to ring. The sexton too had a small bell on his door, like the priest's, and the village boys would often open the door a bit when they passed by to hear the ring of the bell and the swearing of the sexton's wife. When she had sworn for a time they would cry, "Witch, witch, witch!" When Bára and Josífek came in the door and the bell rang, she ran out into the vestibule; since the end of her long nose was pinched by her spectacles, her voice sounded

120

nasal when she cried, "What's that you've brought home?" Josífek stopped short as if he had been scalded, let his eyes fall and was silent. Bára too let her eyes fall and was silent. But behind the sexton's wife the tomcat ran out and, catching sight of Lyšaj, started to arch his back and sputter, and its eyes shone; Lyšaj began to growl, then barked and ran after the cat. The cat jumped under the cupboard, and when Lyšaj tried to root him out of there, jumped up on a shelf among the pots. There he was secure, but every hair still stood up straight with rage. Lyšaj jumped awkwardly up onto the shelf and barked until their ears burned. The sexton ran out; on seeing the fuss, the two enemies assaulting one another and his wife angry, he too grew angry and opening the door, shouted at the children, "March right out again from where you came, and take that beast with you!" Bára did not need to be told twice, she called to Lyšaj, whom the sexton was now lashing vigorously with his cane, and ran as if from a fire. Josífek tried to call her back, but shaking her head she said, "Even if you gave me a heifer, I wouldn't come any more," and she didn't come, though Josífek begged her many times and promised that his mother would be happy to see her, especially if she would leave her dog at home. She didn't go and she wouldn't—from then on she lost all her respect and liking for the sexton's wife—except what she had for Josífek himself. She had always believed that the sexton was the equal of the priest, and held him in great respect when he appeared dressed like the priest: in the church everything was under his authority, and when he would give some idle boy a slap in church the boy did not dare say a word, and the villagers, whenever they wanted something from the priest, would always go first to seek the sexton's advice. "The sexton must be something that's good," the girl had always thought, but since the time when he had shown her the door so unpleasantly and had switched Lyšaj, so that whining the dog had done a good piece of the way home on three legs only—since that time whenever she saw him, she would think to herself, "No, sir, you aren't anything good."

How different it was when Elška took Bára to the priest's, and that would occur on Thursdays and Sundays. As soon as the bell rang, a maid would open and let the children in, even with Lyšaj, who was on good terms with the priest's dog. Quietly the children went to the servants' kitchen and climbed onto the stove, where Elška kept her toys and dolls. The priest, already an old

121

man, would sit on a bench at the table, with his snuffbox and a blue pocket handkerchief lying in front of him, and with his head leaning against the wall, and he was always dozing. Once only was he up; then Bára ran up to kiss his hand, and he stroked her head, saying, "Why, you are a good child; go and play, go, children!"

Miss Pepinka, the priest's sister, was also kind to her. She didn't talk much to Bára, though she was fond of gossiping with the neighbor women, but she always gave her a big piece of bread with honey, or a roll for her lunch, bigger than the one she gave Elška. Miss Pepinka was a person short in stature, and God had stinted in forming her: she was fat, red, had a wart on her chin and weepy eyes, but when she was younger, as she herself said, she had been pretty, which the sexton always confirmed. She wore long dresses like the wives of the gentry, with a short waist, an apron all around with large pockets, at her side an armful of keys. Her gray hair she kept nicely smoothed down, and on her head on weekdays she wore a brown kerchief with a yellow border, on Sundays a yellow kerchief with a brown border. Miss Pepinka was usually to be seen bustling about the house or in the field, she spun, or with spectacles on her nose she mended the clothes. On Sundays after dinner she also dozed a little and after vespers played cards with her brother and the sexton. But she rarely called the priest "brother," and usually "Reverend Sir." Miss Pepinka was the head of the household: whatever she wanted was done, and whatever she said everyone in the house took for irrefutable truth; whomever she favored, they all favored.

Elška was Miss Pepinka's darling as well as the reverend father's, and whatever Elška wished, that Miss Pepinka too wished, whomever Elška liked, on that person Pepinka looked with favor. Hence Bára did not receive a sullen look at the priest's, hence Lyšaj was endured, and even the sexton, though otherwise he could not stand the dog, often tried to stroke him there out of love, but Lyšaj could not stand the sexton and always growled at him.

Bára was happiness itself when she could visit the priest's. Inside the house everything shone, it was crammed to the ceilings with beds and the featherbeds on top of them, fine pictures, inlaid cabinets; the garden was full of flowers, vegetables and fine fruit. In the yard they kept fowls and rabbits, whatever you wanted, and in the shed there were cattle so fine it was a joy to gaze at them. Jakub had his greatest pleasure in taking care of the priest's cattle. And in the servants' room on the stove there were so many fine toys and Elška never made pies of mud, and never sprinkled them with powdered bricks or lime—she always had the real things and whatever she made could be eaten.

Bára could not help but be pleased in such a home, but above all she liked Elška, and it often struck her even that she was fonder of her than she was of her own father, and that if Elška were to live in a shanty instead of the rectory, she would still like to visit there. Not once did Elška ever make fun of Bára; when she had something nice she would always share it with her and often she would put her arm around Bára's neck and say, "Bára, I like you very much." "She likes me very much, and yet she's so beautiful, she's the priest's niece and everybody speaks to her with respect, even the schoolmaster and the sexton—and those others laugh at me," Bára repeated to herself, and in her heart she would always embrace and kiss Elška for her kindness, but in real life she was too shy, though she longed to give vent to her ardent feeling more openly.

When they were chasing one another on the meadow and a lock of Elška's hair would come unbound, then Bára would ask: "Let me fasten it for you, Elška, you have hair as fine as flax, I love to touch it." When affably the girl permitted this, she would finger the fine hair with pleasure, admire its beauty, and then finishing her work she would grasp one of her own rough tresses and hold it up against Elška's, saying, "There's a big difference." Yes, compared to Bára's Elška's hair was like gold against tempered steel. Yet Elška did not like it and longed to have hair as black as Bára's.

Sometimes when Elška would come running to Bára's and they were sure no one was watching, they would go swimming. But Elška was timid and even though Bára kept reassuring her that nothing would happen, that she would hold her and teach her how to swim, she would not venture farther out into the water than her knees' depth. Afterwards Bára loved to wipe Elška's feet with her own coarse apron; clasping the small white feet in her powerful fists, she would kiss them and laughing, say, "Lord, what little feet those are, soft, soft and so tiny! What would they do if they had to go barefoot?" she would add, bringing her own sunburned, skinned foot full of calluses towards Elška's white foot. "But doesn't it hurt?" Elška asked, touching the hard skin on the sole of Bára's foot with a feeling of compassion. "Till it got as hard as leather I minded it, but now I couldn't feel fire itself under my feet," Bára replied almost with pride, and Elška wondered greatly at her.

So the two girls took great pleasure in each other's company, and often Josífek joined them: when they played at holding feast-day celebrations, he had to bring the things they needed, to grate the food and carve it; when they played wolf, he had to be the sheep; when the game turned to bartering he had to haul the pots. But he didn't mind any of it and was most happy to play with the girls.

The children reached their twelfth year and an end came to their childish joys: the sexton sent Josífek to town to school; he wanted him to become a priest. Miss Pepinka sent Elška to Prague, to a rich, childless aunt, to learn good manners and so that the aunt would not forget her country kinfolk. Bára was left alone with her father and Lyšaj.

II

Life in the countryside flows quietly along, without noise or murmur, like a meadow brook. Three years had passed since Elška had gone to Prague. At first Miss Pepinka and the priest could not seem to do without her; they missed her terribly, but when the sexton objected that it was they who had sent Elška away from home, Miss Pepinka replied sagely, "Dear Mr. Wolf, one can't live for today; we must think of the future. We—well, as for us, God grant, we'll get through life somehow or other, But Elška is young, we have to think of her. As for saving money—good God—where would we get that? A few featherbeds, some kitchen utensils— that's the whole of what she'll get after we're gone—and it's little enough. The world values only these (meanwhile Pepinka opened her palm and with the other hand she gave an imitation of count- ing), and her Prague aunt has them—countless ones. Perhaps she'll take a liking to Elška; it's only for her own good that we sent her there to stay." The sexton could only agree with Miss Pepinka.

The Prague aunt had been ill for many years, and ever since her husband had died she always wrote to her brother-in-law and sister-in-law saying that only medicine kept her alive, and that if it hadn't been that her doctor understood her system so well, she would have been dead and buried long ago. But all of a sudden Elška wrote that the aunt had a new doctor and that he had prescribed that she bathe every day in cold water, walk a great deal, eat and drink well and at once she would get well. The aunt had heeded his advice and was now healthy as an ox. "Hm, how things do change in the world! Well, if that's how it is, Elška can come home at once." As Miss Pepinka wished, so it happened. That very day the groom had to pull the buggy out of the shed and take it to the wheelwright, and Miss Pepinka, resolved to go for herself, brought a hat out of the closet to inspect it and make certain it had not come to any harm. Yes, Miss Pepinka also had a proper hat, she had obtained it some ten years before, when she had been in Prague, from the aunt. In Vestec no one had ever seen her wear it, but when she and her brother travelled to the town nearby to visit the dean, then she put it on, and now she also had to wear it to Prague so, as she said, not to bring disgrace on the aunt by wearing a kerchief.

The next day the buggy was fixed, the third day Pepinka ordered them to grease it and have the horses shod, the fourth day she took leave of her household duties and sent for Bára to tell her to watch over things in her absence. Early in the morning on the fifth day fodder was loaded onto the buggy for the horses, food for the coachman and in part for Miss Pepinka as well, a basket of eggs, a pot of butter and other such gifts for the aunt, a box with the hat, a bundle of dresses, and after holy mass, after long goodbyes and injunctions, Miss Pepinka hid herself inside the buggy, the coachman lashed at the horses, and for better or worse they set off on their way. Whoever saw the old-fashioned buggy, which resembled a winged kettle suspended amid four wheels, took off his cap from afar even though Miss Pepinka, wrapped in so many scarves, buried in the depths of the buggy among all the provisions and the piles of hay which jutted out above her, could not be seen. But the peasants knew the buggy, their fathers had known it and had said that that same buggy had known Žižka himself.[2]

No one looked forward to Elška's coming with more enthusiasm than Bára, no one thought of her more enthusiastically either, no one spoke oftener of her; when she had no one else to talk to she talked to Lyšaj: she promised him that when Elška returned he

125

would have things good again, and she asked him whether he had missed Elška. Miss Pepinka and the priest knew how much Bára loved Elška, and they liked her for it. Once when Miss Pepinka had fallen ill and Bára had helped out with the greatest willingness, she had had an opportunity to convince herself of the girl's loyalty and her good heart, so that later she took her on as help whenever there was work to be done, and in the end had so much confidence in her that she entrusted the key of the larder to Bára, a sign of the greatest favor on Miss Pepinka's part. And so she turned over the supervision of the house to her when she went away, which surprised all the village housewives immensely and turned the sexton's wife against her all the more. At once people started saying, "Look, such freaks get their luck from Hell—just see how she's feathered her nest at the rectory." By this they meant Bára. The prejudice against the poor girl did not pass; she did not care whether people liked her or not, she did not force her way among the young people, whether to play with them or go dancing; she looked to her work and to her old father, and the priest's house was her Prague. Voices resounded in the village which said, "You have to give the girl credit: there aren't many boys her equal in agility and strength, and not a single girl. Who else could carry such full pails of water, and do it as if she were playing? And who else is so good with the cattle? Horses and bulls, cows and sheep— they all listen to her, she can do anything with them. A girl like that's a real treasure on a farm." But if any of the lads should have said, "I'll have her for my wife," the mammas would at once have shrieked, "No, no, boy, don't bring her into our family, you can't tell how it would turn out and she's a queer fish."

In fact then none of the boys dared court the girl, nor did they dare trifle with her. Bára did not yield, nor did she let her judgment be clouded with fine words. The sexton's wife hated her the most, though Bára had never in her life done her the least injury; on the contrary, she had done good in defending Josífek from the boys' vengeance. When any of them had received a box on the ears from the sexton, he naturally wished to repay it to Josífek. But the sexton's wife was angry with Josífek because she thought he was a shilly-shallier and because he let a girl protect him, and because he was fond of the girl; she was angry because Bára went to the priest's and they liked her there. She would have been able, surely, to dislodge her from the priest's, had Miss

126

Pepinka not been Miss Pepinka—but Pepinka would not let you blow dust in her eyes—least of all would she let the sexton's wife. Once the sexton's wife and the teacher's wife had invented some gossip at Miss Pepinka's expense, and since then the ladies hadn't seen eye to eye, though before they had been bosom companions. Miss Pepinka often ticked off Mr. Wolf for this, saying, "A pointed nose is fond of prying," which was intended as a hit at his wife, though Wolf was always a lamb at the priest's, and only at home a real Wolf.

Two, three, four days had passed since Pepinka had gone, and Bára couldn't wait. "Good Heavens, Reverend Sir, how far is it to Prague?" she asked the priest; when he had had his afternoon nap he was in the best humor. "Be patient, girl, they can't be here yet. Over a hundred miles—that's a piece of the world—three days to get there, Pepinka will stay there two days, and three days on the way back—just add it up." Bára counted the days, and when four more had passed, preparations were made at the priest's, and now Bára counted only the hours. When for the tenth time she ran out to have a look, the sun had already set and her father was driving home the herd, the buggy of course appeared on the highway. "They're coming!" Bára shouted, so that the priest's whole house shook. The priest came out to his gate, the sexton behind him; Bára would have run to greet the travellers but she was ashamed and ran about from place to place, and when the buggy already approached the house she was seized with anxiety, her heart pounded and her throat was tight; she was hot and cold all over. The buggy stopped at the gate; the first to pile out was Miss Pepinka and behind her jumped out the slender figure of a red-cheeked girl at whom the priest, the sexton and all the young people were staring. If she had not rushed to put her arms around the priest's neck and called him "Uncle!" you could not have believed it was Elška. Bára did not take her eyes off her, but when Elška had slipped from the priest's embrace she came up to Bára, clasped her in both arms and looking up into her eyes said in her sweet voice, "Bára, Bára, I've missed you so. How have you been—and is Lyšaj still alive?" Then Bára broke into tears and wept until her heart almost broke and she could not answer. In a while she finally sighed, "Well, just so you're here now, dear Elška." The priest repeated after Bára, "Well, just so you're here now. We've missed you." "They wanted me to stay another day,"

127

said Miss Pepinka, loading the arms of the sexton, Bára and the maid with all sorts of things from the buggy, "But I was worried for you, dear Brother, that you would be by yourself. And we wouldn't have made do with the fodder," she added. The buggy was returned to the shed to repose again, Miss Pepinka put her hat back into the closet just as unspotted as it had been when she took it out, put away what she had brought with her and distributed the gifts. Bára got pretty ribbons for her skirt and her hair, and a necklace of red coral beads from Elška. Elška had also brought fine clothes with her, but they would have not been enough to please, had she not brought her own unspoiled, good heart back from Prague as well. She hadn't changed.

"Oh, Bára, how you've grown!" was the first thing Elška wondered at when she had a chance to talk to Bára and to look at her properly. Bára was a good head taller than Elška.

"Oh, Elška, you're still just as good as you always were, only you're prettier than ever. If it weren't a sin to say it, I'd say you look like the Virgin Mary on our altar."

"Get along with you, what are you saying?" Elška scolded her, but not sharply, "You're flattering me."

"God forbid, I'm speaking as my heart tells me. I can't get enough of looking at you," Bára said sincerely.

"Dear Bára, if only you'd go to Prague, you'd see so many pretty girls!"

"Prettier than you?" Bára was astonished.

"Even prettier."

"Are the people kind in Prague? Is it beautiful there? Did you like it there?" Bára asked after a while.

"Everyone was good to me, my aunt, and the governess— they all liked me. I liked to be with them, but I missed you and I wished you were with me. Oh, dear Bára, it's so beautiful there, you can't imagine! When I saw the Vltava River, the Castle, the beautiful churches, the buildings, the gardens—I stopped in my tracks. And so many people on the street, it's like a festival, and some of them are dressed every day as if it were a holiday, carriages drive by constantly, and there's so much noise and turmoil a person doesn't know who's with whom. Just wait, next year we can go there on a pilgrimage," Elška added.

"What would I do there, people would laugh at me," Bára gave her opinion.

"Don't think that; there people don't pay attention to one another, they don't even greet each other."

"I wouldn't care for that—it's a strange world," Bára expressed her surprise. The next day—it was Sunday—Elška dressed nicely, on her head she put a red velvet cap, just in style and very becoming, and went to mass. All eyes in the church were turned only toward her, and many of the lads thought, "For you, my girl, I'd serve twice seven years if I had to, if I'd just be sure of getting you."

In church Elška was always very devout and did not look at anyone; so it was then, but when she left the church and walked through the village, she glanced all around, greeting the villagers who crowded about her and welcomed her home from Prague, asked them how they had been all that time and answered their questions. Much indeed had changed during those three years, though the villagers hardly realized it. Here and there an old man or woman was missing, one whom Elška used to see on Sunday sitting at his threshold or in his orchard, warming in the sun. From the young people more than one couple was gone; these were now occupied with housework. Infants toddled in the grass whom Elška did not know, and many a head had turned white which had been only gray—and Elška's girl friends were now going with boys, though they had not been old enough for that previously. But no one addressed her as Elška any more—each added to that name the title of "Miss."

When Elška heard herself addressed so, her face colored even more; with this title the villagers were expressing a fact that she herself did not yet realize—that she was no longer a child. In Prague at first they had called her "Little Miss," and then later "Miss." At first she had supposed they were making fun of her, but learning that it was the usual title for girls, she accepted the custom. But the country honored her more and elevated her more, and she felt this, and so her face flushed with maidenly modesty.[4]

The sexton's wife came out to the threshold as well, and when Elška passed she invited her in. She liked Elška, even though she was not on good terms with Miss Pepinka. She asked Elška how she had done in Prague, how the altar of the Church of St. John looked in the Hradčany Castle, whether it was true that the Prague Bridge was paved with gold, and when Elška was answering all her queries she looked her over from head to toe—not a thread escaped those venomous eyes. Elška asked about Josífek.

"Oh, he's doing well at school, he's first in his class and growing like a fish. Many, many times he's asked about you, Miss Elška, when he's been here for the holidays; he was lonely—there was no one with whom he could enjoy himself. He shouldn't go with the village children, now that he's a high-school student," the sexton's wife opined; Elška had a different opinion, but she kept silent. That afternoon Elška went to visit Bára.

The cowherd's house was a small hut, the smallest in the whole village, but none other was neater than this one, perhaps, with the exception of the priest's house. A table, a bench, two chairs, beds, a chest and a loom—that was all the furniture, but it was as clean as glass. The walls were white as chalk, the scrubbed ceiling shone as if it were made of walnut wood. On the wall a few pictures and in back of them green sprigs; on a shelf there sparkled a few jugs and plates—all from the mother's dowry. The little windows were always open in summer and in them in pots bloomed basil, stocks and rosemary. The floor was not of wood, it was only chaff from threshing pounded down, but Bára covered it with a mat which she had plaited herself.

By the hut was a piece of orchard and a small flower garden which Bára tended; everywhere and in everything it could be seen that the inhabitants of the hut knew few needs, but that the being who ruled here was not lacking in a sense of beauty.

Not a single girl in the village, not even excepting the maid servants, wore such humble clothes as Bára, but not a one of them looked as clean at work all week long as she did. Her blouse was always tucked in at the neck and the sleeves and was very coarse, but it was always as white as new-fallen snow. Her dark skirt of wool and her rough apron of linen completed her costume, and only on Sunday did she wear shoes and wear a bodice; in winter she added a woolen coat. As ornament she wore green trim on the skirt, a red galloon on the apron, and red ribbons in her black braids which hung down in back almost below her knees. The village girls often reproached her for going about all week without stays, but she did not listen to them, she preferred to feel free, and Elška always told her she looked better without them. No one is quite free from vanity, nor was Bára!

130

Bára had great pleasure in Elška's visit; she took her about everywhere, boasted to her of the flower garden, led her into the orchard, the field and out onto the meadow to her father, who could not believe how Elška had grown; in a word they visited all the spots where they had played three years before. Then they sat down in the orchard, Bára brought a dish of cream in which black bread had been crumbled and she and Elška ate of it as they had in former times. Meanwhile Bára told her of her black cow, of Lyšaj and then they came to Josífek.

"And Mrs. Wolf still can't stand you?" said Elška.

"No, she can't, it's as if salt gets in her eyes when she sees me, and when she runs out of other things to talk about, she finds fault with my eyes and says I look like a tadpole."

"That's wicked of her!" Elška grew angry.

"Yes, it's not nice, especially since I don't do anything to hurt her. But the other day I did lose my temper; I sent her a mirror so she could look at her own beauty first before finding fault with others."

"You did well," Elška laughed, "but why is she angry at you?"

"Oh, she's a real horror, she stings everybody with her basilisk eye, not just me. Perhaps she's angry because I'm more in favor with you than her Josífek is, and because he likes me. Poor fellow, he always got a beating when his mother found out that he had been at our house. I tried to persuade him not to come, but he would come; I couldn't help it."

Elška was silent, but after a bit she asked, "Do you care for Josífek?"

"Why wouldn't I care for him—everyone nags at him, poor fellow, the way they do at me, and he can't protect himself; I'm sorry for him."

"Is he really the same as he was? Why, Mrs. Wolf said he had grown."

"Up to Lyšaj's garters," Bára smiled, but at once she said with compassion, "How can he grow, when his mother gives him more clouts on the back than groats in his stomach?"

"But what does Wolf say—it's his son too, isn't he?"

"Wolf and his wife are cut from the same cloth. They're angry because they think he doesn't want to become a priest. Good Lord, how can he answer for that if he doesn't want to—

131

why, an unwilling servant would not be pleasing to the Lord God."

"No, he wouldn't," Elška agreed.

The girls talked for some time, then Bára accompanied Elška home and from that day they visited one another frequently, though they no longer played with the dolls above the stove.

But the two girls' friendship was not pleasing for the villagers, and the women began to ask each other why Miss Elška was friendly only with the cowherd's family, which was unsuitable for her; they said she should rather associate with the elder's family, or the alderman's, or others. On purpose their talk was open—so that it would reach Miss Pepinka's ears. Miss Pepinka was furious. It wasn't wise to stir up the villagers; Miss Pepinka didn't wish to send Elška out to play with the young people, but to invite the girls to come to the rectory wasn't quite fitting either, so she talked it over with Elška. Elška quickly decided that she would visit the village girls every so often, but that Bára would remain her best friend. Miss Pepinka had nothing against this, for she was fond of Bára for many reasons. She supposed that Bára would hardly marry, that then she would stay on as her own right hand, for the time when Elška would get married. Miss Pepinka had a husband picked out for Elška, but no one knew of this, not even the priest himself. It was the bailiff from the neighboring estate; Miss Pepinka liked the man, and she supposed that for Elška it would be a fit provision. The estate's lands bordered on the church property and the bailiff, when he visited that end, always stopped in at the rectory. Elška had no inkling of the happiness which her aunt was preparing for her in her mind, and her head was occupied with plans that were quite different from becoming the bailiff's wife; she had not even told Bára of them so far. But Bára noticed that Elška was often pensive, sad, and she guessed that something was oppressing her heart, but she thought the time would come when Elška herself would speak of it. She was not wrong. In spite of the fact that the village women tried to paint her in a bad light to Elška, calling her loose in her ways, Elška trusted Bára more than them and liked her as much as she ever had.

On St. John's Eve the two girls met and Elška asked Bára, "Are you going to throw a wreath into the water tomorrow?"

"I won't by myself, but if you like, come at sunrise to our house and we'll do it together."

"I'll come."

Just before sunrise Elška was standing in the herdsman's orchard, with Bára beside her; they were tying white, blue and red flowers to hoops twined from willow sprigs.

"Whom will you think of?" Elška asked Bára.

"Good Lord, I've no one," sighed the girl. "I'll toss my wreath in any old way, to see if it floats after yours. I would only wish to go with you, Elška, when you get married."

Elška was silent, and a blush spread over her face; after a bit she gave her hand to Bára and said, "Here's my hand: we will stay together if you don't marry—then I won't marry either," she added with a sigh.

"How can you talk like that, Elška? Few people like me, but everybody likes you. You'll be rich, while I'm poor; you are beautiful and I'm not pretty; you're educated, and I'm a simple, silly girl—should I think about a husband when you won't?"

"Aunt always told me it depended on your preference: one person likes a carnation, another a rose, a third a violet; every flower has its admirer and every one has its own kind of beauty. Don't underestimate yourself, and don't put me on a pedestal—we are equal. You really don't want to think about any fellow—you haven't thought of one already?"

"No, no," Bára shook her head, laughing, "I don't think about any of them, and when they come to court, I send them straight away about their business. Why should I spoil my thoughts, why bind my golden freedom?"

"But if one of them liked you, really liked you, and you liked him, you'd let yourself be bound?" Elška asked.

"Why, Elška, don't you know the way things go? First his parents would talk it over with my father, to find out how much Dad would give before the fellow took me. My dowry isn't big enough for some families to accept, and I won't be taken in on charity; I'd rather tie a millstone around my neck and jump into the river. If I put one on voluntarily, I'd have to call myself a real fool. If they speak badly of me now, they'd say much worse things then. Let me be the way I am, I've got posies in my belt," she added in song, sticking a bunch of flowers left over from the wreath under her belt. But then pointing at the dawn's light, she said, "It's high time!"

133

Elška quickly finished making her wreath and both girls hastened to the nearby bridge, which led over the river to the meadows. In the middle of the bridge they stopped.

"Let's throw them in together," siad Elška, holding her wreath out over the water.

"Now!" cried Bára, throwing her wreath over the water. But the wreath, thrown with a strong arm, did not hit the water but landed on a willow, and for an instant Bára froze still, then she wept and tossed her head saying, "Let it hang there, the flowers are pretty on the willow." But Elška didn't take her eyes off her own wreath: dropped with a trembling hand, it turned a moment on one spot, then a wave caught it and gave it to a second one, that one to a third, they carried it farther and farther until it disappeared from the girl's eyes.

Elška, her hands clasped on the railing, watched the wreath with burning eyes and face as the current carried it far away. Bára, leaning on the rail, also watched it in silence.

"And your wreath got stuck here—you see, you'll be married here!" Elška broke the silence, turning to Bára.

"That means we won't stay together; I'm to stay here, and you'll go far away from us. I don't believe it, though; man proposes and God disposes."

"Of course," said Elška with a voice almost tearful and she lowered her eyes to the water with a sigh.

"Elška, would you really like to go so far away—don't you like it here?" Bára asked, and her great dark-blue eyes looked inquisitively into Elška's face.

"What are you thinking of?" whispered Elška, not raising her eyes; "I do like it here, but. . . ."

" 'But there's someone far off there whom I miss, I'd like to go to him,' isn't it so, Elška?" Bára completed her thought and laying her brown hand on the girl's white shoulder, she looked into her face laughing. Elška raised her eyes to Bára and smiled, but at the same time she broke into tears.

"If something's troubling you, tell me; I'll keep it as secret as the grave," Bára said.

Elška silently laid her head on Bára's shoulder, embraced her and went on weeping. Gently, like a mother clasping her baby, Bára drew her to herself, kissing her blond hair.

High over their heads a lark flew up in song. Over the tops of the green woods the sun was rising and bathing the green valley in a golden glow. Jakub came out of the house and the voice of his horn reminded the girls that it was time to go home.

"We'll talk about it on the way," said Bára, taking Elška by the hand across the bridge and along the meadow way.

"But how did you tell it in me?" Elška asked.

"Good Lord, it's easy to tell. You're thoughtful, sometimes sad, and then again your face will shine up—when I first noticed you, I thought there must be something. I guessed it."

"Just so Aunt doesn't notice it and ask me about it," Elška said anxiously, "She'd be angry, she wouldn't like him."

"Does she know him?"

"She saw him in Prague; he's the one who cured my Prague aunt."

"The doctor? You told me several times what a fine man he was, but then why should Miss Pepinka not like him?"

"I don't know—she only runs him down, and says he seems repulsive to her," Elška said it almost tearfully.

"Maybe he isn't nice?"

"Ah, Bára," the girl sighed, "so handsome a man as he is you couldn't find all around."

"Maybe he isn't rich?"

"Rich? I don't know, but what of it? What good is money?"

"That's true, but Aunt will want you to marry a rich man and be well provided for."

"No, no, Bára, I won't marry anybody else, I'd rather die."

"Well, it won't be as bad as that—Miss Pepinka and your uncle will be won over when you tell them you love him."

"I don't dare tell them, my aunt in Prague forbad me, but she promised us she would look out for our happiness, even if my aunt here tried to prevent it. A week ago he wrote that I'll see him next month."

"You write?"

"This is how it is: my aunt can't write and she's near-sighted. Hynek—that's his name—don't you think it's a pretty name?"

"Strange, I never heard that name before," Bára rejoined, and Elška went on, "Hynek offered to write the letters for her. She wouldn't write—maybe once a year—but he urges her on to write often so he can send along a message. Uncle is surprised how often she writes now."

"But what happens when Uncle reads the letter?"

"We thought of that: we write in a way no one will understand except us."

"It's wonderful when you're accomplished—I couldn't do it."

"You'd learn how easily enough," Elška opined. They had just reached Bára's house, and she took Bára by both hands and looking into her face with her clear gaze said, "You don't even know how much better I feel now—it's as if a stone had fallen from my heart. Now I can talk to you about him. But Bára," she added in a confident tone of voice, "haven't *you* got anything to tell me?"

"Me?" Bára's voice faltered and she cast down her great eyes. "Me—nothing. . . ."

"Not even a single word?"

"Nothing, Elška, nothing, just dreams!"

"Tell me about them!"

"Some day!" Bára shook her head, slipped her hand out of Elška's and pointing to the shed and the kennel, she added, "Look at Lyšaj, how he's fretting, and Blackie's likely to hang herself on her rope. It's time to let them out, and your cows are already with the herd—I can hear their bells. In a minute Dad will be driving them past. Go back along the gardens, Elška, so the women don't notice you and don't spread gossip."

"Oh, let them talk, I'm not doing anything bad. I'm going, I'll do what you say, but very soon we'll have another talk," Elška said as she disappeared among the fences.

III

Two pieces of news were making the rounds of the village: in every house and every cottage they talked of nothing else but the ghost seen in the church woods and of Miss Elška's coming wedding to the bailiff.

"So she's forgotten her first love so soon?" the reader will wonder. Don't do Elška an injustice: she has not been unfaithful even in her thoughts, and she was resolved to undergo anything rather than become the bailiff's wife. Even if she had not been in love with someone else, the bailiff was not the man she could have fallen in love with.

136

He was a short, fat man, a real potato set on short legs. Red cheeks like peonies and a nose of the same sort. On his head he had a bald spot, which he covered however with the red hair that remained to him in back and around the ears. His eyes were grown over with flesh and had this good quality—especially for a bailiff— that they could look in two directions at once. In summer he wore a straw hat with a green ribbon, a cane with a tassel, nankeen trousers, a winter vest buttoned over his chest to keep him from catching cold and from soiling his shirt, around his neck a colored cotton scarf and a frockcoat brown in color with pointed tails and yellow buttons. From his coat pocket there always hung the corner of a blue handkerchief, for the bailiff took snuff. It was said among the Vestec villagers that the peasants on the neighboring estate had more than once dusted out the bailiff's frockcoat in the wind, but it never came to court. The bailiff was a great coward, but the peasants still feared him, since he made up for want of courage with the deceit and vindictiveness with which he paid them back; towards people from whom he could expect some profit he was unctious and well-mannered; otherwise he was a crude man. He was also very stingy, and the one good quality no one could deny him was that he was wealthy. Yes, Mr. Kilián Sláma was wealthy, and that was the good quality that endeared him to Miss Pepinka; nor was she of the opinion that his appearance was un- attractive. She had never liked tall, thin people, and it flattered her greatly that the bailiff kissed her hand. She supposed that Elška would get used to him and in the end get to like him; she told her brother, who did not wish to hear of the plan, that a man like that is far better able to respect a woman than a young swell, that he would go to the ends of the earth for her, that Elška would be a lady and well off, that if he would die she would be taken care of. "And, if Brother should die, I'd have a place to go," she further considered to herself. In short, Miss Pepinka knew how to bring it off: she saw to it that the bailiff came to see them often, and finally the priest had no objection to him; he was used to him. When the bailiff did not come to dinner and after dinner the priest had to play his game of whist with Pepinka and the sexton or with the school teacher, it was as if something were missing. Elška had no suspicion of Pepinka's plan at first: she heard only praises of his kindness and riches, which she noticed however as little as she did the attentions which the clumsy bailiff paid to her. But as things went on, the bailiff made greater efforts and Miss Pepinka became more open, so that Elška comprehended what was going on. She felt like laughing, but when her aunt refused to understand her jokes and began to urge her in the strictest terms, and the priest too advised her to marry the bailiff, she became sad, began to avoid the bailiff, and ran with her troubles to Bára.

Bára knew of Miss Pepinka's plan from that lady herself, for Pepinka wanted Bára to help her and help persuade Elška. But this time she had gone too far; even if Bára had not known of Elška's love, she would not have tried to change her mind. She herself did not value the bailiff more than dust in the eyes, and would not have had him if the estate itself had come with him. She did not commit herself to Pepinka, but secretly she and Elška conspired and she herself carried to the town post office the letter in which Elška described the whole story for her aunt in Prague.

Ever since Elška had learned what was going on, the bailiff had not heard a kind word from her nor seen a pleasant look—and no one would have said that good, kind Elška would have the power to speak curtly or to give evil looks. Every time he came to the rectory he heard mocking songs on the village square, songs apparently composed on purpose for his benefit and sung on purpose for him to hear. Still he did not take offense, until one day he met Bára and she suddenly came out with a song:

> Just a little dwarf
> Toddling on his feet:
> He sees pretty girls
> Whom he wants to meet

The bailiff exploded with rage and his nose reddened like a turkey's when it sees red. But what good was that, when he had already survived all kinds of shame and ridicule—he also survived the village girls' jeers, consoling himself in the thought that, "Just wait, you girl, when I've got you—and your money—then I'll get back at all of them!" But the bailiff forgot that even in Foolstown you can't hang a thief till you catch him.

One morning the report went through the village that there was a ghost: a woman in white had walked from the church woods towards the village, across the village square, over the meadows, and had disappeared somewhere near the cemetery. The sexton's wife took to her bed, for she said it had knocked at her window and when the sexton had gone to the window, not knowing who it was, he had seen a white figure with a skull which grinned at him and threatened him with its finger. It was curious that Wolf too did not fall ill, but his wife thought only that Death had appeared to her, and she must die in a year and a day. The farmhand who had the night watch also swore that it was a ghost and that it came out of the church woods. People tried to recall whether anyone had been hanged there, but when no one could come up with anything, they supposed that someone had buried some treasure there once and that his soul had no rest and was seeking a liberator. There were all sorts of suppositions and the talk was only of the ghost.

"I don't believe it," Bára said to Elška, when the latter came to her that very day on the glade in the forest where Jakub was pasturing the cattle.

"I don't care how it is, I'm grateful because it's rid me for a couple of days of a visitor I could almost hate. He wrote to Uncle to say he had harvest and all kinds of work, that he can't come for some days, but I'd bet my head on it he's heard about the ghost and is afraid. He's awfully frightened of ghosts and he'd have to come through the church woods.

"If only he could be blown away there, so he wouldn't come to Vestec any more. I'd rather see you in your coffin than with that baldpate at the altar," Bára grew angry. "I don't know what Miss Pepinka's done with her brains that she's trying to force you—she's usually so good-hearted."

"She's concerned for me, that I may not be well off—that's the reason and so I can't be angry with her, but I can't marry him, no matter what."

"And you mustn't: God would punish you when you gave your vow to Mr. Hynek, if you didn't keep it. You know what people say: "Whoever won't his love vow keep, he'll regret and oft will weep."

"I'll never, never break it, even if I have to hold out for years," Elška asserted, "but he—he—won't he forget?" In Prague there are lots of beautiful girls who are his equals. Oh, Bára, suppose he forgets me—I'd die of grief!" and Elška began to weep.

"You're like a crazy person, the way you torment yourself. Yesterday you were telling me what a fine man Mr. Hynek was,

139

how much he loved you, and today you're inclined to doubt him?"

Elška wiped her eyes, smiled, and sitting beside Bára on the long green grass said, "It was just a momentary thought. I have faith in him as I have in God. Oh, if only I were a bird, so I could fly to him and tell him my troubles."

Bára thought at once of the song, "If I were a nightingale," and started to sing it, but the song was too merry for her mood, and in the middle she stopped suddenly, as if she were frightened of something. And her cheeks reddened.

"Why did you start just now—and why did you stop singing?" Elška asked, but Bára did not reply, and only looked at the woods.

"Bára, Bára," Elška shook her finger, "you hide everything from me, and I have no thoughts concealed from you—that isn't nice of you."

"I don't know myself what to say," Bára replied.

"Why did you take fright just now—you know you're not afraid of anybody. Who was that in the woods?"

"A forester, maybe," Bára was evasive.

"You know very well who it was—there was no point to your getting frightened. Or maybe you saw the ghost?"

"No, no, that wouldn't frighten me," Bára laughed loud and tried to change the subject, but Elška clung to the same thread and finally asked right out whether Bára wanted to marry Josífek if he didn't become a priest. Already Bára had burst into even louder laughter. "The Lord preserve me!" she cried, "The sexton's wife would cook me a snake the very first day. Josífek is a fine boy, but he doesn't fit here. He's not for the herd or the plow, and you can't give him a spindle. All you could do is put him behind a frame, or under glass, like something to look at."

Elška too laughed at her idea, and after awhile she asked Bára quite frankly, "So you really haven't grown fond of any-one?"

"Listen, Elška," Bára said after a brief hesitation, "Last spring I used to go to pasture alone with Lyšaj. Dad had a sore foot and couldn't make it there. Once I was pasturing there, and then the elder's Blondie and Milosta's Birch fell out somehow and started to butt at each other. You can't let them do that—they'd soon ruin their horns. So I grabbed a pail and ran to the river for water to throw on their heads, but before I could get back to the

140

herd some forest ranger came out of the wood and, seeing that the cows were butting, tried to chase them apart. "Get away!" I yelled at him, "I'll get them apart; watch out or the bull will see you, he's fierce!" The forester turned around but just then the bull caught sight of him. Luckily the cows ran off when I showered them, or it would have been hard for the forester to get away. I had a bit of trouble holding the bull and calming him down—Dad can hardly hold him, but he listens to me when I threaten. The forester hid in the woods behind a tree and watched; when the herd was grazing again he came out to the edge of the woods where I was standing and asked me my name. I told him. He looked at me a bit strangely, took off his cap, thanked me for saving him, and went off into the woods. Since then I've seen him many times, but I haven't talked to him again, only when he'd greet me when he was going by. He'd stop at the edge of the woods, walk near the river in winter, and sometimes come to visit the village, and so it went all through winter and spring. On St. John's Morn, when you'd gone home, I was helping Dad drive out the herd when I saw him come over the meadow toward the bridge. He stopped just where you and I had been standing, looked around, then came off the bridge, crawled into the bushes and I could see how he took the wreath that had got caught on the willow and slipped it under his coat. Just now I saw him go by down by the woods, I don't know what it is, but whenever I see him, I get frightened."

"And you've really never spoken to him?"

"Only that first time, otherwise not a word," Bára asserted.

"But you do like him, don't you?" Elška went on interrogating.

"I do—like any good man who doesn't hurt me."

"But how can you know if he's good when you've never talked to him?"

"He can't be bad; you can see it in his eyes."

"So you do like him?" Elška persisted with her questions.

"There are better-looking boys in the village, but if I've got to tell the truth, then I'd say that I like him better than any of them. I often dream about him."

"Whatever a person thinks about, that he dreams of."

"Not always—there are dreams God sends, too."

"Tell me honestly—if the forester were to say, 'Bára, I'd like to marry you,' would you have him?"

141

"How can you say that, Elška; he'd never think of me, certainly not to marry me. Those are vain dreams and speeches—forget it. Hey, Blondie, where are you getting to? Lyšaj, where are you chasing—don't you see Blondie's after Birch?" Bára cut short her speech and jumped up from the soft grass to turn the cow back. Whenever Elška tried to speak of the forester Bára always became evasive and began to talk of Hynek; she knew that subject would turn Elška away from any other.

In several days the bailiff was back at the rectory; nothing had frightened him away. But he came in the daytime. Even at the rectory they talked of the ghost, though the priest did not believe such superstitions. Still they thought there must be something to it, since every third day it walked about from eleven to midnight, as very credible people affirmed. It menaced people and peered into windows and showed a skull. People were so frightened no one, save the boldest of the men, would venture out across the threshold in late evening. They were sorry for their sins, they paid for prayers for the souls in Purgatory; in a word, fear of death drove them to repent. The priest preached against superstition and error to be sure, but it had absolutely no effect.

The bailiff, though he would not admit it, was so scared he was visibly pale; and if his greed for a fair bride and a rich dowry had not tempted him, they would not have seen him any more at the rectory. He wanted to seal the match as soon as possible; he spoke to Pepinka and the priest and, receiving their assurances, intended to speak to Elška so that the wedding could be celebrated right after harvest. Miss Pepinka informed Elška of the bailiff's coming visit the next day and tried to persuade her to be reasonable and heed the voice of good sense. Elška wept and begged her aunt not to force her to marry that monster, but Pepinka was most indignant with her, and the priest, though he was not so insistent as his sister, none the less reprimanded her for ingratitude and lack of good sense. From Prague no letter came, nor any news, and Elška did not know what to do. She took counsel with Bára, who consoled her and stirred her up against the bailiff, but none of this was any help.

The next day came, a day when the supposed ghost did not appear. The bailiff arrived, dressed up to the nines for the matchmaking. Miss Pepinka had been cooking and baking from dawn so that the guest should enjoy the best, and wine was put out on the

142

table, to be served in celebration of the great day. Bára was also at the rectory, and only her persuasion was able to keep Elška on her feet some way or other. She was quite ill from it all.

When the bargaining began, Elška proposed that the bailiff come for his answer in a week; she hoped that by that time word would have come from Prague. This procrastinating answer and the bride's coldness did not please the bailiff; he saw that things were not going well, but what could he do, he was silent and trusted in his patroness, Miss Pepinka. In spite of his bad mood he found the food and drink excellent, and his cheeks tingled. That day he was wearing a blue frockcoat which suited him much better. Evening was setting in, the bailiff wanted to leave for home, but the priest did not wish to let him go yet, and an hour later, when he tried again to leave, the priest said, "Just wait a bit; Wolf will accompany you with the groom too, maybe; it could be there are some rascals in our woods."

It was as if he had showered the bailiff with cold water: the latter ceased to enjoy his food and would rather have seen himself at home in bed. He would not have stayed had it not been for the offer of companions. But Wolf was a bit tight, and the groom too was sampling the wine as he poured it, thinking, "It isn't every day . . ." and they failed to depart till after nine. Finally they set out on their way. Sobered with fright, the bailiff noticed that both his companions were drunk: they zigzagged as they went, one this way, the other that. There was no talking to them, and the bailiff was in deadly terror, though he still clung to the hope that today the ghost would not appear. Oh, he had so looked forward to this day, he had everything calculated so well, and yet it had all gone sour.

The night was rather clear and one could see from the village as far as the woods; the travellers were already near their goal when suddenly out of the woods emerged a gigantic—or so it seemed to them—white figure—straight toward them. The bailiff gave a cry and like a block of wood tumbled to the ground; the sexton sobered up in a flash and took to flight; only the groom stood still like a post—but when the white figure cast off its cloak with a white arm and showed him a skull which bared its teeth at him, his hair stood up on end, terror seized him and he sank beside the bailiff to his knees. But the figure did not take notice of him and with a mighty arm raised the bailiff from the ground

143

and bawled in a hollow voice into his ear, "If ever again you come courting at the rectory, it's all up with you!" Saying that, it walked off with a long, slow step toward the village.

Meanwhile Wolf, running breathless to the village square, caught the night watch; together they turned half the village out of bed. The more courageous ventured out and took cudgels and flails, while the sexton insisted on going to the rectory to get something consecrated. They put it in their midst and set off toward the church woods. At once they caught sight of the white figure walking slowly, not toward the village but toward the meadows and the cemetery. They stopped short for a moment, but then, screwing up their courage, they all set out in a pack after the white figure which, seeing them, accelerated its pace. Suddenly it too broke into a run toward the river, and on the bridge suddenly disappeared from sight. Those who were more courageous rushed after it. At the bridge they stopped. "There's something white lying here!" they shouted. The sexton made the sign of the cross over the bridge and when nothing responded to his cry of "Every good spirit praise the Lord!" one of the peasants moved closer and saw that it was only clothing. With a stick he turned up the garments and they carried them, thus transfixed, back to the village; along the way they picked up the half-dead bailiff, whom the groom almost had to carry. They went straight to the rectory. The priest was not yet asleep, and willingly opened the door to them. They examined what they were carrying, and all stood as if struck dumb. There were two pieces of white coarse linen and a brown wool skirt with red trim. They recognized the skirt: "It's Wild Bára's!" they all shouted. "A plague on her!" some of them swore, "She's a real devil!" others cursed, but the worst to rage were the bailiff and the sexton; they were beside themselves. Only the groom laughed and said, "I sooner thought to meet my death than see Bára in that ghost—she's a devilish woman!"

At that point Miss Pepinka joined the company; the noise and uproar had lured her from her little room where she was already reclining in bed. She was veiled in a kerchief, on her head she wore a yellow knitted cap (a nightcap); she always had to wear something yellow. She came with a lamp in one hand and a bunch of keys in the other. "For Heaven's sake, folks, what's happened?" she asked in fright. From several mouths at once she heard the unheard of news. "Oh, the godless, ungrateful girl!"

144

Pepinka cried full of terror. "Just wait, she'll catch it from me; I'll read her the riot act; where've you got her?" "Who knows, she disappeared in the middle of the bridge, just as if the earth covered her up." "Perhaps she jumped into the water?" the priest said. "We didn't hear any splash, nor did we find anyone in the water, but what does that matter, Reverend, when a wild child like that knows how to make itself invisible; in the water it's like in fire; in the wind like on the ground, it's the same everywhere," one villager said.

"Don't believe such tales, folks," the priest reproved him. "Bára's a dare-devil and has been up to tricks, that's all, and for that she must be reprimanded. She must come and see me tomorrow."

"Reprimanded severely, Reverend Sir," the bailiff spoke his mind, trembling with hatred and terror that even now had not left his knees, "severely—she should be punished for making fools of the whole village!" "It wasn't that bad, Reverend," the peasants gave their view, "Only the women were frightened!" "My wife, poor woman, fell ill—there's a piece of godlessness you can't forgive," Wolf complained, but like the peasants he did not mention his own terror. Miss Pepinka was so overjoyed at this she was ready to pardon Bára. But the groom stirred her up again when he said, "Why should I deny it, I was really scared, and I don't frighten easily—and we were all scared. You, Mr. Sexton, hardly made it home, and the Honorable Bailiff here dropped like a piece of ripe fruit. When she bared her teeth at me, I really thought it was Death—it's no wonder, I was a bit tight—and I was already thinking she would grab me by the throat, but she grabbed the Honorable Bailiff instead, picked him up and shouted into his ear, 'If ever again you come courting at the rectory, it's all up with you!'"

The groom was all ready to show how Bára had picked the bailiff up, but the latter bent aside and his face became red and purple by turns. This offended Miss Pepinka frightfully, but the peasants forgot their abuse of Bára for what she had done to the bailiff. The whole matter was put off till morning; the bailiff stayed over at the rectory, though by dawn he was across the boundary already.

When Elška heard next day what Bára had dared to do for her sake, she begged her uncle and Pepinka to forgive Bára since she had only done it for her—to rid her of the bailiff. Miss Pepinka did not wish to abandon her plan, however, and could not easily forgive Bára the humiliation the bailiff had suffered. "And if you don't marry the bailiff, you won't get a single thread from me!" she threatened Elška, but the girl only shrugged her shoulders. The priest was not so headstrong; he did not try to persuade his niece, but he could not bring himself to forgive Bára completely. Elška would have liked to go to see Bára, but she did not dare to.

Jakub, suspecting nothing of his daughter's fall, took his horn the next morning as usual and went to call the herd together. But to his amazement it was as if all the cattle had strayed overnight, or all the servant girls had fallen asleep—nowhere did the gates open. He went to the cattlesheds themselves and trumpeted enough for the dead to rise from their graves—the cows bellowed, but no one came to let them out. Then the girls came out and said, "You won't go out today, Jakub, someone else will go!"

"What's this?" thought Jakub and went to the elder's. Here he learned what was up.

"We've got nothing against you, but your Bára is wild and the village women are afraid she'll bewitch them."

"Has any harm ever happened to the cattle?"

"No, it hasn't, but Bára might take revenge."

"Let my girl alone," Jakub grew angry, "if you want me to go on working, I'll go on, if not—that's all right too, the world is broad—the Good Lord won't desert us."

"It just wouldn't work."

"So give the hut to anyone you wish, and good riddance!"

Jakub had never talked so much in his life, perhaps, or gotten so angry. He went home. Bára was not there. He went to untie Lyšaj; his cow and the bull, which he took care of, he left to bellow and went to the rectory.

Bára was standing before the priest. "Did you play ghost?" the priest interrogated her.

"I did, Reverend Sir," Bára said without shrinking.

"Why?"

"I knew the bailiff was afraid of ghosts. I wanted to scare him away so he wouldn't bother Miss Elška; she can't stand him and would die if she had to marry him."

"Remember—you should never put out fires unless they're burning you, even without your help the matter would have been put to rights. How did you disappear from the bridge?"

"I threw off the canvas and the dress, Reverend Sir, and jumped into the water and swam a bit under water, so no one saw me."

"You swam under water!" the priest clapped his hands in amazement. "What a girl! And at nighttime! Who taught you that?"

The priest's amazement was almost comic for Bára. "Dad showed me the movements, Reverend Sir, and for the rest I taught myself. There isn't anything to it. I know every rock in the river to stay clear of."

The priest gave Bára a long talking to, after which he sent her off to the servants' kitchen, to await his decision. He took counsel with the elder, the alderman and the schoolteacher and they came to the decision that, since Bára had created such a public scandal and had been so defiant, she should be punished publicly. They sentenced her to be shut up in the charnel-house in the cemetery for one whole night. It seemed to them to be a frightful punishment, but when she had been so brazen as to fear nothing or no one, let her learn what fear was.

Miss Pepinka was quite displeased with the verdict, Elška was horrified and the women trembled with terror at the thought—even the sexton's wife was willing to forgive Bára, thinking she would have been punished enough with a reprimand. Only Bára was not disturbed—she was more upset that the community was driving her father out. She had already heard what had happened. When the priest told her where she was to spend the next night, she heard him out quite calmly, and then kissed his hand, saying, "What does it matter where I spend the night, I can sleep anywhere, even on the rocks. But it's worse for Dad: where will he go now they've taken his work away? Dad won't last long without the cattle, he's so used to them—he'll die. Can you do anything to help, Reverend Sir?"

They were all surprised where the girl found her self-confidence, and yet they believed that it wasn't natural, and that Bára was not like other people. "She'll be crestfallen, though, by evening," many of them thought, but they were wrong. Bára was unhappy only until she learned that the peasants had given Jakub back his job, a result the priest had brought about by entrusting his own cattle to him.

147

After dinner, while the priest dozed and Miss Pepinka too nodded a bit after the nighttime uproar, Elška slipped out of the house and down to see Bára. She was broken up with weeping and terror: she threw her arms around Bára's neck—and wept again.

"There, be quiet," Bára comforted her. "Only just so that midget doesn't come back—he'd have to be completely without honor to show up now—the rest of it will take care of itself."

"But you, poor darling, tonight in the charnel-house—Good Lord, I won't rest."

"Don't be concerned because of that—I've slept by the cemetery more than once before and I've had it right in front of me for whole days and nights. Just you sleep! But please let Dad know he's not to worry about me, and he should tie Lyšaj up at night so he doesn't follow me. Tomorrow I'll tell you the whole story—how I chased that bailiff away—you'll have a good laugh. You'll soon get news from Mr. Hynek, maybe. But you, Elška, when you get away from here, you won't leave me here?" she asked Elška sadly. But Elška squeezed her hand, whispering, "We belong to each other!" Silently she left—and Bára broke into a song and was content.

When it grew quite dark, the sexton and the night watchman came to take Bára to the cemetery. Miss Pepinka winked at her in signal for her to ask the priest's pardon; she too would have put in a good word for her, but Bára refused to understand, and when the priest himself said that the punishment might perhaps be remitted, she tossed her head in defiance and said, "If you've thought me guilty and deserving of punishment, then I ought to undergo it!" and went off with the men.

People ran out of their houses, and many pitied her, but Bára did not heed any of them and walked with a light heart to the cemetery, which lay at the foot of the woods, not far from the common pasture. They opened a small room where bones and stretchers were piled up, wished her "God keep you," and went home. In the chamber was a tiny window about a palm's breadth from which the valley and the woods could be seen. Bára stood at that window and looked out for a long, long time. Mournful must have been the thoughts which ran through her head, for tear after tear fell from her beautiful eyes onto her brown face. The moon climbed higher, one light went out after another; it grew quieter and quieter all around. Over the graves lay the shadows of the tall

148

fir trees which stood by the walls, over the valley a light mist arose. Only the barking and the howl of dogs broke the night's stillness. Bára gazed out at her mother's grave, and recollected her lonely childhood, the hatred and contempt of people, and for the first time felt all that burden, for the first time there came to her the thought: "If I could only lie here, Mother, beside you!" Thought gave birth to thought, one image followed another—in her mind's eye she was embracing the fair Elška, and on the forest path her imagination conjured up a tall, broad-shouldered man with an energetic face, dressed in forester's clothing. But at last she turned away from the window, silently shook her head and covering her face with her hands, she sank with a deep sigh to the floor. She was weeping and praying. Comforted at last she arose from the floor and was about to lie down on one of the stretchers, when a dog barked at the window and a rough voice resounded.

"Bára, are you asleep?" It was Jakub and Lyšaj.

"No, Dad, but I'll soon go to sleep—why did you come? I'm not afraid."

"All right, girl, you sleep; I'll sleep out here, it's a warm night!" And the father lay down under the window with the dog beside him. They slept well till morning.

When dawn came the next morning, a man was coming through the forest in a forester's dress. Jakub had often seen him walk through the wood and through the valley, but did not know who he was.

"What are you doing here, Jakub?" the forester asked when he came up to him.

"Why, sir, they locked my girl up here all night, and I couldn't stay home."

"Bára? What's happened?" the forester asked in astonishment.

Jakub told him everything in few words. The forester cursed, then he pulled his rifle from his shoulder and hung it on a tree. Nimbly he leaped over the wall of the cemetery and, breaking out the door of the charnel-house with his powerful shoulder, stood in front of Bára, whom the noise had awakened. Seeing the forester before her, she thought she was seeing a dream, but hearing his voice, she wondered how he could have come there and in her distraction could not even thank him for his greeting.

149

"Don't be surprised, Bára, that I've broken in this way; I was going past when I saw your father and heard what's happened to you. I'm very angry that you've been put here. Come away from this place," the forester bade her and took her by the hand.

"Oh, no, sir, I'll stay here till they come for me—they'd say I'd run away. Why, I didn't even mind it so much." Bára said uncertainly, gently extracting her hand from the forester's.

"Then I'll call your father and we'll both stay here," said the forester and called over the wall to Jakub. Jakub too climbed over the wall and came to Bára, and Lyšaj hardly knew what to do from joy when he saw Bára again. When Jakub saw where Bára had slept he almost broke into tears, but he tried to hide them and went to visit the grave of his dead wife. The forester sat down on the stretcher, while Bára played with Lyšaj, though she knew well that the forester was looking fixedly at her; she blushed and turned pale and her heart beat more than it had in the night when she had been alone in the charnel-house.

"But isn't there anyone in the village who might have looked in here to see how you were?" the forester asked after a time.

"Besides Elška and my father there's no one; Father's come, Elška can't come and there's nobody else who loves me enough. And there's you, of course," she said, looking the dog in the eyes. "Everyone's afraid to come to the cemetery at nighttime," she added besides.

"Your courage amazes me, just as your strength did. Why, I told Mother about you," said the forester.

"You still have your mother?" Bára asked confidingly.

"Yes, my aged mother; we live together on the mountain, three-quarters of an hour from here, in the ranger's cottage in the forest. I am the forester. My mother longs for a daughter: she would like to see me happy. I haven't found a wife to my taste anywhere—till I saw you. Bára, I don't like long speeches—I've loved you ever since I saw you—I got to know you, even though I didn't speak to you—and if I didn't say anything to you up to now, that was because I couldn't presume to have your word. Now you know all: tell me if you like me—and if you want to be my wife. You can't stay in Vestec any more: collect what you have here and come with your father to my house in the forest, where people will love you."

Bára stood like a statue and didn't move, nor could she speak. The forester did not know how to interpret this, but desiring to know the truth, even though it might be bitter, he asked Bára once more if she would be his wife. Then the girl burst into tears and cried, "My God, can it be true that you love me?" The forester confirmed this with his lips and by giving his hand and only then did she confess her long nourished love for him.

Having reached an understanding they came out, knelt before Jakub and the forester said, "You know me, Father, you know I can provide for a wife—for a long time now I could. But I didn't care for any until I saw your daughter and then I fell in love. We've just agreed in that: now give us your blessing. Even though it's in the cemetery—everywhere is God's earth, God is everywhere!"

Jakub did not ask the details, just so Bára was happy: he gave them his blessing and then they agreed on the arrangements.

How surprised the sexton was when he came for Bára after angelus and found her in the company of her father and her intended, for such the forester at once proclaimed himself to be.

There was still greater surprise at the rectory, and throughout the village. People had thought: the Lord knows how tamed Bára will be, how humiliated—and she had come back engaged, and to such a bridegroom! They could not believe it was possible, that anyone could come to like Wild Bára—and it had happened. "She has Hell on her side!" the girls told one another. But Elška had great, true joy when Bára brought her intended. "You see, God has repaid you the service you did for me and for which you underwent so much. I knew you would find a man who would love you. Only love her well, she deserves it," the noble girl turned to the forester and gave him her hand, which he pressed in sincere feeling.

The forester would have liked to take Bára away with him at once, but things did not go so quickly, and Miss Pepinka did not wish to let her go when a wedding was in the offing; rather let there be all three announcements at the same time, if her intended was in such a hurry. Nor could Jakub tear himself away from his duties so quickly.

Bára was sorriest for Elška. But the very next day the priest received a letter from Prague in which the aunt wrote that she would leave Elška her whole estate, but only on the condition she marry the young physician who had cured her (the aunt); the

151

priest should ask his niece if she were willing or not. There was an enclosure for Elška, full of the fairest hopes for a quick reunion, and so Bára had no more objections.

Before the wedding everyone made peace with her, and even the sexton's wife wished her happiness and gave her a letter from Josífek. Elška read it to Bára and learned only then what Elška had known for a long time: that Josífek loved her, and it was because of her that he had not wanted to become a priest. But now that she was getting married, he would gladly fulfill his parents' wish.

In a week Miss Pepinka gave Bára her wedding. The forester's old mother came too and took her daughter back to the forest, the daughter whom she had looked forward to meeting for so long. Jakub went with them.

When the forester conducted his young wife through the house and brought her to the bedroom where his bed was standing, he took down a now dry wreath that was hanging above it. "Do you recognize it?" he asked Bára. It was the very one he had untied from the willow on St. John's Day. Bára smiled.

"Whom did you think of when you threw it into the water?" the forester asked, clasping her to his heart.

Bára did not reply, but embraced him and raised to him her sweet, smiling eyes, which people had called an ox's, but which, for the forester, were the most beautiful in the whole wide world.

NOTES

1. *Polednice,* Noon Witch, a spirit regarded as evil and harmful to humans; she is imagined as covered from head to toe by an enormous white kerchief.

2. Jan Žižka (died 1424), leader of the Hussite armies in the Czech struggle against the German King Sigismund for religious freedom.

3. The village title *panna,* "maiden," implied that the girl was a virgin; the city title *slečna,* which became the standard Czech form, respected the girl for qualities such as her beauty.

4. St. John's Eve and Morn were times of divination among the European peasantry: at this time a girl could learn who her husband would be, or what he would be like. Here the wreaths, floating on the water, are used to reveal whether the girl will wed in the village or go away.

BOŽENA NĚMCOVÁ

LETTER OF AUGUST 26, 1856, to JOSEF LUDIMIL LEŠIKAR

Among Czech writers, Božena Němcová was outstanding for her personal letters. These give a spiritual portrait of her as a woman: the youthful letters full of spirit, hope and enthusiasm; the later letters eloquent and touching portrayals of the poverty-stricken life she and her family were forced to lead. Her style is straight-forward and affecting, yet without artifice or pretension. And although her life was hard, Němcová never lost her essential optimism and faith in mankind and never ceased, in spite of official persecution and the political reaction that followed the abortive Revolution of 1848, to stand for the Czech national cause.

The present letter was written to Josef Ludimil Lešikar, a young Czech patriot who had taken an active part in the revolutionary movement of 1848, when he had become acquainted with other Czech patriots, including Karel Havlíček and Božena Němcová. After 1848 he was harassed by the Austrian police for his political activities, and found it impossible to support his family. He finally emigrated in 1853, going to Texas. From there he wrote letters to acquaintances in the home country begging them to send him Czech books to read. Němcová replies to one such letter: the book she sends is most likely Pohorská vesnice *(A Mountain Village), which had just been published a few weeks before, and which Němcová reportedly considered her finest work.*

August 26, 1856

Dear Friend!

With this letter I take the liberty of sending you a copy of my new book. I know how much interest you take in my work and in Czech literature generally, and I hope that you will accept this gift with thanks. I am very glad to hear from you, since recently both my husband and I have thought a great deal about you, especially now that our circumstances are becoming more and more unbearable.

153

You know perhaps that in July our dear friend, the great Czech patriot Karel Havlíček died; he was staying at his brother-in-law's.[1] I visited him often during his illness and, together with his other numerous admirers, my husband and I took part in his public funeral: there I placed a wreath on his coffin. It may be that all his faithful admirers, both from Prague and from the countryside, were there, but I have a feeling that the authorities cannot forget my husband's part in the funeral. When one official came right out and accused him of a wrongdoing—the distribution of death notices—my husband grew very upset and spoke harshly to him, for which he was sentenced to eight days in prison. At the trial the talk was mostly of my husband's "provocative" behavior at the funeral; of the alleged insult no one spoke.[2] Of course my husband made an appeal, but we fear that he will never be permitted to re-enter the civil service, and perhaps will even have difficulties finding a position in business, though he has made application. I fear even worse: that they will take away his pension and forbid us to reside in Prague.

My friend, you can hardly even guess how hard our life is here in the home country. I do not think of myself—I was born to misfortune and poverty—but I am thinking of my children. I have only my work to help feed my family, but consider: how can I write when my head is full of worries about each piece of bread—it acts like a dense fog on my mind. How can I use my spiritual gifts to earn a livelihood for my children and give pleasure to people when life is killing me and the world drives me to my death? It's easy to say: he who does not work shall not eat. An idiot can imagine that if a cobbler can make a shoe on an empty stomach, then a writer can forge a novel for which he will be offered a paltry recompense. Believe me, my friend, were it not for the children I would go and take service somewhere, but so long as my children are not provided for, I must endure it all. How painful it is for me to see my children go in patched clothes alongside the children of the rich!

Forgive me that I make so many complaints concerning our unfavorable circumstances. It was a lucky move, and until death I will never cease to regret that I could not resolve to go to America, when you were going and my husband too was willing to come. I would have spared myself so much bitter experience and avoided this miserable situation. Today I no longer care how things will turn out for us: I am resolved on everything; if I could only bring my children to a more assured future, I myself would be content even with stale bread.

Be well, dear patriot and friend, greet your dear wife and children for me, and all our fine Czech people around you. And please, remember to write to us. Live happily in that new world and never regret having left your own land and going to live abroad—our country is everywhere where there are people who speak our language and share our customs and longings.

Your devoted Božena Němcová

NOTES

1. Karel Havlíček (1821-1856), a Czech national leader who had worked as a journalist and critic to educate his people and help them win political autonomy within the Austrian Empire. He had been arrested and tried several times for his political activities; in 1851 the police exiled him (without trial) to Brixen in the Tyrol, but released him in 1855 when his health was undermined.

2. Josef Němec, Božena's husband, had been dismissed from the Austrian Civil Service because of the part he had played in the Revolution of 1848, and was kept under police surveillance. Apparently the police regarded the publicity given to Havlíček's funeral by Němec as an act of political provocation, intended to create a demonstration. It must be remembered that the period of the 1850's was one of harsh political reaction in Austria.

Němcová seemingly wrote the present letter within several days after her husband's interview with the police and trial.

KAROLÍNA SVĚTLÁ

Johanna Rottová, who later took the pen-name of Karolína Světlá, was born in 1830, the daughter of a Prague tradesman. She married Professor Petr Mužák in 1852; her husband helped to strengthen her already awakened sense of Czech patriotism. She grew very fond of her husband's birthplace in Northeastern Bohemia, the village of Světlá in the shadow of the Ještěd Mountain Range, and spent several months there every year: the locale, people and their dialect were to serve as material for her writing, and she took her pen-name from the name of the village. In 1862 she had a love affair with the writer Jan Neruda, but gossip and her own feelings of duty and guilt led her to break off the relationship, a pattern of self-abnegation often to be repeated in her novels and stories. Her last years were filled with chronic illness and given over to mystic religious and philosophical speculation. She died in 1899.

The Rott family was acquainted with Božena Němcová, whose literary career and writings had a great impact on Světlá. She resembles Němcová in her strong ethnographic influence and use of details of village life. Like Němcová's tales, Světlá's show a strong influence of the fairy tale in their conception of character and construction (the present story can serve as an example). But Světlá lacked Němcová's strong optimism, her hope and her faith in dreams; Světlá's heroines are strong and devoted, but their way leads them ultimately to sacrifice of their own happiness from a sense of duty. Such is the moral of her novel A Village Romance *(1867); in* The Cross by the Brook *(1868) the heroine gives up her own love but accepts her husband's extramarital relationship; ultimately she redeems her husband, however, through her love. Besides the wealth of accurate ethnographic details, Světlá's work is striking in the strength and integrity of her characters, especially the women.*

The present story was first published in Světlá's Sketches from the Ještěd Country *(1873).*

POOR DEAD BARBORA

People found it very funny that Matýsek and Barbora were going together. She towered almost to the ceiling, while when he sat down at the table his head was scarcely visible; she laughed all

157

day long, while he continually pouted; she would have taken on ten Prussian troopers all at once, while he lowered his eyes immediately and grew red if anyone stared at him. Barbora, or Barka as she was known familiarly, was always contented with everything: however things happened, so they happened. If matters were at their worst, she would remark nothing more than "Well, so be it" and would forget it as if it were out of sight and under water. Matýsek on the other hand remembered everything a long time, and at the smallest trifle was already whimpering, "It's too much, it's too much for me!" Whenever people saw them together, they were always surprised at the fact that these two could have taken it into their heads to keep company. It had started when the two of them were in the pasture and had driven their animals into the same part of the field. As soon as Matýsek's two goats were grazing, he turned his back to the field and sat down under a bush, found a bit of wood, pulled out his knife and started to work.

But the other lads wouldn't put up with this; they insisted that everyone who shared the pasture with them should share in their devilment. If Matýsek wouldn't listen—and often he wouldn't—they would grab the knife away from him, throw it away and break whatever it was he had just carved. The more he pouted the more they would grin, as is the way with such fine young fellows.

But the moment when Barka, from a distance, caught sight of the boys preparing to make trouble for Matýsek, she ran straight to the tree, tore off a branch and chased after them. Hardly did they look around when she had caught up with them, and wherever her branch landed, there it landed—why couldn't they leave Matýsek alone?

"This is for a keepsake—whoever isn't satisfied can come back and I'll give him more if he wants," she would shout after them when they were routed, squealing, to all four corners of the earth. With that she set the whimpering Matýsek back in his place under the bush, found him his knife and watched him as before. After this Matýsek would enjoy a fine week or more in the pasture.

It's obvious the boys weren't going to let Barka get away with it, always sticking up for Matýsek.

"Yes, yes," they shouted at her, when she was comforting him, "tuck him nicely in his little box, so the birds don't mistake him for a fly and eat him up, or a grasshopper trample him to death—you couldn't get married then, and we'd lose out on our wedding gifts!"

But the instant they saw Barka raise her branch, they were up and running from her, till their heads shook. They already had proof Barka had the strength of fifteen men, and they knew they wouldn't change her even if all of them went after her together.

* * *

Matýsek worked for an elderly, childless widow who couldn't get around and whose eyes were dim. What he did, he did, and he did it well, and she didn't cheat him on his food: she was happy to have someone work for her who wouldn't cheat her. But still Matýsek would whimper that things were harder for him than for anybody else, and that it was all too much for him to take. Barka worked on the farm of the worst bloodsucker in the whole region, and her fingers were hard as pegs from the work, all the veins on her neck were swollen, and her face was burned so by the sun and wind that the skin peeled off in one piece. She worked for ten ells of linen cloth a year for a blouse and a jacket, and shoes to wear in wintertime only. In place of pay he would give her tips whenever he sold one of his cattle from the shed or when she hauled grain to the mill to be ground. But still she praised the life.

"My farmer doesn't let me go a single day without eating," she bubbled over to Matýsek, "and I've always got shoes to wear to church. Since I've worked there I've bought two kerchiefs, one made of silk, a real skirt and a coat; I don't have to wear homespun to church if I don't want to." Barka had spent over nine years already with her farmer.

Sometimes people would laugh at the idea that these two might be keeping company, and sometimes they would say, laughing of course, that the two of them were as well suited to one another as two pigeons might be. By that they meant that the one was as weak-minded as the other.

If anyone whispered anything of that sort in Barka's hearing, she would always let it go by without saying anything other than her usual, "Well, so be it." But God preserve that anyone should say it about Matýsek—in a trice she was up and at him.

159

"You let Matýsek alone," she would cry, all flushed, "he has enough good sense for his own affairs and doesn't need any for other people's."

Matýsek, of course, didn't fly out at anyone so, should anyone hint at anything against Barka or himself, but still no one could ever efface it from his memory. Should he have to pass by anyone of that sort, he would at once turn his eyes to the ground and never raise them until he was well past, even if he thought the person were going to fire a gun at him. Oh, Matýsek had his own head and knew how to hold it; he also knew how to punish people when he didn't like them.

No girl would go dancing with Matýsek; they said he wasn't fully grown and his looks put them off, and that his mouth puckered so, and he had nothing to wear besides the jacket he had from his dead father, beneath which peeped out a vest of more than ample cut, set with buttons as big as fists, and Lord knows what else they found fault with in him. Let them find fault—he didn't care for them; he danced his fill without them. Barka always came for him by herself to take him dancing. She would take him by both hands, like a mother teaching her year-old child to stand on its feet, and dance with him as long as his wind held out. Her wind was up to spending the whole night dancing.

It wasn't much fun, either, dancing with Matýsek; he knew nothing about music and was too timid to step out in time properly. He fumbled along as best he could, at the same time hanging his head and leaning forward with his whole body; if his partner had not held him so firmly, who knows how many times he might have kissed the floor in an evening. But at his side Barka would jump all the higher and all the more merrily, as she looked out over the whole room to see if everyone was paying attention to what a good dancer Matýsek was. She would smile so that her white teeth shone into every corner. People would hold their sides laughing when they danced.

"Why do you dance all the time with that clumsy? You're a born dancer—we'd like to dance with you!" the boys shouted at Barka, but only for a laugh; what could she say to them, anyway? None of them would have taken her dancing for a fortune, only perhaps if he wanted to insult his girl friend and make her angry.

160

But Barka always knew how to snap back at them.

"Dance with anybody you like, I won't give Matýsek up and I won't hear him slandered like that. He can plait things from brush, make brooms, and carve toys too. Not everybody needs to bang his head against slabs to be beautiful, or crush rocks in his hands, after all."

And she was back again dancing with Matýsek, and if anyone didn't turn quickly enough to suit her, she would take him by the elbow and push him out of the way: didn't he know which life he was in or how he got there? Barka's agility pleased Matýsek enormously, and he was always whispering to her on the sly which of the dancers she should cut out next, cackling at that till he almost choked to death. He told Barka on the way home that he would not choose another girl for all Jerusalem, and that he would remain hers even if the brides in Prague were to send their match-makers to him.

*   *   *

If the widow gave Matýsek bread and cheese on Sunday, he would eat the bread and keep the cheese for Barka. If Barka got a white roll on Sunday from her farmer, she would at once set it aside for Matýsek. As soon as Matýsek had washed his wooden spoon after supper, he would take off his long jumper and put on his father's red vest and blue jacket, which the girls hated so. Scarcely had Barka finished milking in the afternoon than she would throw on her starched skirt and put one of her kerchiefs on her head, the other around her neck, and go off to meet Matýsek.

She knew precisely the moment when he would come, though they never made an agreement, and he was quite certain she would be on her way, even guessed exactly each time at what point on the road she would come into view between the trees.

"You weren't on your way to see somebody else?" he asked when they met.

"Not for seven golden castles," Barka reassured him. It was terrible how fond they were of each other: no other boy and girl were so fond of one another as these two; what the one wanted the other did too—it was as if they had but a single soul.

If it was cold or rainy, they would sit in the shed together; if it was warm and sunny, somewhere on the edge of the field. He

161

would reach into his pocket and hand her the cheese nicely wrapped in a hazel leaf; she would open her white kerchief and shove a white roll into his fist. They would eat and sun themselves, and on some days, if it was very hot, they would doze a bit there. On other days they would go on talking so much they were not able to stop. Matýsek could talk marvellously of strange things, and often he got far ahead of Barka in that; she didn't know from where the ideas came to him. If from the edge of the field he were to see a coach, for instance, driving past along the highway, then he would try to guess who was in it, the steward from the estate, or the brewer from town, or perhaps even the lord prince himself.

"They really ought to put a stop to that, some people riding around all the time and others going only on foot—some people owning everything and others nothing," Matýsek argued amid his speculations.

"I don't think the authorities would put up with that," Barka opined.

"They sure wouldn't—the gentlefolk aren't about to try that," Matýsek cackled. And people said he had a weak mind!

"Maybe if the Lord God wanted it that way, then it would come about," Barka considered, "but most likely not—it wouldn't be good for some people's health."

Matýsek stuck to his opinion, that everyone should be allowed to ride in carriages, and he wouldn't budge. But Barka found a trap for him.

"And who'd take care of the horses then? Who'd feed them and water them?"

To that, of course, Matýsek had no ready answer, and he stared at Barka for a long time with eyes and mouth wide open. He avoided a direct answer by expressing a wish to have so much small change it would jingle in his pocket with every step he took.

"Oh, that will come," Barka consoled him.

"No, it won't," he whimpered, though he really wanted Barka to reassure him once more.

"It will come," she said, "hasn't it started to come now already? And I've started to get some too. We've a fine couple of guilders people are keeping for us, and if we live long enough, we'll have them to spend."

"But where do we have them?"

162

"Our farmers keep them for us. If we stay healthy and work for them another twenty years, then they'll have to pay us a hundred, at least. Just count it all up!"

"You count it up," Matýsek pouted, "you're just teasing me." But he couldn't pout for long, and he even had to smile just a little at the way Barka had turned things around: she seemed to be teasing him, and yet she was right. Yes, she was right, if one went at the matter from all sides and from underneath. Barka, seeing that he was on the point of laughing, began to laugh herself, and she laughed irrepressibly for more than an hour, thinking of all the money they had and how rich they were.

But at the height of her laughter tears came into her eyes.

"One thing came true for my poor dead mother, at least," she said, weeping and laughing together, "She always told me, 'I can't leave you anything, child, but at least God may grant you should inherit my character from me. I don't know how to get angry, and everything I come across I know how to turn to the bright side, no matter what.' "

Matýsek's eyes overflowed just as Barka's had: he couldn't see her laughing without laughing himself, and so he couldn't see her weep without weeping along with her! I said, you remember, that it was as if they had but a single soul.

"I don't ask for anything in the world," sobbed Barka, "but one thing I do ask for: to go some day and have a look around Vamberice.[1] My poor dead mother went there to sacrifice to the Holy Virgin, and there she prayed for me to inherit her character."

"But you'll get to go some day," Matýsek consoled Barka, "and maybe you'll get much more besides," he added and was happy he had remembered to say this and thus make her leave off her tears.

"Do you think I could get a green jacket with a sulfur-yellow trim?" Barka sighed, wiping her eyes with her hard, callused hand. "I must say, I'd like to have something fancy to go to communion in."

"But wouldn't you rather have your own goat and your own little house?" Matýsek interposed.

"Why wouldn't I want a goat and a house too? Of course I would. And believe me, just as soon as I have my own sitting-room, I'd insist on getting a spoonbox to hang up by the stove, painted

163

red as blood, with eight sizes of spoons—four pewter spoons in each size."

"Oh, if only I had my own sitting-room," Matýsek cried, and now he looked a whole head taller, "I'd know what to do. I'd give up all this field work and take up plaiting brooms. That's something for you, and you can sit indoors, warm and cosy, do your own work; people ask about you and have heard of you. No one can do without a broom-maker these days."

"That's true," Barka nodded, "it's a fine thing to be a broom-maker, I think that's a fine trade."

"But, Lord, I wouldn't just make brooms," Matýsek boasted and again he grew by a whole head, "I'd make wooden lanterns and fit them out with glass myself, and if anyone wanted a quail cage made to order, I'd make one and hang a bell on top of it. I'd even make a dog kennel. I'd paint it green and, so everyone would admire it, I'd put a blue star and a yellow moon on it. Don't think I couldn't do it—I could!"

If anyone from the village were to go by and see them sitting there deliberating so eagerly, he would not fail to stop and question them.

"When are you folks going to get married?"

"It will happen some day," Barka discouraged the curious passer-by.

"You've been some time at it already. Why, you were going together when I was courting, and now look, my son's ready to get married himself. . . ."

"Not everything can be done in a hurry; things come to people when they come."

"That's true, of course, but still one has to fix a time for things."

"Well, then, it will happen when our farmers suggest the idea."

"You'll wait some time for that."

"That's the way it is, then. We don't lack for anything, anyway."

Matýsek said nothing, but he took close note of everyone who interrupted them in this fashion: later the man might pass him a hundred times and even call to him, but Matýsek would only drop his eyes to the ground and never raise them until the mocker was past.

*   *   *

How was it Barka guessed that things that are to come to people come of themselves? All that which they had ever wished for and which they had discussed on Sunday afternoons came to pass precisely so. Had anyone told them it would be possible? No one!

Barka's cousin died, a woman to whom she had never even claimed kinship. She had been a strange woman. She had one daughter with whom she had been on bad terms ever since the daughter had married, a thing the mother did not wish. She let the daughter move off to live with her husband somewhere across the frontier,[2] never inquired about her and, should a letter come from her, never accepted it. The mother and daughter had had no news of one another for many years.

When the court officials wrote the daughter after her mother's death to come and claim the inheritance, it turned out that the daughter too had been dead for a long time and her husband as well. They left no children or other relatives, and so everything went to Barka. All at once she owned a little house, an orchard, a tiny field and a small pasture, two goats in a shed, tools and materials for carpentry and cooping all about, and in a closet two full chests, one with the clothes of her late cousin-in-law. He had been a carpenter and had dressed quite properly. He left a furskin cloak and a blue coat, the latter as fine as if the tailor had just finished work on it. And when Barka opened the other chest, the first thing she came on was—a green jacket with sulfur-yellow trim!

Underneath the jacket in the chest there were so many skirts Barka might have worn a different one for each day of the week, but such a thing she never could have done for the world. She feared God too much.

The first news of her inheritance had so staggered Barka they had to pinch her arms to bring her back to her senses. And why not, for it was most incredible. She stood and stood there, unable to realize that everything which had belonged to her cousin was hers now, and that she need never again work as a servant until her death, or Matýsek either.

"Just get some sense," her farmer told her. "If you're foolish, people will soon take it away from you, what God had saved up for you. I can already see you, letting yourself be cheated until you won't have anything left. I must give you help with it, otherwise you'll be complaining that I had no more sense than you had. The best thing would be if you got married, and right away. I can tell you a husband right off who would know how to farm that place of yours so you wouldn't have to take care of anything yourself."

And he named his own brother, who had lost his own wife about a year before. People said he had beaten her to death. He was a brawler famous far and wide; you had only to brush up against him, ever so lightly, without intending any harm, and already you were in trouble; people went a hundred paces or more out of their way to keep away from him. His children took after him, and were every bit as mean as their father. The farmer was afraid his brother would kill someone and be sent to prison, and then he would have to take care of the wretched children. He preferred to wish them onto Barka.

Again they had to bring Barka back to her senses, she was so frightened by his talk.

"How can you speak about your brother, when you know I've got Matýsek?" she reproached him, trembling all over.

"You aren't going to marry that hungry little dwarf, now you've got a house and lot? He's got nothing and his whole life he won't have anything. He was good enough as long as no one else wanted you." You should have seen Barka then, how she got her dander up! She flushed all over, and every nerve throbbed inside her.

"If I wasn't good enough for someone then," she exploded, "then he isn't good enough for me now. Matýsek's been going with me for a long time, and he never wanted to go with any other girl, even if some lady in Prague were to send matchmakers to him he wouldn't receive them for all Jerusalem—and now you'd have me go with someone else? Not for seven golden castles, even if my own patron saint were to make the match for me! Why I wouldn't even do it for Our Lady—give him up—and that I swear. . . ."

And Barka felt sick, she was so pained at the thought that they were trying to take her away from Matýsek. When she recovered her breathing she began to wail so for Matýsek it could be heard as far as the village square. She could not be repressed, and the farmer, though he spoke fiercely and insistently, trying to provide a living for his brawling brother and his worthless children, couldn't manage it. In anger he left her, seeing at last that she wouldn't budge, but he did not speak another word to her so long as she stayed in his house.

For his part Matýsek was not the least surprised how things had turned out. Hadn't Barka promised this all the time? They had been expecting it, they had kept talking about it, and at last it had come to pass—what was so strange about that? He was even surprised that it hadn't come sooner. Nor did it ever occur to him that he might now not be a match for Barka. Here and there people did hint at this to him from envy, but he laughed in their faces. How could he not be a proper match? For her no one else in the world would suit.

Barka stood staring at him when he announced to her he would go to see the parish priest to arrange for the wedding bans. She could not comprehend where he had found so much courage. As soon as she asked him if he didn't think he should go, he assumed a weighty air, set out and walked across the entire village to the priest's so that, when he entered the latter's receiving room, the reverend sir could not even be sure it wasn't some fine gentleman pressing toward him. From the time he heard the bans announced in church, Matýsek never got out of anyone's way, and everybody else had to get out of his. God can only judge, where and how he learned to make a change so great. People who had not seen him for a long time and then met up with him were at a loss to know how to talk to him. In a word, he was a totally different person.

Along with the house Barka had inherited a hired woman with four children.[3] She was pleased with this, for she thought of her own widowed mother and her own orphaned childhood, and at once gave the children her love.

Not so Matýsek. He looked the woman and her children over with a glance so strict the woman took refuge behind Barka and the children began to tremble, at which he asked them whether they had a proper awareness of who he was? When the poor children did not know what to say to him, he told them that he was the master here, that they all must obey him, and that should he order anything in the house or in the field or in the shed, it must be done just as he commanded. To confirm this teaching with an example, he sent each child out five times or more for something no one needed, and each time it had to be taken back again.

167

The children did not even dare breathe.

"You'd like it," Matýsek continued, "being idle all day long, not minding anything or afraid of anyone? I'm going to change all that. I'm going to exercise you and drill you till I teach you some order."

Speeches like this pleased Barka very much: why shouldn't he bawl at the kids if he wished? He couldn't hurt them by shouting at them, and playing the master he made a fine figure of a man. The first day after the wedding she gave him kreutzers to put in his pocket, enough that they made a jingle there; the children weren't even allowed to approach him or they might lose the coins for him, and when he donned his long coat on Sundays they were not even permitted to look at him, lest they dirty it.

Oh, now Matýsek could spin on his heel in the warm, cosy sitting-room, where he summoned the children ten times a day in order to question them and learn from them who was the master, and from which he banished them ten times again for the most varied crimes, to which in first place belonged impolite coughs or sneezes, but even more than that for silence in reply to his questions dealing with his own person, importance and significance. Sometimes they accomplished no more than devoting the whole morning to opening and closing doors.

Barka did not cease to be amazed at the good fortune that had come to them, especially when she fixed her gaze on the wall by the stove, where they hung a spoonbox painted red, for eight sizes of spoons and with four pewter spoons in each size, like she had always wanted. Sometimes she would gaze at it for a whole hour. She and Matýsek now ate with no other spoons than the pewter ones or with other dishes than porcelain; in the whole house not a single wooden spoon or wooden dish was to be found. Nor could you have found such a thing had you searched from attic to cellar and turned everything upside down. Indeed, there was no reason for surprise that Matýsek should play the lord, or that Barka permitted him to do it. Matýsek began what he had already said he would: he gave up all farm work and took to making brooms. Barka wasn't permitted to go to pasture either, nor would he let her go out to the thicket for wood; all that was for the hired woman to do, and Barka could only busy herself about the stove or spin at his side. He wanted her to spend her time watching and admiring him.

And Barka gave him her admiration, not only because he so wanted her to but because she really did admire his skill. He made not only brooms, but lanterns and cages, whatever anyone might order. Many people now knew about Matýsek and came to see him. But he had known all the time that one day he would be famous. He often told the children how he had known that and had thought of it long ago, when Barka was still taking his part in the pasture with her branch. And he kept reminding them to pay careful attention to his every word and deed, so that some day they would come to be like him, though he expressed many doubts that this would really come to pass. In them, he said, he couldn't see a single vein of himself.

All day long the children had to jump around Matýsek, run out and back in again, speak and not speak, at one time hand him everything, and at another just stand there and not give a whimper or budge, whatever he took into his head to make them do. Meanwhile Barka would often give them food to taste, tidbits their mother couldn't offer them, just so Matýsek's good advice should seem more appealing to them. Matýsek was never to see this, and she always had to make her gifts secret so he would not find out. The moment he noticed anything he would pout and whimper, "Why couldn't you have given it to me—I'd have put it to good use, and the children will only drop it when they're on the run."

The kennel with its star and moon which Matýsek had looked forward to for so long and with such joy he now built.

"Why shouldn't we have something special too?" he told Barka and bought a dog for the kennel. Though it was white, they named it Gypsy. His old mistress had a dog named Gypsy and he could not forget the name.

When it was windy out, Matýsek would lose himself in thought and not talk for two hours together.

"What have you got in that head of yours?" Barka would ask, at the same time smiling with pride. She knew he was working something out, something that no one else would have thought of. And she was right.

"I'm considering that if a man were to make a cage for the wind, then he could catch it and keep it in there. That would be an advantage in our mountains, wouldn't it, our Barka?"

Ever since they had been married, they called each other nothing but "our Matýsek" and "our Barka."

169

Barka agreed that it would be a very advantageous thing for people if they could catch the wind in a cage so that it could not harm them.

"Well, who knows if you won't hit on it," she opined. "When people got the idea of trapping thunder—and it was caught too—why shouldn't you make a cage that would catch the wind?"

Sometimes out of a clear sky Matýsek would throw down his broom and stretch out on the bench at the table.

"I don't have to work if I don't want to, do I, our Barka? No one can give me orders, or you either. Leave that spinning and come over here, sit down beside me at the table. We can play cards a bit, while we have a smoke and something to drink."

"Well, so be it," Barka agreed, got up from her spinning-wheel and went over to the cupboard for pipes, cards and glasses. Each of them lit his pipe, and Barka filled the glasses with home-made cordial and shuffled the cards; they played, drank and smoked to their hearts' content. Actually Matýsek had never learned to play cards before, nor had he smoked, and the cordial was hard for him to swallow without choking; he had never drunk anything stronger than whey. But Barka had been telling him for so long that he would be missing something if he didn't learn, so finally he gave in and consented to try. But she had to try it with him, for without her he would scarcely have ventured to do it, and if she wished him to keep at it, as befitted a proper farmer who wants to pass for something in the world, then she had to join him in the smoking and drinking.

Scarcely had Barka set up her new household, than she thought about Vamberice. She believed that her continual good luck was due to the fact that her mother had consecrated her there.

Matýsek couldn't wait for her to get home from the pilgrimage; the very first day he kept running every so often to the window to look out and see if she weren't back yet. To make the time pass quicker, he would advance the hands on the clock, walk part of the way out to meet her, and make marks on the door to show how many days she had been gone and by when she was sure to return.

"It's too much, it's too much for me!" he whimpered, going back to the sitting-room himself. The whole time he didn't touch cards or his pipe or the glass, he even lost his love for making

170

brooms. The woman couldn't do anything right. Barka had told her to cook for Matýsek in her absence, but whatever she made and set on the table had something wrong with it.

The children had it the worst: the moment they crossed his path he would run after them with a switch and drive them away. If they were not near him, he would run after them with the switch anyway and demand to know why they weren't in the sitting-room. And so it all went as in a farce. The sun could still be shining brightly, and he was already calling to the woman, "Have the kids say their prayers and get to bed so I can have some peace!" As soon as she had heard their prayers and sent them off to sleep on the hay, he would lay into her again and ask why she was raising her kids to be loafers who would never learn anything but how to sleep and would most certainly come to a bad end in this world. He so upset the woman with his talk of a "bad end" that she herself would grab the switch and chase the children from their loft. Sleepy, they had to sit beside her in the corridor around the upturned sauerkraut barrel and flake chicken feathers for pillows for the winter. Usually they did this for so long that both children and mother would slide from the barrel down to the floor, where they all slept till morning, exhausted with fear, running about, and with the ceaseless disturbance; when they got up in the morning, the mad dance would begin again.

When Barka returned she had many things to tone down and straighten out. They were all careworn and ill, from all sides she heard nothing but complaints, and the accusations were such that it was difficult to judge. Finally she put an end to it all by taking an oath: she would never go on a pilgrimage again. The poor woman did not realise that soon she would take another pilgrimage, one from which there is no return.

*   *   *

Suddenly out of a clear sky Barka's hand began to swell.

"That's because I don't do anything," she told Matýsek. "All the strength's staying inside the hand—that's why it swells. Not everyone can stay idle, I said it to you more than once when we were still single and you would talk about everyone riding around and doing nothing."

The woman didn't like the look of the hand, and thought it might be in the bone.

"As soon as the snow melts, I'll go over the mountains and bring the healer. He's famous, and he doesn't charge you very much."

"Just let him say whatever he wants—I'll count it out to him right on this table," Matýsek boasted, jingling the coins in his pocket. It saddened him that Barka was ailing, and that every so often she had to lie down to rest. He grew lonely the moment she wasn't with him. She had to have her bed moved out and put right under the window, so that she could have a good view of him and he of her.

The woman did not wait for the snow to melt, but the first day the sun shone warm and from the windows looking onto the orchard a trickle of water could be seen piercing the snow, she gave no heed to the drifts and set out over the mountains for the healer, bringing him back to Barka without mishap.

The healer looked over the swollen hand, took out some sort of oil and told her to rub it on hard and often; should the oil not help, she should send to him again and he would give her medicine, after which she would certainly get better. But he did not deceive Barka.

From the expression in his eyes as he glanced at the woman, Barka realized that no oil, no ointment would help her; she knew that she would never get up again well—the woman was right, and the bone was rotting in her hand.

The woman went out to see the healer off, and Matýsek went too, to hear if his coins, to which Barka had to add quite a few more, would jingle in the healer's pocket the way they had in his. Barka was left alone in the sitting-room.

For a while she sat on the bed not realizing where the ideas in her head had gone; it was empty all of a sudden. She could not imagine how Matýsek could be left here without her, who would tell him what clothes to wear on Sunday: his furskin cloak or his coat; who would go along with him to church wearing the green jacket, with whom he was to talk, drink and smoke, who would stay with him here in the world till old age, who would wait on him, cater to him. . . .

She glanced through the window at the orchard, where Matýsek, leaving the woman to finish the task of seeing the healer off on his way, had stopped and begun to drill the children again. Today was the first day they had ventured outside.

It was a lovely evening; on the summits of the mountains crowns of roses were on fire, and the heavens looked like a golden sea that was slowly turning pale until the first stars of evening shone. They smiled at the mountains and the thought of the time when these would be green and happy again, when the fir groves would be heavy with the scent of trees and the blue violets, when they would hear the nightingale sing beside the brook, when from each craggy rock a flower would bud and in each furrow a lark would hide. They too felt sad, seeing nothing but snow, hoarfrost and frozen ground below.

Barka's eyes grew damp and great drops fell on her clasped hands: spring had come for her for the last time—but at once her thoughts turned to Matýsek.

"He must not be left a widower; with the house any woman would marry him now, and not just any one at all, but a good woman of the proper sort . . . the best thing would be if I were to pick one out for him . . . it's too bad he doesn't care for our hired woman—she wouldn't harm him in any way. . . ."

At that moment a young woman ran into the orchard to return an axe she had borrowed from Matýsek. She started to joke with him.

"When are you going to get a divorce from that wife of yours so you can marry me?" she laughed at him. All the girls spoke to him that way when they caught him by himself.

Matýsek always took them seriously. "Would you?" he stretched himself till he was a whole head taller. "I'll bet you would! And others would have me too, I've got to watch out for them. Just remember I wouldn't marry anyone else than Barka for all of Jerusalem. I wouldn't give her up if the brides from the seven golden castles sent their matchmakers to me, even from Prague itself."

"And what if you became a widower?"

"Get away!" Matýsek tramped toward her all flushed with anger and raised his axe to her. The girl laughed all the harder, but still she had to run.

And weeping in the bed, Barka felt as if all the nightingales which were preparing to celebrate the coming of spring in the mountains had begun to sing in her breast, as if all the violets

173

which were going to waft their scent in the green groves had blossomed in her heart. . . . Matýsek wanted her as no other boy had ever wanted his girl; no other husband and wife were so happy as they, even if you went round the whole world to look for them.

And meekly she hung her head and admitted that she had dwelt here long enough in joy, in plenty and happiness, that it was entirely just that her lot should pass on to another. . . .

"It wouldn't work to pick out a bride for him; he wouldn't take another, whatever might happen to him. I must arrange it some other way, so things go along without me," she said, wiping her eyes. "If only he wouldn't be here when they carry me out. I'd certainly turn over in my coffin before they put me in the ground when I saw what he'd be up to. They say a dead person sees and hears everything that goes on around him till the priest sprinkles holy water on his grave; what I'd see and hear—Lord! He won't want to give me up to death, but the way he'll anger God with that stubborn head of his!"

And from then on Barka thought of nothing but how to arrange things so that Matýsek would let her go without fussing too much, and so he wouldn't miss her too much after she was gone.

"If I can just last till cranberry time, then I'll clear out without his noticing," she prayed. She prayed so zealously and so earnestly that, though her hand was now nothing but one enormous wound, and her body nothing but skin and bone, still she lived through the spring and the summer. Everyone who came to visit her took the last farewell of her and departing, knew that he would never see her alive again; only Matýsek noticed nothing. He was already used to seeing her in bed all the time, and if he ever began to ponder it more seriously, Barka would pull him out of it with some joke or other. We know how she was able to turn everything to its bright side, and this ability remained with her until the very end.

One afternoon in early September Matýsek was finishing work on a cage for a rare bird for the priest. He was pleased with it, and kept dancing around it. Again the idea came to him that it would be a good thing to invent some sort of cage not only for birds, but for the wind.

This time Barka did not reply that there could be no doubt that, if people had invented a trap to catch thunder with, he could succeed as well.

He noticed this and went over to her.

"What's wrong, our Barka, that you talk so little nowadays?" he asked, stroking her bandaged hand and sadly gazing into her sad eyes.

Today for the first time he noticed how careworn and pale she looked. She had scarcely any breath left. For the first time, perhaps, he had an inkling of what was in store for him.

"But that's just because it's taken so long," Barka consoled him and tried her bright, welcoming smile at which she was so successful. "It will turn very soon now. I think I might get well quickly if I could just eat my fill of cranberries."

"You can have all you want of them, in the grove the ground looks like a red carpet. I saw it this morning on my way to get sticks for the cage."

"Those wouldn't help me or refresh me. If cranberries are to do any good, they must come from Bezděz itself.[4] Our Lady Mary sprinkles them with dew, on purpose for sick people."

"Someone from here can set out for there tomorrow."

"That's what I thought too. I'll tell the woman to let the kids go."

"What good could they do?" Matýsek objected, "They'd make a fine mess of things. They'd bring back leaves and stems, ripe ones, unripe ones, green ones—all mixed up together. You'd like those! And who knows if those rogues have ever been as far as Bezděz. They'd loiter around wherever they might take a fancy, and then say brazenly they'd been to Bezděz. They'd be good for nothing except carrying the load; someone mature, wise, reliable has to go with them. You know, I could go with them myself, no one knows how to drill them and put them through their paces the way I can."

Barka had him where she had wanted to put him: he was thus made ready for the three-day trip, in which time she could set out on her own journey—to eternity. Her peaceful eye had already gazed into its depths, but her lips still smiled. For she had dwelt here long enough in happiness, joy and plenty with her husband, who wanted her as no husband had ever wanted his wife.

"Of all people it's you who are the best," she whispered to him, "Since we've been together I've never heard a single harsh word from you, or had a single blow, you haven't even snapped at me once; God bless you a hundred thousand times for that. . . ."

175

Matýsek smiled in self-satisfaction, jingling the coins in his pocket.

"Such a good character as yours no other wife has, you can turn everything onto the bright side, and whatever a man has in store for him that's good—you know about it beforehand and promise it to him. Only stop being so thin and pale, and your lips are so blue and they quiver so."

And again Matýsek stroked her bandaged hand and again as before he gazed at her with the same uncertain, concerned look.

"I'll be well again, as soon as I eat your cranberries—I'll run around like a chicken to get them!"

"If only you were well now!"

"I will be, for certain, the Virgin has promised me. But if I do get well, I must go and visit her in Vamberice. She asked it of me in a dream last night and I promised to go."

"You shouldn't have promised," Matýsek whimpered and hung his head, "why, you gave your oath to us all you wouldn't go on any more pilgrimages."

"This time it will be different," Barka calmed him, "the woman will take better care of you, and the kids, too, behave better now. It will all work out just as if I were here."

"No, no, it won't," Matýsek grieved and clutched her feather-bed like a child whose mother seeks to give him the slip.

"You'll see it will work out," Barka smiled at him, but within herself she felt that she was already standing at the gate of Heaven. "Just give the woman orders for whatever you want, so she'll do it; she's not a bad person, you know, she'll gladly do everything for you just the way you want and she'll keep house for you in my place. She knows the house will be hers some day if she serves us both well till we die, she has it in writing. Don't stay home all the time, go out sometimes, look around and visit the neighbors so you'll know what's going on among folks in the world, and so you'll have something to laugh at. Go to church too and pray there for me, it's good for people who are making a journey if we pray for them at home. . . . I'll remember you too in my prayers. . . . I won't even do anything there but pray for you!"

"If you'd just stay here instead!"

"Keep your things in good shape, so they'll last. Wear your furskin cloak whenever you want, but spare your coat, you won't buy another soon again. Those new shirts for which I spun

176

yarn last winter—you know, the ones with the tiny red hearts on the collar—don't wear them all the time. Wear them only on Sundays and holidays, so they won't get worn out right away, then you wouldn't have anything I made to remember me by—and I'd feel sad. . . . Don't give up work, carve something every day; that way you'll chase away your loneliness. The best thing would be if you started working on that cage for the wind, and when you get tired of that, call in the woman, play some cards, drink and smoke. . . ."

"Oh, I couldn't drink away being lonely without you, and I couldn't smoke it away either, I know that like I do my catechism," poor Matýsek lamented and kept clutching the featherbed tighter and tighter. Tears as big as peas flowed from his eyes. And no longer could Barka behold his grief with dry eyes; she too relieved her feelings with tears.

"Well, do you know what," she sobbed, putting her good arm around his neck, "if you're too lonely here and things don't go well without me—you needn't leave me all alone there. You can run over there and fetch me."

You should have heard what joyous laughter Matýsek fell into when Barka suggested how he should best deal with his loneliness. He would let her go on the pilgrimage and he would no longer try to prevent her, but when the days weren't counting off quickly enough and when he'd feel just the least bit sad, then he could run and fetch her. Barka on her pilgrimage wouldn't even expect him, and all of a sudden he would take her by the apron and then he wouldn't let her go—she'd see. . . .

*   *   *

If Matýsek had let the children go by themselves to Bezděz for cranberries, they would have done to a hair's breadth what he had predicted to Barka. The journey to and from was occupied with constant promptings and drill. When they took a liking to a place they wanted to stop there and pick, no matter where. They would have been a fine help to Barka. They had no other concern for their trip than to eat as many black raspberries and blackberries as they could, their faces and hands constantly looked as if someone had painted them; at each well he had to stop them and make them wash so that people who met them would not be too frightened. He told himself how he would complain to Barka about what he had gone through with them during those three days, trouble such as he had never undergone before this, so much so these cranberries must certainly do her good.

He drove the children forward like a flock of young goats, each with a load that would have cured ten people, not to speak of one. They too knew what reports they would give of their trip to Bezděz and the things they had learned, things they had never known previously.

Before the woman could stop him, he rushed through the door of the sitting-room with them so that Barka might have the joy of gazing at that bountiful harvest—but he stopped short on the threshold as if he had grown fast to it—the bed by the window was empty, and Barka was nowhere in the room.

It took quite a while until the woman's tears had abated and she could come up to him. He asked her nothing, did not even look around at her, though he felt her beside him.

"You're surprised, aren't you, Matýsek?" she finally forced the words, though she felt as if her heart within her would break. "You were hardly gone when the mistress felt well enough to get up. She didn't want to delay—she left on a pilgrimage! She said she had already spoken to you about how you were to manage everything if you didn't find her at home."

Barka had died a few hours after Matýsek's departure; she had felt her hour coming and had disappeared, fortunately, before he returned, as she had fervently asked of God. She had provided for the funeral, given the money and made all the arrangements, asking each person for God's sake not to betray her secret to Matýsek—that she would never return home again—until he himself should hit on it. She hoped that he would gradually grow used to the idea that she was tarrying too long on a pilgrimage.

He—how could he get used to doing without her!

The woman slowly led Matýsek to the table, without his resisting. She brought him something to eat and took care of him as she had promised Barka on pain of her salvation. Matýsek did not answer her. Not touching the food, he sat there in silence, without moving, with his gaze fixed on the bed, as if there were not a drop of blood in him. . . .

178

No power could persuade him to go to bed; the whole night he stayed sitting at the table, staring constantly with his empty gaze at the empty bed. . . .

When the woman came in next morning, he was still sitting at the table. It seemed to her that he had aged twenty years and that his hair had suddenly turned white, but this time he spoke to her. "It's too much, it's too much for me!" he said in a strange, hoarse voice, "to go away like that and stay away, who ever heard of such a thing. But since she felt like going, let her stay there; I'll do my own work, things can get along without her."

"That's right," the woman praised him, "let her go on the pilgrimage if she feels like it, and we'll stay here. If you're sad that she's gone, the best way to punish her is not show it. She'll think twice then before she chases off like that again. Have a drink and drown your sorrow."

And the woman brought Matýsek glasses, cards and pipe, all as Barka had ordered. Matýsek eagerly seized the glass and the cards and the pipe. But the glass stayed full, the pipe went out in his mouth, and all of a sudden he had forgotten the names of the cards. Ah, he had told her it wouldn't work without her, and still she had gone! Was it any wonder, then, if again he didn't go to bed the whole night long, but sat at the table and muttered in a dark voice that was not his own, "It's too much, it's too much for me!"

His work went no better. He carved, smoothed the wood off, and glued, but when he tried to put it all together, he didn't know what went with what, he missed her bright smile, her loving words which always made everything clear for him and which, should his mind wander, set him back on the right path again. Since she was no longer there to admire him, he mixed everything up, so that no one could make heads or tails of it. Even the humble brooms no longer turned out smoothly, and his new brooms were not in the least like the old ones.

"It's too much, it's too much for me!" he lamented in his corner, from which he had such a fine view of the bed. "So long as Barka's gone, I can't manage anything because of the grief she's made with her leaving."

And he remained sitting passively at his place for whole hours, not taking his eyes from the bed, as if by staring at it he could force her finally to show up there.

179

Sometimes he got up and walked over to the clock, evidently wishing to push the hands forward so it would run faster, but after a while he would go back again with his head hanging. At other times he would seize the chalk as if he wanted to make lines on the door to show how long Barka had been gone and reckon when she would return, as he had done before when she went off on a pilgrimage; often he went to the door as if he wanted to look out to see if she were coming, but he never carried out his intention. To himself he appeared as if he believed in her pilgrimage, but at the same time he must have known quite well that she had undertaken another kind of journey from which no one had ever returned, no matter how people waited for her and advanced their clocks in order to bring more quickly the time when they would see her again, or made on the door God knows how many chalk marks. . . .

Matýsek convinced himself only in his own eyes and in other people's; but when he came to meet God, he suddenly confessed the truth. No longer in church did he turn with the married men to the benches on the right, but he cowered in the vestibule among the beggars, who had nothing and no one. There he knelt, pressed the rosary to his lips and those who stood beside him heard nothing the whole mass long but his whispering, "For poor dead Barbora, for poor dead Barbora. . . ."

But when he had left the church, again he sought to ignore the fact of her death, and whomever he met he would stop and ask whether he had seen Barka anywhere, and complain to him that it was too much, it was too much for him, when his wife wouldn't come back home to him from a pilgrimage!

And people let him have his way and agreed he had a cross to bear with a roving wife. Many counselled him to leave her where she was and not let her in, even if she should come home right away. He nodded to them that he would do so and looked forward to the way she'd have to beg before he would let her in again. He decided that he would let her plead a long time at the door before he'd open it—but the moment he entered the sitting-room where her empty bed stood by the window, the bed from which she had smiled at him so that his work flew along as if it were play when she looked at him with such joy, so that he could make anything people requested of him, even perhaps that very cage in which the wind could be trapped and held—there he sank

180

down again on his stool, staring dully and emptily into space, and his poor mind did not know how to cope with what fate had sent him.

One morning he arose early with a bright face. It was Sunday and the bells were just ringing for matins.

"Bring me one of my shirts with the red hearts from the closet, and my blue coat too," he commanded the woman with his old voice and manner.

She was very surprised, for since Barka had died he had not worn the coat. He was saving it, as Barka had told him, and the shirts with the red hearts for which she had spun yarn he was saving as well.

Oh, he knew by heart each word of hers she had said to him that evening before she had sent him off to Bezděz.

"Don't expect me back from church today," he told the woman.

"Why not?"

"I can't stand it here any more; I've got to come to terms with it. I'm going on a journey. I'm going to Vambeřice. She told me if she should stay there too long, I should run and fetch her, and that's just what I'll do. She'll look surprised when I come up to her all of a sudden and say, 'Here I am, our Barka!' "

The woman supposed he was no more serious about that than he had been when he said he would lock the door on Barka should she come back home again. Approving of his proposal, she brought him his rosary and cane.

For a long time she watched how he walked along by himself and tears came into her eyes. She had so liked to watch the couple walk to church together, you could tell by their gait how happy they were to walk at one another's side, how happy they were to live in the world together. . . . True, people laughed at them and whispered all sorts of things about them, that they were feeble minded, for instance, but so few sins as they had on their consciences you couldn't find in any other home in the whole county.

But the woman waited in vain for Matýsek to come home for dinner. The children came running back without him, out of breath, hot and terrified. Matýsek had knelt as always in the vestibule, they told her, and prayed with his rosary for poor dead Barbora, but when people stood up at the end of the mass, he

181

alone did not rise; when they all went out of the church, he alone did not go. The children had tapped him on the shoulder, he did not stir, though he gazed at them in a strange manner. Terror came over the children and they began to shout. People came running, raised Matýsek, tried to revive him, but he was stiff. . . .

Matýsek in truth had gone off to join Barka, since he could not wait for her; he had come to terms with his loneliness.

And no wonder: it was too much, it was too much for him!

NOTES

1. Vamberice (German Albendorf), a celebrated place of pilgrimage in Silesia.
2. Across the frontier, i.e., in German-speaking Silesia.
3. The Czech term *podruh* (fem. *podruhyně*) denotes a kind of tenant farmer who is dependent on the farm owner and works for him.
4. Bezděz, an ancient village with castle ruins in Northern Bohemia.

JAN NERUDA

*Jan Neruda was born in Prague in 1834, in the Malá Strána, the pictur-
esque old district lying beneath Hradčany Castle on the west bank of the
River Vltava, a quarter of the city he was to celebrate in his writings. His
father was a retired soldier who opened a small food shop, and the family's
circumstances were modest. He went to high school there, and later to the
Academic High School in Prague. An acquaintance with many older writers,
such as Erben and Božena Němcová, as well as comradeship with aspiring
writers of the young student generation, especially Vítězslav Hálek, helped
to inspire Neruda's literary interests. He entered Prague University in 1853,
in the Faculties of Philosophy and Law, but did not complete his studies
because of lack of funds. Around 1856 he took a position as reporter on the
German daily paper* Tagesbote aus Böhmen *(no Czech newspapers had been
permitted to appear during the 1850's). Starting in 1859, he worked for
several new Czech magazines and newspapers, finally ending up with the
newly founded Národní listy in 1865. More and more he devoted himself to
literary and dramatic criticism; at the same time he wrote and published
poetry, and he became the leading Czech poet of his generation. A short-
lived relationship with the writer Karolína Světlá in 1862 ended with her
breaking off the affair.*

*Neruda's prose grew out of his newspaper work. He specialized in
writing daily feuilletons or columns which, written in an informal, chatty
style, he employed systematically in order to interest the reader in his own
concerns for national development, education, and self-improvement. He
stood for democracy, equal rights for women, social justice and economic
amelioration of the conditions of life of the workers. Still it is perhaps something of a surprise to find him seeming to make common cause (though not
without certain apprehensions) with the workers in the celebrated Prague
May Day demonstration of 1890.*

*Neruda's feuilletons developed into literary sketches and finally a vol-
ume of stories, his prose masterpiece, appeared, the* Tales of the Malá Strána
*(1878). Pictures of the self-satisfied middle-class burgher life in the ancient,
settled, almost stagnant Malá Strána quarter he recollected from childhood,
they are incisive masterpieces of genre realism and, at times, caustic satires
directed against a staid bourgeois existence which stifled progress and brought
needless sacrifices in the name of a self-satisfied, bourgeois Philistine morality.
The first story below, "How Mr. Vorel Broke in His Pipe," is an example of
this satirical, anti-bourgeois type which is typical of most of the stories.*

183

One or two of the stories are essentially childhood reminiscences; the long humorous story given below, "How It Happened . . . ," is of this second type: the exaggerated, romantic patriotism of the schoolboys is close to factual reminiscence, even though the patriotic plot they fabricate is of course an invention. Neruda is criticizing here not the patriotic cause as such (he himself had labored to promote the same), but a patriotic cause which had no tie with practical reality, which had no chance of success without long patient labor and the establishment of national institutions on which a strong democratic political movement could be based. In this story he also protests against a romanticism which looks back to a glorious past (in this case the great time of the Hussite Wars, when the Czechs held off half of Europe), without coming to grips with the reality of the present.

Though Neruda's career was long, and in many ways he never outlived the positivistic, anti-romantic mood which prevailed during the 1860's when he first came to literature, still he himself grew and developed over the years, and his talent, in particular his poetic gift, never dried up but found ever new forms of expression. Illness confined him to his apartment during the last years, however, and he died quite alone, in 1891.

TALES OF THE MALÁ STRÁNA

HOW MR. VOREL BROKE IN HIS PIPE

On February 16, 184_, Mr. Vorel opened his new flour store in the building known as "The Green Angel."[1] "Du, Poldi, hörst,"[2] the captain's wife said to her unmarried daughter on the floor above us; the daughter was just leaving for market and was already on the sidewalk outside. "Buy groats from that new man; we can try him."

Many casual readers will perhaps suppose that the opening of a new flour store was in no way anything special. But to these I would respond merely, "Oh, you poor fellows!" or I would even shrug my shoulders and respond nothing at all. In those days when a country person who might not have visited Prague for a good twenty years or so and who would then drive in through Strahov Gate and on down to Ostruhová Street[3] would find the clothing store on the same corner where it had stood twenty years before, the baker under the same signboard, and the greengrocer in the same building. In those days everything had its own fixed place, and to set up, all of a sudden, a flour store where a clothing merchant had once been was a thing so silly that it would not even have occurred to anyone. A shop was handed down from father to son, and if it should sometimes pass to someone who had moved in from another part of Prague or from the countryside, the natives did not regard this as too strange, for still it had in some way obeyed their sense of accustomed order and had not confused them by innovation. This Mr. Vorel, however, was not only someone quite foreign, but he had set up his shop in the building known as "The Green Angel," where there had never been any shop before, and what was more he had had the ground floor apartment broken out so that it now opened directly onto the street! Where previously there had always been a bay window at which sat, all day long from morning till evening, a Mrs. Staňková with a green shade on her eyes and a prayerbook in her lap, so that everybody who walked past could see her. The elderly widow had been moved away three months before to Košiře and now—but what good was such a shop, anyway! There was one flour dealer in Ostruhová Street already, all the way down the hill to be sure, and what was the point of another one? In those times people still had some money saved and could buy the bulk of their supplies directly from the mill. Perhaps Mr. Vorel thought, "Anyway, it will work!" Perhaps he thought with self-satisfaction that he was a young, good-looking fellow, with round cheeks, dreamy blue eyes, slender as a young girl, that he was a bachelor and that the cooks would come to his shop to buy. But such things are still all very dubious.

And it was also just about three months since Mr. Vorel had moved to Ostruhová Street; he had come from somewhere in the country. Nothing was known about him save that he was a miller's son; perhaps he would have told people more, and even willingly, but they didn't ask him. They displayed toward him all the arrogance of natives, and he was a foreigner to them. Evenings he would sit at the "Yellow House" with a jug of beer on the corner of his table beside the stove, utterly alone. The others did not even notice him except to nod their heads when he greeted them. Whoever came in after he did looked at him and could have supposed him a total stranger, come here for the first time; if it was he who came in afterwards, the conversation would quiet down when he made his entrance. Even the day before no one had noticed him, and yet such a hearty celebration was in progress! Mr. Jarmárka, the postal clerk, was celebrating his silver wedding anniversary. It was true that Mr. Jarmárka was still a bachelor, but on February 18, twenty-five years ago today, he had almost been married. His bride had died the day before the wedding; Mr. Jarmárka thought no longer then of marrying and had remained true to his intended, and he was quite serious in suggesting that today was his silver anniversary. His neighbors too, all most worthy folk, saw nothing strange in this either, and when at the end of the customary daily beer-drinking Mr. Jarmárka had produced three bottles of Mělník wine, they were sincerely glad to drink his health. The glasses made the rounds—the innkeeper's wife had no more than two of them in her whole stock—but neither of these reached Mr. Vorel's table. And yet today Mr. Vorel had a brand new Meerschaum pipe, bound in silver, and he had equipped himself with it just so he could look like one of them.

On the sixteenth of February then, at six o'clock in the morning, Mr. Vorel opened his new shop in "The Green Angel." On the preceding day everything had been made ready, and the shop sparkled, new and white. In the compartments and sacks the flour shone whiter than the freshly whitewashed wall and the dried yellow peas stood out brighter than the orange-painted counter. The natives, when they went past and on down the street, took a good look inside, and some of them even went back a step or two to take another look. But no one ventured inside.

"Anyway, it will work," Mr. Vorel said to himself, clad in a short gray rough jacket and white trousers, at seven o'clock.

"If only the first sale would show up," he said at eight, lit his new pipe and smoked.

Around nine he moved closer to the door and looked out impatiently onto the street to see if the first sale might now finally appear. Miss Poldýnka, the captain's daughter, was just then coming up the street. Miss Poldýnka was a plump, short lady, with powerful arms and hips, well past twenty. Three or four times people had said that she was about to get married, and her bright eyes now possessed that expression of indifference, actually of languor, which creeps into the eyes of all ladies when the married woman's bonnet is too long in reaching them. Her gait was more like a waddle, but besides that it had another special characteristic: at precise intervals Miss Poldýnka would trip and then reach down for her dress, as if she had stepped on it. To me her gait resembled a long epic poem, divided into fixed lines with an equal number of feet to each line. The flour merchant's gaze rested on Miss Poldýnka.

The young lady came up to the shop with a basket in her hand. She looked inside as if she were surprised, then tripped up the stair and stood in the doorway. She did not quite go in, but at once pressed her handkerchief to her nose. Mr. Vorel had had a real hard smoke and there was plenty of smoke in the shop.

"I humbly kiss your hand.[4] What can I do for you?" Mr. Vorel asked eagerly, retreated two steps and set his pipe down on the counter.

"Two pints of medium-size groats," Miss Poldýnka ordered and turned back and stood halfway outside the door.

Mr. Vorel filled the order. He measured out two pints, added almost a half-pint extra and poured it into a paper sack. Apparently he felt it was necessary to say something while he did this. "Please be fully satisfied, gracious lady," he stammered. "Please—here it is!"

"Does it cost very much?" Miss Poldýnka asked with her breath held back, coughing into her handkerchief.

"Six hellers. That's right! I humbly kiss your hand! My first sale to a beautiful young lady—that will bring me luck!"

Miss Poldýnka looked at him coldly and with amazement. A foreigner like that! He could be happy if the miller's daughter, that red-haired Anuše, would have him, and now he presumes— — — She did not answer and went out.

Mr. Vorel rubbed his hands. He looked out into the street again and his eye rested on Mr. Vojtíšek, the beggar. Just at that moment Mr. Vojtíšek, his blue cap in hand, stood on the threshold.

"Here are two hellers," Mr. Vorel said magnanimously, "Come back every Wednesday." Mr. Vojtíšek thanked him with a smile and went on. Mr. Vorel again rubbed his hands and thought: "I have a feeling that if I look real hard at people, then they must come in. It will work out!"

But just at that moment Miss Poldýnka was standing by "The Deep Cellar," telling Mrs. Kdojeková, the counsellor's wife, "He's got so much smoke in there, the goods are like smoked sausage." And when at noon the groat soup came to the table,

187

Miss Poldýnka insisted that "you can smell tobacco smoke in it," and put down her spoon.

By evening all the neighborhood was saying that everything in Mr. Vorel's shop reeked of tobacco smoke, that the flour was scorched and the groats flavored with smoke. And Mr. Vorel was now called nothing but the "smoked meat merchant"—and his fate was sealed.

Mr. Vorel suspected nothing. The first day had gone badly, all right. The second, the third day—well, anyway, it would work out! By the end of the week he had taken in no more than two gold pieces in all—but that was – – – !

And it went on and on the same way. No one came from the neighborhood and only an occasional country dweller wandered into the shop. Only Mr. Vojtíšek came regularly. Mr. Vorel's one consolation was his pipe. The gloomier he became, the more powerful the smoke rings which twined from his lips. Mr. Vorel's cheeks turned pale, his forehead wrinkled, but day by day the pipe grew redder and sparkled more prosperously. The Ostruhová Street police looked murderously into the shop at that indefatigable smoker—if, pipe in hand, he had stepped at least once out over the threshold and into the street! One of them, little Mr. Novák, would have given I don't know what to get a chance to knock that pipe out of his mouth. Instinctively they shared the natives' dislike for the foreigner. But Mr. Vorel sat gloomily behind his counter and did not budge.

The shop grew poor and empty. After five months or so suspicious figures began to visit Mr. Vorel—Jews. Each time Mr. Vorel half closed the glass doors of the shop. The natives told each other quite confidently that the Malá Strána would see a bankruptcy. "Once he's brought in the Jews!"

By St. Havel's Day[5] they were saying that Mr. Vorel would be moved out and that the landlord was going to turn the shop back into an apartment. Finally, the day before the moving, the shop was now closed for good.

But the following day, from nine in the morning till evening, there were masses of people in front of Mr. Vorel's closed shop. They said that the landlord, when he could not find Mr. Vorel anywhere, had had the shop door forced open, that a wooden stool had fallen out on the street: above it there dangled the unlucky flour merchant, hanged high up on a hook.

Around ten o'clock the court commission arrived and entered the shop through the door leading from the house. With the help of Mr. Uhnmuhl, the Malá Strána police captain, they took down the suicide.

He reached into the dead man's jacket pocket and extracted a pipe. "Just look at that—I've never seen a pipe so beautifully broken in!"

NOTES

1. At this period, when there were still no street addresses, buildings were often known by their proximity to a church, shop or tavern, or by some feature of the building itself. Presumably "The Green Angel" was named from a decorative feature on the building.

2. "You hear, Poldi."

3. A steep street in the Malá Strána, climbing the hill toward Hradčany Castle and the Strahov Gate. Neruda grew up on this street, which today is called Nerudová ulice in his honor.

4. An expression of politeness toward women, borrowed from German. The formula often substituted for (rather than accompanied) the actual kissing of the lady's hand.

5. St. Havel's Day, October 16.

HOW IT HAPPENED THAT ON AUGUST 20, 1849, AT HALF PAST TWELVE IN THE AFTERNOON, AUSTRIA WAS NOT OVERTHROWN

On August 20, 1849, at half past twelve in the afternoon, Austria was to have been overthrown, or so it was decided in the Pistol Society. I don't even know any more what it was that Austria had done to offend, but I don't doubt in the least that the decision was taken after long deliberation. There was no help for it, the matter was agreed upon, sworn to and the execution entrusted to the experienced hands of Jan Žižka z Trocnova, Prokop Holý, Pokůpek and Mikuláš z Husi,[1] that is, to me, to the son of the smoked meat dealer Josef Rumpál, to the shoemaker's son Frantík Mastný, and to Antonín Hochmann, the one who came from somewhere near Rakovník and who studied on money given him by his brother, a peasant. Our historical cognomens had not been given us through any play of chance, but quite according to our merits. I was Žižka, for I was the darkest of the lot, I talked most forcefully, and right after the first meeting of our society (it was held in the Rumpáls' loft) I had equipped myself with a black patch over my left eye, which created a general sensation.[2] That black patch I had to wear at all the meetings: it was not any too comfortable, but of course I had no choice in the matter. The others all had claims to their cognomens that were equally convincing.

The plot was prepared with a circumspection that was truly staggering. For a whole year we had used each outing for practising together at sling throwing. Mastný-Prokůpek supplied excellent material for slings, and at a hundred paces we could hit any treetrunk, so long as it was at least as thick as a man. Of course we did not confine ourselves to that. For a whole year we had put back every Kreutzer, whether acquired honestly or dishonestly, into our common "pistol treasury," from which came the name of our group. The total finally came to all of eleven guilders. For five guilders we had purchased, a week before, in a shop on Na příkopě,[3] a pistol of "Lutych workmanship,"[4] as the

191

salesman put it. We spent whole meetings looking at it: now that the holidays were coming we held these daily; it passed from hand to hand, and each of us confirmed that indeed it was real "Lutych workmanship." We had not fired it yet even once, first of all because we had no powder, and second, because the state of emergency which had been proclaimed was still in force, and we had to be careful.[5] In general we were extremely circumspect not to betray ourselves, and this was the reason why we did not take anybody else into our society: we were only four freshmen,[6] but we knew this was enough. We could have bought a second pistol for the remaining six guilders and thus doubled our arsenal, but we had designated that sum for powder, since we did not have a very precise idea of how much that might cost. One pistol was quite enough for the plan we had adopted. We had some other property which belonged to the society, including a porcelain pipe which Prokůpek smoked at our secret meetings in the name of us all: it was an elegant, impressive-looking pipe with a painted chalice, flail and spear,[7] but for the time being we did not place any special emphasis on it. We also had our own special little electric generator. Brother Prokůpek had made it for us—he was an apprentice locksmith—from an old two-groschen piece, but the machine did not turn out right. We left it at home.

I give the details of our plan here so that all can give their admiration. Our chief purpose: to overthrow Austria. Our first requirement: to take control of Prague. An essential means to our end: to seize the Belvedere Citadel at the head of the Marian Ramparts, where we would be masters of Prague and where, according to our view, we could not be bombarded from any direction.[8] Calculated details: the citadel would be stormed exactly at noon. If one consider that in taking various fortresses the custom has always been, from time immemorial, to do it at midnight, but that at midnight the guards are most likely to be at their most vigilant, he must recognize that our plan was conceived in a fiendishly clever way. At that time the citadel was guarded only lightly, by from six to eight soldiers. One of these stood on guard right by the iron gates which led to the courtyard: these gates were always slightly open and we could see the soldier there, leisurely pacing up and down. Another soldier walked back and forth on the Prague side, where several cannons stood. We would slip up to the gate innocently, the four of us and one other—we

192

will soon see who this was—throw ourselves on the guard, knock him down, take his rifle, knock out the windows of the guard-room with a double round of fire from our slingshots, rush inside and at the lolling guards, knock them down and take their rifles. There remained the other guard. He would most likely surrender, we would tie him up and take his rifle. But should he not be willing to surrender, it wouldn't matter—we would knock him down anyway. Then we would at once roll one of the cannons up to the gate, light the pitch ring which is there on a pole, and shout to the people of Prague from the ramparts that it was a revolution. Then the army would come, of course. But they could not reach us over the wall, and we would open the gate suddenly every so often, fire at them from our cannon and at once shut the gate again. We would knock down the first soldiers, the rest of the garrison would probably surrender, since they would be threatened on all sides by the revolution, and, if they would not surrender, it still would make no difference. We would rush out and join the people of Prague, and the first thing we would do would be to liberate all the still groaning political prisoners on Hradčany.[9] The rest of it was as natural as growing rye. Our first victorious battle would be won at Německý Brod—we would lure the army there.[10] Our next would be won on the March Plain—precisely on the March Plain, where the spirit of King Přemysl Otakar cried out for vengeance.[11] Then we would take Vienna and overthrow Austria. The Hungarians would be helping us at that point. Then we would knock over the Hungarians. Marvelous!

A very important part at the commencement of this bloody drama was to be played by the fifth person. He knew nothing of this and was not to know anything until the very last moment. He was the poultry vendor Pohorák. He came from near Jeneč on the far side of Bílá Hora,[12] and made the trip to Prague with his cart and his draft dog three times a week, hauling chickens and pigeons to market. It was our Rumpál-Prokop Holý who brought him to our attention when we were discussing a most important matter, the procurement of powder. At that time procuring powder was extremely difficult: merchants could sell it only to customers who had permits, and Prokop Holý, from whose parents Pohorák bought his smoked meat, informed us that he always bought powder in Prague for the storekeeper in Jeneč. Prokop Holý had asked him if he would buy powder for him as well, for

193

an especially good price, and Pohorák had agreed. On August 19 Prokop Holý had turned over to him the whole six guilders, of which two were a regal gift and four were designated for powder. The next day he had promised that he would hurry up with his sales and purchases and that, instead of going toward Strahov Gate, he would come out through Bruska,[13] and there he would give the powder to Prokop Holý. Then he would learn that we were a whole force, he would unhitch his white dog from the cart, leave the cart on the highway and join us. That he would join us there could be no doubt—why, he had received two guilders, and then the honor of it! In any case, we would make much of him, of that he could be sure. Prokop Holý informed us that Pohorák had told him the year before, just after Pentecost, how he had pulled a husar off his horse out in the fields.

"Beyond Bílá Hora live the strongest people in Bohemia," said Prokop Holý.

"And that includes Rakovník," Mikuláš z Husi added and waved his mighty fist in the air.

If I should say so, Pohorák's cooperation was an extremely pleasant thing. And I would wager that the other commanders had an entirely similar reaction. The question at issue in our plan was, as outlined in detail above, the matter of the guard at the gate. And there was something that had occurred only a few months before, the traces of which still had an effect on each of us. We four were playing—and there were more of us than four— we were playing ball in the moat by the ramparts. For several hours the ball was kept rolling in our military game. We had a first-rate rubber ball, which we had purchased for half a kreutzer. We were playing splendidly, no doubt, for a grenadier who was passing by stopped to admire us. He stood there a long time, and even sat down in the grass to admire our game in greater comfort. Suddenly the ball happened to roll right past him, the grenadier stretched lazily until he turned over on his stomach and seized it. Then he got up very slowly—his getting up seemed to have no end—and we anticipated that he would hurl it back to us with his powerful right arm. But his powerful right arm stuck the ball leisurely into his pocket, and his powerful body plodded lazily along the hillside upward. We surrounded the grenadier, begged, bawled, threatened him—the result was that Prokop Holý received a slap in the face and Mikuláš z Husi another. Then we threw stones at him, but the grenadier ran after us and history must justly note that we all ran away.

"You know, it's a good thing we didn't take him on," Jan Žižka z Trocnova explained later. "You know what it is we're after, and who knows what could have happened! When there's a conspiracy you never know what can happen—I know that! I was all atremble—with rage—I felt like grabbing the fellow—but I thought, 'Just wait a bit!' " This logical explanation was unanimously accepted with gratitude, and each of us confirmed that he too had been atremble with rage and could hardly hold himself back.

In the first days of August, when we were dealing with the most subtle details of our plan, I asked suddenly: "Does Pohorák's dog bite?"

"He bites," Prokop Holý confirmed. "Yesterday he ripped the maid's skirt at the gingerbread shop."

It was extremely important that Pohorák's dog bite.

*　　*　　*

The morning of the memorable day arrived. The unerring chronicle of the heavens marked it as a Monday morning.

I had seen the first glimmer of dawn, then an ashen-gray sky, then all of a sudden light shone, growing ever brighter and clearer— all at intervals which were endlessly long. Yet my whole soul thirsted with a strange longing for dawn not to come and for the sun not to shine and for nature to leap over this single day. I anticipated that something unpleasant would surely occur, I prayed and prayed, and my soul, I confess, was perishing in dejection.

I had not slept the whole night. Sometimes, just for a moment, a feverish drowsiness would settle on me, but at once I would twitch on my hot bed and it was all I could do to refrain from groaning aloud.

"What's the matter with you—you're breathing so heavily?" Mother asked me several times.

I pretended to be asleep.

Then Mother got up, made a light and approached my bed. I kept my eyes closed. She put her palm on my forehead. "The boy's burning like fire. Come here, husband. See, he's got something."

195

"Let him alone," my father advised, "yesterday he was off somewhere with his craziness. They're up to no good—those club meetings have got to stop: he goes around with Frantík, Josef and that Rakovník kid—"

"Why, you know they all study together—that way it's easier."

I am writing the truth. I really was sick. I had been sick, in fact, for a number of days, worse and worse as August 20 approached. I noticed something similar in all the other commanders. At the last meetings the talk had sometimes gotten confused. Inwardly I attributed this to fear on the part of my fellow commanders. I had gotten hold of myself and two days before I had made a strong speech. They had denied the charge in the most heroic terms, we had all fired one another up, never had our speeches been so strong and emphatic. The next night I slept, but badly. Yes, if I had sensed heroism in the others, I would have felt quite different myself.

That I should have felt fear, I could not admit at any price. I thought to myself, and the thought sounded like a heavy complaint to fate's account: why should this frightful task have been allotted to me? Austria's overthrow suddenly seemed to me to have become a cup full of ineffable bitterness. I would have been glad to pray, "Lord, take this cup from me," but I felt that there was no way out, and the height of glory was for me to climb my Golgotha. My oath was binding.

At ten o'clock we were to be there, at eleven Pohorák was to come, and at half past twelve our action was to be carried out.

At nine I left home.

A pleasant summer breeze freshened my temples. The blue sky smiled like Márinka, Prokop Holý's sister, when she was trying to tempt others to some piece of roguishness. In passing I should say that Márinka was my love. I thought of her, of the respect she always showed my heroic character, and suddenly I felt easier, my chest swelled and my soul grew strong.

A magic transformation had occurred by the time I reached the Stag Moats,[14] and twice I observed that I was hopping on one foot.

I tried to think if everything was in order. It was, in the very best. Two slingshots were hidden in my one pocket. In the other was hidden my black eyepatch. Under my arm I carried my school

196

books, a piece of military deception. I walked along the Marian Ramparts past the soldiers training and did not even shiver. I knew that by the time appointed they would have long since been back in their barracks.

There was plenty of time, and so I made the round of the whole strategic position. I crossed the Chotek Gardens where, next to the road leading down the hill, Mikuláš z Husi was to take up his post. I looked down toward Bruska Gate, where Prokůpek was to stand, awaiting Pohorák's arrival so that, overtaking him by taking the steep sunken road, he should bring us the news quickly. I came out to the citadel and from there went along the ramparts to Bruska Gate. When I came near the citadel, my heart began to pound; when I left its vicinity, the pounding stopped again. The ramparts stretching from the citadel to Bruska Gate form two projecting bastions. The first of these was quite elevated and had at the top in its compass a small level space: in the middle of this there was then a little pond with an edging around it, with thick rushes and bushes all around—the scene of many of our revels. Under one of those bushes we had buried a fine pile of stones for our slingshots. The compass of the lower bastion was a rather deep ravine. Today in that notch stands the Panorama Cafe—at that time it was a place overgrown with thick bushes. A few paces farther on is Bruska Gate, my post as that of chief commander.

I sat down on a bench under the gate and opened a book. A light quiver ran through my body, at times shivers went down my back, and I don't think it was fear. I felt quite good on the whole. Much of my feeling was derived from the fact that so far I had not caught sight of a single one of my fellow commanders. I had the pleasant suspicion that they were afraid and would not come. My heart kept urging me to throw out my chest in pride so that I could feel this—but my mind was superstitious and counselled me not to call attention to myself thus, and so I did not throw out my chest.

Drums and trumpets sounded in alternation on the Marian and Belvedere Fields. People and carts were coming past me and going in the gate. At first I had not paid any attention to them, but now superstition began to enter in, imposing its own game. Should one of them turn off here at the end of the little bridge toward Bubeneč, things would turn out badly for us—if he would

197

turn left towards Podbaba, things would go well. One—three—four—five—all of them were heading towards Bubeneč—now trumpets sounded from the Belvedere Field as if for retreat—I leaped up.

Just then the clock in the tower of St. Vitus Cathedral sounded ten. I looked around and saw Mikuláš z Husi tripping through the alleys of trees to his post. A noble, courageous heart—a daring champion—he had even given up his holidays for the great cause—he could have been at his brother's home for two whole weeks now—but I felt that it troubled me a bit that I saw him. Now I had to make my rounds, according to my orders. I walked slowly through the fortifications, holding the open book in front of me. Nowhere did I see a man coming up the hill.

I reached the little pond. Here Prokop Holý was lying on the grass. When I caught sight of him, I began to take loud, heavy steps, as if my heavy foot clad in armor were thundering along a fortified wagon encampment.[15]

Prokop Holý also held a book in his hand and was looking at me. His eyes were red.

"Everything in order?"

"Everything."

"Have you got it?"

"I've got it." He meant the pistol which had been entrusted to him.

I cast a look towards the bushes, beneath which our stones were lying. Prokop Holý looked too and evidently tried to smile at that, but he could not bring it off. At that moment a soldier came out of the citadel with a jug in his hand. He was dressed in a long blouse with a fatigue cap. He was assigned there to do odd jobs. We had completely forgotten him in our calculations—well, one more of them! He slowly walked toward us, and when he had reached us, he put the jug down on the ground. Inside us both there was a rattle like a clock works.

"Do you have a cigar, young gentlemen?"

"No, we don't—" but I did not finish the answer; obviously I could not say that, except for Prokůpek, none of us smoked.

"But you must have two Kreutzers—give me something for baccy! I'm from the last year's Revolooshing"—a fresh rattle, a real electric shock—"and every day gentlemen give me change for baccy."[16]

I took out two Kreutzers and gave them to him with a shaking hand. The soldier whistled, picked up his jug and walked away without even saying thanks.

I waved my arm and walked down to the highway. I entered the Chotek Gardens and approached Mikuláš z Husi, who occupied a bench by the "fine panorama." He looked over his book down at the ground. A heavy, prolonged step, again as from a foot clad in armor.

"Is everything in order?"

"Everything," and he smiled a little.

"Is Prokůpek at his post?"

"Yes, and he's smoking." Down below sat Prokůpek on the railing, swinging his feet and smoking a cigar.

"Tomorrow I'm going to start smoking."

"Me too."

A wave of my arm and departure with heavy steps.

I sat down again at the gate. The soldiers were coming back in detachments from their combat training—fine! But, strangely, I looked at them today with a kind of painful distaste. At other times the sight of them had stirred me up, and the mere rattle of drums was sufficient to unleash the most glowing fantasies: in my playful imagination I would supply whirling, intoxicating strains of Turkish music, even when there was none; I saw myself at the head on a snorting white horse, on my way back from victorious battles, behind me soldiers singing merrily of victory, around me the exulting crowd, myself with motionless visage, only occasionally inclining my head. Today that fantasy was like yesterday's beer, well aerated and stale, from which my mother made a soup which I hated. No longer did my head yearn for those victorious heights, and my tongue felt as if it had a light covering of clay. Whenever any of the soldiers happened to look up at me, my gaze would jerk suddenly to one side.

I looked out over the countryside. A silent joyfulness, as if a rain of fine gold were falling on the hills and vales. Still the landscape had its own special elegiac tone—I shivered in spite of the warm air.

I looked up to the blue sky. Again I thought of Márinka. Dear girl! But it seemed to me that again at that moment I was a bit fearful. The thought passed away. Yes, of course—Žižka had defeated a hundred thousand Crusaders with a handful of men[17]—the knight Percival had killed a hundred armed men in an hour—but God knew what it was: not even history had the power to convince, to drive away aerated beer or clay on the tongue.

No—it was out of the question—retreat was impossible—so be it!

Now more people than ever were coming out of the gate. My gaze followed them without thinking. Then again the game of superstition involuntarily began, and this time, equally involuntarily, I introduced a deceitful trick. I bet only on those who were wearing country clothing and who could therefore be judged in all likelihood to be going to turn to the left, toward Podbaba.

A sudden fever seized me—I got up with effort.

Better make the rounds again! In any case inexorable duty called.

When a second time I approached Prokop with heavy steps—but this time I felt they were not very heavy—the inspecting officer was just entering the citadel. In any case we would wait until he came out again.

But on Prokop Holý I observed an alabaster whiteness.

"Pepík, you're frightened," I said with genuine sympathy.

Prokop Holý did not reply. He placed the index finger of his right hand on his right eye and pulled the lid down so that I could see the red edge underneath. It was a well-known gesture of Prague youth, signifying a complete negation.

Why hadn't he said that he was afraid? Austria could still be—

"It's eleven," Prokop Holý shrieked.

The sound of eleven strokes floated through the air, slowly descending. Each knell quivered for a long time around our ears and involuntarily I looked up to make certain the sound was not actually visible. The blows were mighty ones, tolling the passing of one of the oldest and greatest states of Europe!

Slowly I made the rounds of Mikuláš z Husi's military position and then with slow step went down to Prokůpek. It occurred to me that I ought to inspire his attentiveness somehow with a gesture of supreme command.

Prokůpek was still sitting on the railing, but no longer was he smoking a cigar—he now had a cap full of plums in his lap. He was eating them with great appetite and, taking each stone with great care from his mouth, he would place it on his index finger, bring one finger of his other hand into play, flick the finger—and one of the hens promenading on the other side of the road would run off screaming. By now almost all of them had escaped to a safe distance, only one black hen was still pecking the earth in rather risky proximity. Prokůpek was just taking aim at her when he caught sight of me. His trigger finger took a somewhat different direction, and, instead of hitting a hen, the stone struck my chin so sharply and painfully that it felt as if someone had lashed it with the end of a whip. Prokůpek's face shone with bliss.

"What are you up to? Why don't you watch out?"

"Me? You think I don't have eyes? Do you want some?"

"I'm not hungry. How much were they?"

"Eight Kreutzers. Take some."

"I'll take four for Pepík. And keep a watch! He can come any moment now."

And I walked back up the hill. For a second time I felt a seed lash me painfully across my ear, but I did not look back and walked on with dignity.

It was half past eleven when I reached Prokop Holý's post again. He was still lying stretched out on the grass.

"Here are some plums for you—from Frantík."

Prokop Holý pushed my arm away. I set the plums down beside him and lay down on the grass myself, on my back.

A sky without a single cloud. But when one looked aloft, suddenly his gaze turned weak and it seemed as if the air were swarming with lashing white worms. Not only was the air full of them but my body was nearly full of those worms, my blood raced and then stopped again, this muscle would suddenly jerk, then that one. As if melted lead were dripping from the skies.

I turned on my side, facing Prokop.

Three-quarters of the hour sounded.

"You—listen here—" Prokop turned toward me all of a sudden and his eyes were white and dead—" Pohorák must have betrayed us!"

"No, maybe not—" I stammered. But I couldn't rest: I got up and walked up and down. The most frightening ideas of black betrayal billowed through my mind.

Then I looked through the bushes down toward the sunken road—Prokůpek was running up the road, as fast as his legs would let him.

"Prokůpek!" My first thought was: Take flight!

Prokop Holý was also on his feet. From the other side Mikuláš z Husi raced up. He too had seen Prokůpek running.

Prokůpek could hardly catch his breath. "The farm hands drinking there at the tavern are saying the police picked some poultry vendor up in the marketplace!"

No one said, "That's Pohorák!" But, as when a heavy stone falls among a flock of birds, we were already rushing to the four winds.

I raced down the road until my head shook. In a flash I was in Valdštejn Street,[18] but instinct urged me on. I turned into Senovážná Street, and the cobblestones flashed past under my feet. Now I was at St. Thomas' Church and headed into the arcade around the square in an uphill direction. The first pillar of the church flashed by—suddenly I checked my gait and pressed against the second pillar.

The police were just bringing Pohorák past, on the way to the station house, with his cart and his dog. I could see well how moved Pohorák was. His face expressed ineffable pain.

The world's history would have an awkward lacuna if we did not recount what had happened to Pohorák.

That day he had come into the city a bit later than usual through the Strahov Gate, indeed it could be said, a great deal later than usual according to vendors' customs and Prague habits— it was seven o'clock. Down the hillside streets the going was rapid: the near draft animal, the white dog, did not have to pull and ran along happily; the far animal, Pohorák, held the cart back and his left hand, placed on the shaft, jerked aloft in regular, almost rhythmic intervals.

"How is it you're so late today, Pohorák?" the baker in Hluboká Street asked him; he was smoking on the sidewalk in comfort and had his coat off.

"I made some stops," Pohorák smiled and stopped the cart with a long "prr." He reached into his right pocket, pulled out a straw-covered bottle containing cumin brandy and offered it to the baker. "Should we have one?"

"Thanks, I've had mine this morning already."

"Me too, but it's better to say five prayers than just one." And Pohorák drank to the bottom, stuck the now empty bottle back in his pocket, nodded and jogged on.

202

The Selský Marketplace was already full of people. The policeman was leading Pohorák and his cart this way and that, trying to find a vacant spot. Pohorák kept arguing tirelessly with the police corporal; at last a space was found. Sometimes Pohorák would bring rabbits, butter and eggs as well as poultry, but today he had only chickens and pigeons. Poultry was his main business. Pohorák was saturated with that special odor, not especially pleasant, which poultry possesses, so that the air for a few paces away around him had a special character.

Pohorák was already well past fifty. Should the reader have involuntarily gotten the impression from anything said earlier that he excelled in the hugeness and power of his figure, I regret that I must now set definite limits on the reader's powers of imagination. Pohorák did not have the look of one who would wrestle Hercules in the arena for the prize. His figure was slightly taller than average, a bit bent over at the shoulders, and more bony than powerful. His thin face was so adorned with pockmarks that the person with the best heart in the world might not have stopped short of advising him to have his cheeks paved over. Pohorák wore a bluish coat with a fine check; in some places, especially on the back beneath the collar and on the left sleeve, the coat already resembled unchecked dried mud; then smudgy gray wide trousers, well tucked up down below, though it might not have rained for a good two months. His head was covered both in winter and summer by a dark-colored cloth cap, from the edge of which there peeped out a food tax receipt which had been lodged there.

Pohorák spread the straw under the wagon in the shade and the dog curled up there. Then he took his goods out and distributed them on his cart. And then he settled down a bit and looked about.

"Girlie," he addressed a woman of almost sixty, "watch out for my things a bit, can you? The trip's given me an empty stomach—I'd like a mug of beer!"

He went off to the nearest cafe and drank a mug. Then he went on three paces to the tavern and downed two drams of schnapps and stuck a bottle in his pocket as a reserve supply. Then he brought two poppyseed rools, one for himself and one for the dog, and again he was back by his cart.

"Right side or left?" asked the woman who rented stools. Pohorák pointed silently, gave the woman a Kreutzer and sat down on the stool. His hand slipped into the left pocket of his jacket and took out a pipe and tobacco pouch. The pouch cord spun around, the pipe was packed, from the right pocket of his vest there appeared a box of matches, and Pohorák smoked.

A muscular brewer appeared. A brewer or his wife could be recognized infallibly by the fact that behind them a servant-girl would carry a large copper-hooped kit on her back.

"How much are those chickens?"

"How much?" Pohorák considered the question at his own pace and shifted his pipe to the other corner of his mouth. "That's a strange question. But I might sell them for forty Kreutzers."

"Get on with you, you're crazy. Thirty-three. All right? I want six of them."

Pohorák silently shook his head, sat down again and smoked. The brewer withdrew.

"Pohorák, you won't sell for that today," said the woman next to him, the one whom earlier he had addressed as "Girlie." "Don't wait—there's a lot of that kind of goods in market."

"What business is that of yours, old hag? I'll sell for any price I choose. Look to your own rotten preserved eggs, you can't teach Pohorák anything about selling!—Even if I don't sell anything today, I still have my profit made here in my pocket," he added after a while, took a couple of gold pieces out of his vest and shook them.

"Girlie" was silent. Pohorák was silent as well, for he was washing down his anger with schnapps.

A lady with her servant.

"How much are the chickens?"

"Forty each."

"So dear! Thirty-five!—Isn't that right?"

Pohorák was silent.

"Well—don't be so stubborn."

"I can't help it—I'm like that when I take it into my head—and that's it!"

"Let's go on, Ma'am," said the servant. "They're practically green, anyway."

"What do you mean—green—you're green, you cabbage stalk! My chickens change all colors," he took a couple of chickens by the feet and spun them in the air. "Ekkkekkkekkk!"

All the "girlies" around broke out in loud laughter. Pohorák flushed down his anger.

And so it continued.

The market was thinning out. Pohorák's pigeons and chickens were still untouched. Sometimes Pohorák would look, almost inquisitively, at his cart and then mutter, "Can I help it about my head?"

The schnapps was slowly beginning to take effect.

A sausage vendor came past. "Hot dogs! Hots!"

"Let's have one here! Pohorák took a frankfurter and ate it. The vendor was engaged meanwhile in selling to the other wagons. After a minute he came back to Pohorák.

"Dad, three Kreutzers for that frank."

"Which one?"

"The wagon woman opposite him said, "The one you ate up already."

"I ate one up? You're all carzy!"

An argument began. Pohorák cursed them. The vendor fenced with his hook in the air and called the police.

Policeman: "Did you eat a sausage?"

Pohorák rolled his eyes at him, "I did."

"Then pay for it!"

"Sure! Now I just remembered—you know, corporal, I'm an old man—I've got a queer head."

Around him laughter broke out. But Pohorák sat there confused, and several times he lamented to himself, "That head of mine!"—then finished the bottle and smoked.

The sun burned mercilessly. Pohorák felt not himself. He looked at the dog, at how he slept in the shade under the cart—slowly he pulled himself together, covered the chickens and pigeons with a canvas—and crawled under the cart—

By now "Mrs. Totter," the last daily purchaser, had already carried away her purchases. Baskets and lids were disappearing, the wagoners carried off their egg crates. The policeman was making the rounds with the invitation, "Clear out!"

Now he stopped at Pohorák's cart.

"Clear out, whoever owns this cart," and he grabbed the cart. Beneath the cart a dark grumbling could be heard. The policeman looked down there and saw Pohorák, with his cap for

205

a pillow, sleeping peacefully on the straw. "Pohorák, get up!" and he pulled him by the foot.

At that the dog jumped up and jerked the cart to one side so that the wheel ran over Pohorák's arm. Pohorák went on sleeping. The policeman smiled.

"Listen, pour some water on him," called one of the street-sweepers, who had already begun their task. Splash! And half a can of water spouted onto Pohorák's unlucky head.

Pohorák shook himself, sat up and rubbed his eyes.

"Get up!"

Pohorák slowly arose. "I've gotten lazy for some reason. I'm too old for all this work—"

"Well, come along, then, old man. You can sleep it off there."

"Well, you give the orders." And Pohorák grabbed the shaft of the cart and went where the policeman led him, with deep sorrow in his heart.

*　　*　　*

In the Rumpáls' loft an agitated meeting. To swear that we would never, never betray one another. The speaker was Jan Žižka z Trocnova: "I saw him there, as I stand here—it plucked at my heart, but I could not help him!" Only Mikuláš z Husi was absent: he was already on his way to the Rakovník woods.

An end came to our deadly anxieties around six in the evening. With effort Pohorák dragged his cart up the hill and stopped at the Rumpáls' shop. Prokop Holý listened with pounding heart behind the glass doors which led from the shop to the living quarters.

"It went badly with me—they had to take me in and there I slept it off a bit. I'll have to stay the night at the Broadcourt—today's market was miserable—maybe tomorrow will go better—"

A few days later a new pistol was found in a corner beside the fountain. No one knew how it got there, and strange things were said.

But only some four weeks later did Prokop Holý go up to Pohorák as he was pulling his empty cart home from market and ask him, "Pohorák, what did you do with the six gold pieces?"

Pohorák stopped. "What six gold pieces?"

"You know—the ones I gave you to buy some powder."
"Six gold pieces—to me? Josef, Josef—I think you're trying to tempt old folks—tempting old folks—that's a sin!" And he raised his right fist in reproach.

NOTES

1. These are all names of heroic Czech leaders from the times of the Hussite Wars of the early fourteenth century.
2. Jan Žižka was blind in his left eye, and is always depicted wearing this patch.
3. Na příkopě, "On the Moat," the name of a short Prague street on the edge of the Old Town, at the foot of today's Václavské náměstí or Wences laus Square.
4. Lutych, a town in Belgium noted for the fine quality of the small arms made there.
5. This state of emergency, i.e., of martial law, was a second one, proclaimed in May, 1849 in Prague when a plan for a new uprising was allegedly detected and the leaders arrested and imprisoned. This state of emergency lasted until 1853.
6. I.e., freshmen in *gymnasium* or academic high school.
7. These were symbols of the Hussite Reformation and the armies that fought to defend Czech religious freedom.
8. The Marian Ramparts lay behind the Hradčany Castle (see the following note).
9. Hradčany, the hill which is the site of the Prague Castle, above the Malá Strana (Small Side) and overlooking the River Vltava. The prisoners had presumably been involved in the so-called Whitsunday Uprising which began on June 11, 1848, or in the planned Uprising of May, 1849.
10. Německý Brod, today Havlíčkuv Brod (renamed for the Czech patriot Karel Havlíček, who was born there), in Southeastern Bohemia. The town was the site of a major victory for the Hussite armies in 1422.
11. The March Plain, near the border of Austria and Hungary, was the scene of a historic battle in 1278 between Přemysl Otakar II, King of Bohemia, and his chief antagonist, Rudolph of Hapsburg. Since the Hapsburgs subsequently became rulers of Bohemia (though only some centuries later), the battle and its outcome foreshadowed later Czech history and the domination of the Czechs by the Austrians.
12. Bílá Hora (White Hill), scene of the famous defeat of King Frederick and the Czech Protestant forces at the hands of the Austrian Catholics in 1620, lies in back (to the northeast) of Hradčany Castle.
13. Bruska Gate stood at the head of Chotkova silnice (Chotek Road), at the northern edge of the Malá Strána Quarter. It was closer to the Belvedere Citadel than was Strahov Gate.
14. The Jelení příkopy, or Stag Moats, lie down the hill from the Marian Ramparts behind Hradčany Castle.
15. An ironic reference to the Hussite Wars, when the Hussites under Žižka used wagons in formation for defensive purposes.
16. See Notes 5 and 9.
17. The reference here is to the First Crusade against the Hussites; the Crusaders, led by the Bohemian King Sigismund, occupied Hradčany Hill at the end of June, 1420,

and attempted to take Prague. Their enormous army, numbering perhaps a hundred thousand or more, was repulsed by Jan Žižka and the city was left untaken.

18. Valdštejn Street and the following places are all located in the Malá Strána, near Valdštejn (Waldstein) Palace.

On May 1, 1890, occurred the first mass demonstration staged by the workers of Prague, one which, though peaceful, did stir apprehension among the upper classes and the bourgeoisie. As the 1890's went on, the radical cause gained momentum, culminating in the mass trials of 1894 that followed the so-called Omladina movement. In spite of this setback, the Social Democratic (Marxist) Party continued to grow throughout the 1890's and the first years of the twentieth century.

The feuilleton below, one of Neruda's last and possibly his most celebrated, was a classic of the genre even before the Communist years which made it required reading for Czech and Slovak schoolchildren. The non-Communist reader today will be intrigued not only by its somewhat infectious enthusiasm—the effect Neruda no doubt wished to produce—but also by signs of ambivalence in the writer himself, as well as by those historical ironies which the passage of time and further political developments were to bring.

Still, if Neruda's infectious optimism, only partly tempered by apprehension, seems ironic today, we can still read the feuilleton as an expression of liberal intellectualism and its nostalgia for union with the working classes in the cause of social and economic justice. The style, particularly in the first part treating Czech holidays, is typical for Neruda and, in its warmth, intimacy and infectiousness, is close to that of Karel Čapek, a writer whom Neruda influenced profoundly.

MAY, 1890

" 'Twas the first of May. . . ."[1]
Forgive me if I begin with this still beloved poetic phrase, one that in other respects is unfortunately quite outworn. On this occasion I cannot begin otherwise! Year after year these words of Mácha's concerning the First of May have been said in Bohemia thousands and thousands of times, but this year—and now permit me to employ another quite common, quite outworn phrase—I would gladly have a gold piece for every time these same words have been pronounced by our people this year alone, often only involuntarily—as if in sleep—in a low whisper. . . .

209

Yes, it was the First of May, 1890! And whoever lived to experience it as a grown, reflective and mature person will not forget it to the last days of his life!

It would be interesting to read some mystery play, written in Czech, illuminated with real poetry, full to overflowing with the true thoughts of the common people, a play in which the different holidays of the whole year appear and debate among themselves as to which of them excels over all the others, as to which of them is the first.

Let New Year's Day step out first, for instance. But not that empty New Year's imported from abroad, with its head twisted and heavy, with its barren and repellant ceremoniousness, full of lies and full of importunate egoism! Rather our own Czech New Year's, as it still breathes in the village. When in the home all is so peaceful, so sacred. When everything is so clean, when all has already been set out and prepared the day before and when only the most unavoidable, the most essential work need be done. When everyone converses so peacefully, almost in half whispers, and people avoid anger or irritation. When they put on their finest clothes to go to church, and there pray so fervently, and then until the next working day they all feel so blissful, so beautiful!

Let Christmas Eve appear, that time full of marketplace bustle, that time of extraordinary, rich feasting, that time of surprises when gifts are exchanged—in the village it is the image of our impecunious life, but also of our golden family happiness. When after a day given over to everyday bustle there comes that quiet evening, people come together on tiptoe so as to make no sound, and they take their places at the table; contentedly they eat their mushroom soup, their buttered groats, their rolls made of coarse flour, their steamed dried fruit—but then at once they sit still closer to one another and tell all sorts of wonderful tales about bygone times, about far-away lands, wonderful tales of how the Savior was born and how the holy night was suddenly filled with the splendor of daytime, and the angels sang, and how the poor people hastened to Bethlehem and were the first to pay homage to the Redeemer, the first who recognized that human salvation lies in human equality—and when everyone listens and tells his own feelings, as if over their heads that very salvation indeed gleamed and shone, and they get up and cross themselves and go off together to midnight mass, to greet the new morn. . . !

210

Or let Shrove Tuesday come forth, accompanied by music and song, letting all eyes sparkle with merriment, legs gather strength, hearts leap up and mouths let out a whoop! Let it come forth, and let April First come with it, jocular, waggish, full of pranks and trifles, its emblems the clapper and the mocking, whistling pipe.

Let the First of May come forth. Crowned in new bright greenery. With scented lilies-of-the-valley in its sparkling hair. With the nightingale's song on its quivering lips. With a glowing spark of love in its wistful eyes.

Thousands of poets have already sung its praise. It has helped millions of human hearts to beat more quickly, more blissfully. Yet it would hardly know what arguments it could bring in its own behalf. Its place is the wide realm of beauty and love, but its effect can only work in quiet, in silent woodland thickets, amidst the burgeoning buds, in opening hearts. It does not like shouting or bustle. It is not for a lively company or a mass entertainment; it is for the tender gaze of two pairs of eyes, for the sweet whisper of their mouths.

And hence naturally and by chance, the heavy step of human history has so far hardly stopped to mark it, the First of May. Or rather, not till very recently! When the First of May, 1851, came and marked the opening of the First World Exposition, and in it all the peoples joined together in a single circle.[2]

And not forty more years passed, and the First of May, 1890, came. Truly it is we who have waited for and come to see the most memorable May First in man's history. Perhaps, even, the most memorable day in all human history!

With a peaceful yet iron step there marched on the First of May, 1890, endless and boundless legions of workers' battalions, formed in a human file so that forever they should march on with us others in pursuit of exalted human goals, equally justified, equally responsible, equally happy.

It was a mighty march, irresistable, as when the waves of the ocean rush forward. Whoever saw it comprehended what "elemental force" means. And when it is applied in a cause that is spiritual, moral.

An extraordinary day! A marvellous mood! Not fear—oh, no, the possibility of fear did not even cross my mind—but a wonderful expectation of something vague, something completely

211

unknown quivered through all my nerves. A feeling that was not quite pleasant. I recall only two moments in my life when—though they had absolutely nothing in common with this present moment—I had a similar feeling of "something vague, unknown." The first time was in 1848, during those hours when Prague was under bombardment; then a similar feeling awoke in me and persisted during the individual shots from the heavy mortars.[3] And the second time was in 1866, on that afternoon when the Prussians were approaching Prague.[4]

An extraordinary day! So quiet, heavy, so "choked." The streets with a quite different look. Some defiant student caps. Not a single carriage, not even a fiacre. No ladies and gentlemen. Only those who had to toil, and among them we whom the poor workman erroneously considers "gentlemen," though a real gentleman would correctly place us among the "workers."

Then all of a sudden people began to flock in from the direction of the Powder Gate: these were workers coming from a Karlín meeting to join the common Prague gathering.[5]

On purpose I walked against the current of the moving crowd.

Red badges, red neckties—in a twisting flash there raced through my brain the memory of the Commune, the red banners of the anarchists![6] For the first time I had seen it among the people, that dark red color of the world socialist movement: I trembled. On display—on display! The very colors—black on a dark-red background—which had flown over the heads of the Hussites, those fighters for religious freedom,[7] the same colors fly today over the heads of those who fight for full social equality!

The crowds flocked on. Not heavy but deliberately thinned out, and hence all the more endless. Everyone in holiday attire, clean, shining. With light holiday walking-sticks in their hands. Some hands, very likely the most calloused, were today wearing their Sunday best and, not wishing to reveal their coarseness, were fitted out in leather gloves.

The crowds flocked on without cease, but the bustle was only slight. The workers walked on almost in silence, as one sees them coming home together in the evening from work: silent, sparing of words, with a serious face—today it wears an iron seriousness! Just look and see: there you have it marked on the face, that "elemental force!" But it will not turn you to stone! You sense that that force is controlled by deliberate intention. And all at once—as if by a miracle—all at once you have comprehended the meaning of this year's First of May, all at once you see that the whole social and political situation has changed this day in a single stroke, and not only for this day!

And in an endless stream the crowds flock on farther and hasten to Střelec Island, to their public meeting.[8] There they would discuss together for an hour or more, first of all the question of a reduction in their daily work. They suppose that the Lord, when he has his hands full of work for them, has nothing more, naturally, with which to bless them. Well then, so let the Lord now bless you!

But on the streets the stream coursed on, in spite of the meeting, and did not diminish. Not during the day and not during the evening. Hour by hour the number of people everywhere grew greater. A dignified, unassailable holiday picture! Workers came proudly past with their wives on their right, on their faces a contented smile, in their eyes a spark of joy. And with them and among them the rest of Prague, also contented, also joyful.

An extraordinary, yet, a most extraordinary day. In truth even Nature all around appeared to be governed by a similar law. The early morning had been foggy and humid, the air gray and heavy—and then all at once the sun shone forth and it was so bright, so golden, so blissful. . . .

It was the First of May, 1890!

NOTES

1. The celebrated opening of Karl Hynek Mácha's long romantic poem, *May*.

2. The reference here is to the Great Exhibition held in London in 1851, the so-called "Crystal Palace Exhibition."

3. The bombardment of Prague began on June 16, 1848, under the Austrian General Windischgrätz; with this the uprisings that had broken out in the Prague streets were finally suppressed, and an end brought to the whole national movement for liberation.

4. This occurred during July, 1866, in the brief Austro-Prussian War, when Bohemia was occupied by the Prussian forces.

5. Karlín is an industrial suburb of Prague.

6. The reference here is to the revolutionary Paris Commune of 1871 when, at the end of the Franco-Prussian War, Paris was controlled by the radical workers.

7. The Czech Utraquist forces who resisted the invasions of the Catholic Crusaders into Bohemia in the fifteenth century. In linking the modern socialist movement

to the traditional image of struggle for national independence. Neruda is implying that social justice is as important and essential a goal of the national struggle as is national independence itself.

8. Střelecký ostrov (Marksman's Island) in the River Vltava, today a park.

ANTAL STAŠEK

Antonín Zeman, who took the pseudonym of Antal Stašek, was born in 1843 in the Krkonoš mountain country of Northeastern Bohemia, the child of peasants. He attended high school in Jičín and for a time in Krakow (today's Poland), and later the Law Faculty of Prague University. After teaching for a time and working for a short period on the staffs of several newspapers, he completed his university education in Krakow in 1866. For most of his life he practised as a lawyer in Semily in Northeastern Bohemia; he served for some years in the 1890's as a deputy in the Austrian Parliament. His political views were self-acquired and non-conformist, but he tended to support the so-called Realists, led by T. G. Masaryk. Later he came under the influence of Anarchism, and in many respects sympathized with the Marxist Social Democrats as well.

Stašek's most celebrated work, The Shoemaker Matouš and His Friends *(the germ of which was contained in a long story published in 1876 as "The Shoemaker Matouš"), appeared posthumously in 1932. It is a collection of character portraits, figures conceived very much in their author's own likeness, full of inner turmoil and conflict, and of a keen sense of social injustice and of looking forward to a future struggle for liberation, both social and economic. Eccentrics and solitaries, they cannot find a place in the society against whose background they stand out. Yet as literary portraits they are often vividly realized. The present story, taken from the collection entitled* Our Mountain Enthusiasts *(1895), portrays such a figure, also a shoemaker.*

Stašek's work was underestimated by the literary critics until the Communists came to power in February, 1948. In spite of his strongly individual and non-conformist ideology, his radicalism proved attractive to the Communists and he became a favored classic during the 1950's. On balance, it should be said that his work has a secure, if rather limited place among the nineteenth-century Czech realists. His writing is rather rough and unpolished, but few of his contemporaries could match the portrayals of his leading figures in power or conviction.

Stašek was the father of the writer Kamil Zeman, better known under his pen-name of Ivan Olbracht.

Brabanec had been the shoemaker in Vysoké,[1] and in his youth he had been a rash one, but now on his last legs he turned into a sober old man. He had given up his trade and was now living with his Vichová daughter.

So long as he was still cobbling, he had four uncurbable passions. To take part in plays, to catch songbirds, and to meddle in the doings both of the gentlemen who ran things and in the world order of God.

In amateur theatricals he liked best to play the parts of Žižka and of Sultan Sulayman in the play about Nicholas Zrinyi.[2] In Vysoké they had staged plays from time immemorial, and Brabanec was one of the pillars of their theatre. He was a sight to behold when, finishing his role on the stage as Žižka or as Sultan Sulayman, he went off to the cloakroom still dressed in his theatrical costume, settled comfortably in a chair, pulled his short pipe out of his right pocket and his tobacco pouch from his left, calmly filled his pipe and lit up and, waiting until the director would call him back on the stage, would smoke with a dignity truly befitting the hero he had just portrayed. If people had smoked in Žižka's times, then Žižka himself could not have held a pipe or have extracted smoke from it with greater seriousness or with a more realistic heroic air.

Žižka he played not only on the stage, but in life. He did not like priests and would have preferred to deal with them in the manner which, as he had heard and read, his beloved hero had treated them. Whenever anything happened in the village, the district or the whole country which rubbed him the wrong way, he would storm and vituperate, "Send Žižka after them with his mace!"

The mace was his ideal weapon: Žižka was inconceivable without it, either in life or on the stage. When once at the inn the student Haba had tried to point out to him that the mace was a weapon used by riders against foot-soldiers, and hence a crude weapon, that a knight never employed a mace against another knight, and that without question Žižka himself would never have carried one, Brabanec was terribly offended, even exasperated; he considered the speech to be blasphemy against the sacred idea of the mace as he had conceived it. For him the mace had become a symbol of strength and victory over all the injustices of the world. So he let go with strong words at our student who, fearing worse might come, took to his heels.

"Just don't gibber," the shoemaker spat after him as he ran. The mountaineers say of anyone who is uttering anything stupid that he is "gibbering" or "bungling."

From then on no one ever tried to disillusion Brabanec concerning his views on the sacred and inviolable nature of the mace.

His passion for the theatre or his ideas concerning Žižka would never have brought the shoemaker into conflict with the authorities or the police. It was worse with his other passions and with his politics. At the beginning of August, 1868, a notorious camp meeting took place near Vysoké, in the Petrušek Hills; it was one of the stormiest such meetings to be held in those times.[3] Without Brabanec it would not have been possible. He had to be there, and not just as a foot-soldier, but as a cavalryman. He borrowed a gelding from a neighbor, joined some other men on horses and rode in true cavalry style onto the plateau where a thousand heads or more were teeming in the fine summer air. The main thing was that the meeting not be disturbed and—in spite of the fact that it had been prohibited by the authorities—that the speakers be permitted to speak in quiet. For this purpose it was essential to get rid of four district officers who had made their way there and were concerned about order. The shoemaker Brabanec took on this task. He lined up ten riders, gave them suitable commands and charged at the uneasy guardians of public order. Actually it wasn't an attack, but rather an encircling manoeuvre in which he surrounded them with his cavalry and very politely, even humbly, begged the officers to move on a little, saying that those ten cursed geldings might possibly bite or kick, that otherwise some accident might happen to them. With this the cavalry pushed the officers, who were surrounded on all sides, far away from the campsite, where the stormy speaking was going on. It goes without saying that Brabanec got into trouble for this. The army came to Vysoké and the surrounding countryside, and with it an examing magistrate who evaluated the whole popular "action" strictly according to the lawcodes and had the shoemaker locked up together with many of the other participants. He was hauled away to Prague to the Central Court, where such cases were decided at that time. At first they were considering a charge of high treason, but finally agreed that Brabanec had committed the crime of assault and battery according to Paragraph 81 of the criminal code, and that he would be brought to trial only for that.

He considered how he would defend himself. He weighed carefully each word he would pronounce, and even pondered whether, when they would ask him, he should describe himself as a shoemaker or a cobbler. Cobbler struck him as more democratic, but shoemaker seemed weightier and more significant.

He was a great reader: he wished to know everything thoroughly, and according to books. Hence he provided himself with a copy of the criminal code, the one book which was allowed without obstacles to political prisoners, and memorized that unfortunate Paragraph 81. He walked up and down the cell in which he was confined, held the book in his hand and repeated aloud, "When someone by himself, or more than one person, but not in unlawful assembly, shall resist any lawfully constituted authority. . . ." The heavy, concentrated style of the code did not come easily: it took him an entire day to learn that one paragraph by heart, but from then on he knew it as well as "Our Father," so that at his next interrogation he surprised the examining magistrate. He surprised him in another way as well: by his insistence that he was not guilty according to Paragraph 81, because he, Brabanec, had not resisted official personages, but on the contrary, the officials had resisted him. . . .

From that time on a duel began between him and the examining magistrate, the course of which did not see the light. God alone knows what went on between them, but in the end the cobbler or, as he was now to call himself by that more significant and weightier word, shoemaker, was placed in the examining ward of an asylum; after a time he was released from there with a certificate stating that he was mentally deranged, that this derangement was of long standing and must have already obtained at the time when, sitting on the gelding, he had humbly begged the officers to move on.

The examining magistrate cocked his head skeptically and, to tell the truth, he didn't have much faith in that rot, but expert opinion carried more weight even than the lawcode. So just before his trial came up Brabanec was released from prison. His fellows, who remained there, were rather surprised at this, and some even suspected him of having bartered his freedom at the price of

218

betrayal. But they wronged him: the truth was simply that his wiliness and artfulness had helped him out of a ticklish situation; these are qualities which characterize many of our mountaineers and which have deceived even experts. In any case, there were people who asserted that Brabanec actually did have a screw loose, and they were soon confirmed in this belief by something that occurred.

He came home at the beginning of February, 1869, having passed five months in prison. The mountaineers have a proverb to the effect that "at Candlemas the lark must squeak even if he freezes." This year the lark was heard without freezing, for the weather in the mountains was unusually warm and fine. Brabanec was delighted by it, and in any case he did not have much wood for heating; he forgot a second proverb, that the bear repairs his shelter when it is fine at Candlemas, and that he demolishes it when it is cold or very windy. The proverb proved true: a new winter commenced and the shoemaker, at that time already a widower, was compelled whether he liked it or not to provide himself with a great deal of fuel at a high price. It vexed him, indeed his rage reached its peak when at the beginning of April it not only did not turn warm, but there came snowstorms and with them bitter cold, till the shingles on the roof crackled. He cursed horribly, and in his rage he called the cold out to a duel. He opened all the windows of his cottage, shook his fist through the openings and shouted, "Just wait—I'll give you some heat. We'll find out who'll come out ahead!"

And now with the windows opened he kept the fire going for two days and two nights without stopping, and put twigs, logs, stumps on the fire—whatever he had. He might even have cut up the roof and the walls with his axe and burned everything in the cottage that was made of wood if on the third day his stove had not cracked. He wanted to have it fixed at once and continue the battle, but in the whole of Vysoké there was no one who would take on the work, for they feared he would lose his wits. So he had to give up, and, wonder of wonders, the cold too gave up. Right after the end of the duel came a thaw, the sun shone, and spring resounded.

"For Heavens' sake, Dad, what have you done? Everyone in the mountains is saying you've gone crazy," his daughter Růža, now married and living in Vichová, said in horror when she came to visit.

219

"I drove away the cold," he answered and was silent.

Růža would not give up: she went to see the doctor and asked what her father suffered from and whether there were any cure. The doctor, himself a mountaineer, knew his countrymen better than the Prague specialists did, and gave his expert opinion concerning Brabanec.

"Dear Růža, your father has a terrible disease: it is called 'shoemaker's madness or frenzy,' and there is no remedy for it. It is incurable, but one can live another hundred years with it. Just set your mind at rest: he won't die of it."

So the daughter was put off. But misfortunes did not come singly, and another mishap now occurred to Brabanec that same summer. Below the town he owned a piece of meadow, and irrigated it using water which ran from his neighbor's land. The spiteful neighbor cut off his water supply, Brabanec went to law and the case reached the district authorities. The restless shoemaker could not wait for the decision: he went to see the officials nearly every other day to urge them to give him the verdict at once. But it did not come. This seemed to him to be a terrible injustice. One morning he arose early, grabbed an old tin lantern and ran with it to the district office. People were amazed to see him carrying a lantern about in daytime, and supposed that indeed, perhaps, he had a "screw loose." But they were wrong: Brabanec had a clearly determined purpose. He bought a small candle, placed it inside the lantern, lit it and trudged off to the district office, strolled in with his lantern and cried out that he was looking for justice. They sentenced him to two days in jail and handed him over to the court to be imprisoned. The guard, a crabbed old musketeer, put him in the jug and, shutting the door on him, muttered into his whiskers: "Fool! He's trying to get justice from the penpushers! It's the court that administers justice!"

The shoemaker sat out his two days, but he had achieved his goal: in a short time the decision came in his favor, a result which, in his view, the lantern had helped achieve.

But a few months later he had new troubles. He was a passionate birdcatcher: in fall he caught migratory birds in nets and in spring songbirds with birdlime. For nightingales he would have given his life, and since there are none in the mountains, he would go down to the valley on the other side of Jičín for them.[4] From his knowledge of bird habits he would even criticize writers of

220

literature. When he was reading a description of nature in some book which happened to say that in late July at harvest time a nightingale could be heard somewhere in the bushes in early evening, or a thrush in the woods, he would bang the book shut and never look into it again, even if it was full of marvellous thoughts. What sort of rhymester can it be who doesn't know when a nightingale or a thrush sings!

His sitting-room was full of cages and in them swarmed the most varied assortment of birds: thrushes, blackbirds, warblers, starlings, finches, but in first place always nightingales.

At the beginning of May, 1870, his neighbor Jíra, who often went birdcatching with him, came to see him.

"Listen, Florýán, people are saying we can't catch birds any more; they say a new law's come out about it." The shoemaker jumped up from his stool as if a wasp had stung him.

"Who told you that nonsense?" he asked.

"A trooper said it last evening at the tavern."

Brabanec let fall something about laws that, had the state prosecutor heard it, might well have landed him again on the defendant's bench, and walked up and down the sitting-room as if possessed. He could not believe that there was a human power on earth which could prevent him from catching birds.

"Foolishness," he consoled himself and his neighbor and went to feed the nightingale some ant eggs, of which he always kept a supply for his darling. His delight dispelled the unpleasant news and the very next day he went off to Staroves Copse to catch thrushes. He was lucky and caught one songbird, which he brought home. But a trooper, one who had been lying in wait for him, caught him on the road, took the thrush away from him and let it go, and then turned the offender over to the officials. The trouble-burdened shoemaker had another brush with the law.

"You see, I told you, but you wouldn't believe it," Jíra reproached him when he met him that evening.

"Well, it's not the end of things," Brabanec fretted and added, "Parliament must have bungled matters again!" He recalled his months in Prague, obtained a copy of the new law, the literal knowledge of which seemed to him to be the most essential condition for birdcatching, and walked back and forth in his workshop reciting from memory: "Law given the 30th. day of April 1870 for the Kingdom of Bohemia. On the

221

preservation of several species of animals useful to agriculture. . . ."

In a few days time he knew it by heart, and even knew that the nightingale's Latin name was *silvia luscinia,* the blackbird's *turdus merula.* He was amazed that the thrush, that sweet bird, was known to the lawcode simply as "thrush."

"That's how stupid those lowlanders are," he whispered to himself and was greatly surprised to find that all his favorites were on the list of those the catching of which was prohibited. He probed, he reflected, he considered, but all his efforts were in vain: no saving thought occurred to him, whether he twisted the meaning this way or that. It was quite evident that he was not supposed to catch songbirds. He pressed his case before the law to the limit, he made a complaint even to the Viceroy in Prague, but in the end he lost, received a fine and worse: the trooper came to his cottage and released all his birds. During his other misfortunes he had raged, rioted, pounded the table with his fist or kicked the chairs, vented his rage on all the objects which happened to be in his way. This time, however, he hung his head and was sad. The empty cages yawned worse for him than a peasant's empty barns when his cattle have been sold off to pay his debts. He was deeply convinced that a great wrong had been done him, and he missed his songbirds terribly, as if the better part of his soul had flown off with them.

Autumn came and he grieved still more. But then he cheered up a bit, bought a few birds and hung their cages on the walls of his dwelling. With the birds there he felt more cheerful.

With advancing age our shoemaker was growing more serious, quieter, and he checked his thoughts and feelings with a bridle. From his repertoire of plays he eliminated Sultan Sulayman and now played only Žižka. His spiritual life contracted in scope, but it grew weightier and more concentrated. He ceased to intervene with God's order of things; concerning politics he still philosophized, to be sure, but now he restricted himself to Bohemia. Before this he had known in detail which cabinet was helping or harming England, what mistakes France was committing, in what matters he disagreed with the United States, what the Russian tsar ought to do and what it was the Italians were failing to win. At his stool all the threads of world politics came together; from his stool his ideas ranged out over the whole globe. But now within himself he was concerned only for the present and future of his own country. The mountaineers have a proverb that if anyone isn't handsome by twenty, married by thirty, strong by forty, prosperous by fifty and wise by sixty—that after then he can rarely amount to anything. But Brabanec was wise already in his forty-fifth year and at that age he associated only with old people. His workshop was the place of their meetings, where they went "to pass the time." They smoked, philosophized, complained of hard times, sometimes gossiped about their neighbors and their wives, sometimes they read the newspapers, and so the rash, hot-blooded shoemaker gradually became the settled, thoughtful leader of the old people from the whole town and its surroundings.

So it went on with him until the end of the 1880's; this was the time in his life when he was, comparatively, the happiest, if one can speak of happiness in a man who day after day comes up against the cares of life, even sometimes against poverty. He had only the most essential things: a cottage, a bit of meadow, two goats and his business, which did not yield much.

In the housekeeping he was helped by his younger daughter Apolena, who had been his favorite from childhood. Somehow they supported themselves; at times they were in want, but they concealed this and never asked for anything from their neighbors; often they would live for whole days on nothing more than dry bread. Brabanec was one of those people who would rather have committed brigandage than ask for anything or beg for it. His poverty aroused in him a profound bitterness toward the rich men of this world; he hated them deep within and in his old age became a complete socialist. He did not conceal his convictions and acknowledged them quite frankly, if he had the opportunity. But he did not make a public show of them. According to his views he recognized only two kinds of people: rich and poor. All the poor were good people for him; all the rich evil and hardhearted.

In the world he loved most his daughter Apolena. The elder daughter Růza he loved too, but for Apolena he was a tender father. It is said that love leaves a house where there is poverty. This was not the case with the Brabanec family, though gossip Want often visited their house and made herself at home there.

Apolena was a pretty, even beautiful girl of about twenty. She had a slender figure, blue eyes, rosy cheeks, red lips, a light complexion and blond hair, and her tresses fell below her knees. She had inherited her beauty from her dead mother, and was famous for it all over the region. The boys call her the "shoemaker's pretty daughter," and wore their legs off running after her. But her father guarded her more closely than anything.

There is a proverb about girls: "Comb them till ten, guard them till fifteen, and from fifteen to twenty thank the fellow who'll take them off your hands." Brabanec did not follow it: he was displeased at the thought that some day he must find a match for his daughter and take leave of her. His distaste for suitors was of course in vain. The beautiful Apolena loved the handsome Vojta, and the handsome Vojta loved the beautiful Apolena. Vojta was a peasant's son from a village near Vysoké. His parents were looking for a wealthy bride with land, but Vojta had found a poor maid for himself. A quarrel broke out between the son and his parents, a quarrel such as is repeated wherever greedy reason comes into conflict with the impulse of a young heart.

"Girl, let him go. Believe me, he won't marry you and he'll cause you grief for nothing," her father would say.

"I'd rather die," the girl would answer.

Love is like beer poured into a glass: you must drink it before it stands too long, or it will lose its suds. Vojta did not understand this and procrastinated in the manner of all good-natured, indecisive persons. He wrangled with his parents a whole year, and in the end his love grew cold. Apolena no longer appealed to him. At first he kept on coming to see her, but more from a sense of obligation than from desire. The girl sensed this and became unspeakably unhappy. Like her mother, she had a delicate spiritual and physical organism and a gentle nature. Such people for the most part follow the unpropitious law that they cling all the more to those who desert them; they even let themselves be drawn along, as if their weak hearts were fettered or welded by a magic charm that binds them to those who run from their love. The more Vojta turned cold, the more Apolena burned; the farther off he withdrew from her, the more she was drawn to him. Finally he stopped coming; day and night the girl shed bitter, bitter tears. With each tear she let fall, a drop of her beauty vanished. It could be seen how she grew old and wasted away until sick, she took to her bed.

Old Brabanec's heart ached for his daughter and rage against Vojta boiled up within him. His hatred for the rich, among whose numbers he included the faithless lover, reached its zenith. He would most happily have broken the boy's shanks for him. But he cared more for the daughter than for the faithless suitor, and so he went from one physician to another. It did no good. Apolena never rose from her bed again, and people said of her that she had "the wasting sickness," for which there was no cure. When at last she learned that Vojta had announced his engagement, and that he would marry the rich Hanka girl from Jablonec, she became deathly ill.

From Vichová came Sister Růža to stay, she sat down by her on the bed and began a conversation. Their father sat by the door on his three-legged stool, but he did not work; he watched his daughters. Outside the windows the sun was shining on the spreading appletree, just then at the height of its bloom. In its foliage a concealed finch brought piercing sounds forth from its thin little throat and stretched them out at the end of each bar just as the mountaineers around Vysoké draw out the final syllable of each sentence. His voice was assisted by the birds Brabanec kept in cages in his dwelling. The sitting-room was full of chattering and twittering. It was spring. Růža, sitting at the sick girl's feet, wept.

"Why are you crying?" her sister asked.

"Because you are going to die."

The simple folk of the mountains had the custom of telling the sick the whole truth. In this they showed a certain want of feeling, but they were not cruel; it was a kind of thoughtless frankness.

Apolena was hardly surprised at her answer. Evidently she too had considered that death must be waiting for her. She answered calmly, "I know, I know . . . but I don't like leaving you. If only I could stay here in this room like a bird in a cage, or a fly on the wall, and see what you're doing."

At these words her father got up from his stool, turned toward the door and went out into the corridor, where he broke into bitter tears. He sobbed until his whole body shook and, unable to check his weeping, he went to the window beneath the appletree, where there was a bench, and there he sat down.

225

The town stood on high ground, and from almost every household there was a broad view either toward the east and the steep Krkonoš Mountains, or toward the open country. Brabanec's view looked toward the west, where the sun was inclining toward the horizon and where the far-off mountains, Tábor, Kozákov, Bezděz and Ještěd, stood out in their sharp lines against the blue sky. But he did not look at them; rather he gazed down at the floor and in his ears hummed the words, "If only I could stay here in this room like a bird in a cage, or a fly on the wall!"

Finally he grew calm, but he did not go back to the sitting-room. He was afraid. For a time he listened to the finch, which sung to itself on the top of the appletree, then he gazed into the distance and his head was crowded with a swarm of varied thoughts. At the sight of Mt. Tábor he recollected how he had gone there on a pilgrimage with Apolena when she was a little girl; looking at Mt. Kozákov he remembered that the mason Holata had moved there to Komárov village from nearby Třič, and that he had never paid him for a pair of new boots and that he should send the man a reminder; that brought the thought of how hard it would be to provide money for the funeral when Apolena would die; then he turned his thoughts to what they might have for supper that day, and whether Růža had tended the goats. But along with all that tangle of thoughts there resounded con-stantly: "If only I could stay here in this room like a bird in a cage, or a fly on the wall."

Twilight was setting in when he got up and returned to his daughters, who were conversing quietly. The sick girl was asking about the Hanka girl from Jablonec: would she have much of a dowry, when would the wedding take place, if she were pretty and whether she and Vojta loved each other.

Her sister begged her not to think of such things which would make her worse, but Apolena was tormented with a fright-ful jealousy, and it was hard to distract her.

"Růža, go and milk the goats for us," her father commanded her, and Růža obeyed. Brabanec lit the fire and made ready a humble supper: a pot of potatoes flavored with dill. It was the last supper when the whole family would be together. By morning Apolena was dead; people said her heart had burst, but the doctor wrote on her death certificate that it was a stroke. They buried her, and with her the strangled pain of a heart cut down in youth.

People and the world went on in their own accustomed order; only Brabanec was muddled in his course like an old clock that runs fast. He did not seek work, he even avoided it; he walked over the fields and woods with his head hanging; an ineffable grief gnawed at his whole being. His old friends and neighbors who visited him were much surprised at this and often tried to persuade him to take hold on himself, telling him that death was death and to mourn too much for the dead was vanity and craziness.

"They don't understand me, they don't understand me," Brabanec whispered, and in his head there flashed a special thought which had taken root there and grew until it possessed him.

He philosophized thus: "When a man *thinks* something, he is always able to communicate his idea to others with enough clarity that others can share the idea. That is fortunate, but it is not everything. When a man *feels* something, whether it is pain, grief, or anything else, he is unable to communicate his feeling in a way that others can feel the same thing or anything like what he feels. That is a total misfortune. If a hungry man could communicate his hunger, a grieving man his sorrow, a suffering man his pain to others as he can his ideas, views and experiences, there would be less hunger in the world, less sorrow, less pain."

In his brain the shoemaker Brabanec constructed the very special and faddist idea that all human unhappiness rests in the fact that people can communicate only a tiny part of their mental life, their ideas, their understanding, their knowledge, while that other enormous and powerful side of inner life, human feeling, is condemned to prison and to mute silence; it is not communicable. If we tell another: I feel pain, we will not awaken a similar feeling in him, but at the most sympathy. He firmly believed that this was an imperfection, and even believed that in the distant future there would come a time when it would not be like that and when people would be able to communicate everything that dwelt within them. Then the world would be a paradise: there would be neither hungry nor sorrowing nor unfortunates. The well-fed man would feed the hungry, the cheerful man would gladden the grieving, the happy man would console the unhappy.

His head was full of this, and he even hit on the idea that there are poets in the world who have already learned this art, and they are the giants of this world who break a path through

227

to the future. They teach man that which will bring him salvation.

He was not backward with his new ideas and expounded them in detail to his acquaintances who came to see him and "pass the time." But they were not up to understanding him. For that reason Brabanec would get angry at them: his finest ideas were falling on stone and among thorns.

"Listen, neighbor, I think that fellow's got a screw loose," old Valha said of him when he left him on St. Anthony's Eve along with other old folks.

"I think so too; since Apolena died, he's muddled," Jíra agreed, took his old pipe out of his mouth, knocked the ashes out and stuck it into the pocket of his checked jacket.

They left off coming and began to avoid our shoemaker, who the longer he went on, the more he turned to his ideas and his solitude. In fact he *was* muddled in a way—by grief and loneliness. Mornings and evenings he walked in the woods where the birds were singing. It was still spring, and as soon as he heard a thrush somewhere he would stop, listen and whisper, "Maybe it's Apolena . . . she wanted to be a bird." In the daytime he would sit at home but he worked very little, almost not at all; either he dug through old chronicles, or he spent the time thinking, gazing meanwhile for a long time at the same spot. As soon as he caught sight of a fly on the wall, he would say, "Maybe it's Apolena . . . she wanted to be a fly."

His outer life too was changed. He sold the goats, mortgaged his cottage and started to go to church, both to mass and to preaching. On St. Peter's and Paul's Day the priest preached about reason and faith: he compared faith with the spring sun which gives light and warmth, reason and human knowledge with a will-o'-the-wisp which twinkles in the twilight of a summer eve. Brabanec was pleased at this. He had been a pure rationalist who had sought to fit the whole world like a boot onto the awkward foot of his reason: now he scarcely attributed to human knowledge any importance at all. Ever since grief at the loss of his daughter had taken hold of him he was grief itself, and he reflected continually about how fine life would be if people would understand one another not only in their thoughts but in their feelings as well.

He philosophized and at the same time he incurred debts. Růza soon found out about his new way of life; his woolgathering

228

did not bother her, but his debts fired her like a redhot coal on the hand. She feared he might woolgather away the cottage; she rushed to collar him and raged at him.

"What are you up to? You'll soon lose the cottage! And what have you done with the goats?"

In his new frame of mind Brabanec feared his daughter like a schoolboy his teacher. He apologized and behaved to her like a lamb. No one would have recognized the once rash, tenacious sly fox of a shoemaker who had played Žižka and Sulayman. He let himself be led about like a child and made an agreement with Růza that he would sell the cottage, give her whatever was left to him and then come to live with her in Vichová in retirement.

He did so and lived there with her and his son-in-law, a small farmer named Kučera. On the whole they got along quite well. He did a bit of cobbling, helped around the farm and the cottage, and read a bit from the books he had brought with him, but for the most part he only reflected. Philosophizing was in his blood. The communicating of feelings kept driving through his brain, but besides this crazy idea another one possessed him: he now noticed how the whole world worked and slaved to the point of exhaustion, and that only a few lazy, fat rich men, a few crude louts and a few exhausted and weary old men could indulge themselves and rest. Otherwise the age-old curse clung to the whole race of man: "Cursed is the ground for thy sake; in the sweat of thy brow and in sorrow shalt thou eat thy bread!" He noticed that all labor in the world seeks worldly goods and is what learned men call economic labor; that even those who assert that they work for religion, for art, for science, or for the whole of man's society, such as priests, teachers, officials, lawyers, physicians, artists, journalists, ministers and others, actually strive for the most part so that they may live and have abundance and plenty. He noticed that even for those who aspire to power and fame, power and fame are only a stepping-stone to worldly possessions, that this striving is the chief cause of destitution, suffering, pain, murder, fighting, hatred, and of everything with which the human race is afflicted and that yes, there are few crimes which do not have their roots in it. He noticed that even human ideas and feelings are intertwined with this striving, and that they revolve in it one's whole life long as in a closed circle. He could not express it all so precisely, but the idea was in him, though it was not yet clear.

And he reflected further that all drudgery, all craving for property is actually humanity's curse and its misfortune, and that extrication from this would be the world's redemption. He considered how it might be possible to achieve this salvation. After long intellectual somersaults and neck-breaking balance acts he came to the conviction that this redemption could come only when there would be no one in the world but poor people, who did not live in luxury or excess, and when it would be forbidden by law to have wealth or to indulge oneself in plenty.

As soon as this conviction had seized hold of him he began to proclaim it to his acquaintances, and it was no wonder that his needy contemporaries grasped it much better than they had his views about the communication of feelings. Of course they had considered him an eccentric, but a wise and prudent person as well.

But alas, there is no prophet in his own land, and all the less one in his own family! Both his daughter and his son-in-law were sworn foes of his views on poverty. When once toward evening he started to teach his seven-year-old grandson the well-known song, "Blessed is he who has nothing," Růža grabbed the child by the arm, tore him away from his grandfather and lit into her father with dogged words.

"If only you wouldn't spoil the boy—you can go off to burning hell and gibber there!"

By "burning hell" she meant merely the blacksmith Novotný's hut where Brabanec went to pass the time; but by "gibber" she meant her father's proclamation of a new faith, that some day would come a time when there would be only poor people in this world.

"Oh, well, it won't be so bad—I'm on my way already," the old man replied calmly, took his cap off the nail, filled his pipe, lit it and went out.

His daughter thought he was going to see the neighbor Novotný, where his chums and contemporaries often met, but looking out of the window she saw that he was trudging off on a walk up the hill to the woods.

It was early August and a warm day; Brabanec liked to walk to the young underbrush to listen to the robins chirping at evening there. Smoking his short porcelain pipe he dragged slowly along toward the top and muttered, "Růža's mean; Apolena . . . there was a child!"

He thought of her, and loneliness and melancholy took hold of him. He came along the wagon road to the woods, before which a green pasture spread out, sat down on the thick August meadow grass which had not yet been mowed, and turned his gaze toward the undergrowth of firs from which a young robin could usually be heard. He had to wait longer than usual. The sun was already inclining toward the west when the first chirp sounded forth; it seemed to him to be prettier and sweeter today than on other days; it seemed to him so because he felt sad and was agitated. At such times everything affects one more and penetrates more deeply to one's inner being; grief opens the mind's doors wide.

It seemed to him as if that sweet bird, whose delicate little voice sounded so pleasing to him, had a soul of its own, as if it wanted to tell him something. "I understand it, I understand it—it's my Apolena," the old man said and began to weep like a little child.

The sun had already set behind the mountains when he went back. He did not return home, but stopped at Novotný's house, where the usual meeting was going on. But today he was taciturn and did not converse; he let the others speak and himself listened to old Potočník explain how the day before he had attended a séance in Jestřabí. He told of wonders.

Brabanec had long since heard of these people, and had been tempted to go to see them. Hearing the end of Potočník's story, he left for home earlier than usual and on his way he took it into his head to see them with his very own eyes. On Sunday he set forth; after his very first meeting he became an ardent convert to the new doctrine and one of the most noted members of the St. Václav congregation. He was drawn to their meetings by an irresistible force: there his beloved Apolena appeared to him. He firmly believed that he could speak with her through the intermediaries and that her spirit often passed him and visited with him. It was a sweet consolation for him and a great joy.

From the once stormy rationalist he had become a calm and staid spiritualist. He was firmly convinced of the truth of the new science, since the spirits which appeared to him confirmed him in his views of the future poverty of all people.

1. Vysoké, a town in Northeastern Bohemia, near the Silesian border.

2. There are a number of Czech classic plays about the Hussite military hero Jan Žižka, including works by V. K. Klicpera and J. K. Tyl. Nicholas Zrinyi (1508-1566) was a Hungarian general who in 1566 held the city of Szigetvar against the Turkish sultan Sulayman I, but who was himself killed during the action.

3. The years 1868-1871 were a time of widespread political agitation and disaffection in the Czech lands. The Czechs were displeased by the *Ausgleich* or settlement of 1867, under which Hungary had become independent of Austria under the Hapsburg Monarchy, from then on known as the "Dual Monarchy." No political concessions were made to other parts of the Empire, including the Czechs, who had been hoping for autonomy.

4. Jičín, a provincial center about fifty miles east-northeast of Prague.

JAROSLAV VRCHLICKÝ

Jaroslav Vrchlický (the pseudonym of Emil Frída) was perhaps the greatest Czech poet; certainly the total of his poetic oeuvre forms a body of work unmatched not only in Czech but in many national literatures. Vrchlický was born in 1853 in Louny in northwestern Bohemia, the son of a shopkeeper. His childhood was passed with his uncle, a priest, under whose influence he attended high school and then a divinity school in Prague, but he soon gave up his intention to enter the Church and enrolled in the Faculty of Philosophy of Prague University. Meanwhile he had begun to write poetry. He spent a year in Italy as a tutor to the children of an Italian count, and was there struck by the beauty of the Italian landscape, the sea, and the visible signs of the antique classic and Renaissance worlds. In 1877 he was named secretary of a Czech technical school, and in 1893 Professor of Comparative Literature at the newly founded Czech University in Prague. His marriage to the daughter of his friend the writer Sofie Podlipská proved unhappy, and the two ultimately separated. During his final years Vrchlický suffered from a brain tumor, and was a helpless invalid. He died in 1912.

Vrchlický's poetic production was immense, and includes a vast body of narrative and lyric poems, as well as many translations of verse. He knew most European languages and literatures, and his aim was to bring Czech literature up to date and make it more cosmopolitan by introducing foreign poetic themes and by making translations, both of classics (Dante, Shakespeare, Molière, Goethe, etc.) as well as contemporary poets (Poe, Whitman, Rostand, etc.). He raised Czech verse to new heights of subtlety, sophistication and verbal melody, and in some ways his Parnassian verse forshadows the coming movement of Symbolism.

Vrchlický's stories, like his plays, run the risk of being totally overshadowed by his much richer poetic legacy. But his fiction has its own character and, unlike Mácha's or Sova's, is real prose narrative and not the lyricized prose of a poet. The principle of stylization is not lyrical, but rather ironic; the stories are constructed ironies about life, and the consistent application of the ironic principle gives them a somewhat patterned quality. The milieu depicted in the present story, which was published in 1887, is taken from the rich tradition of the Czech village novel and tale, and Vrchlický was especially influenced by the writer Karolína Světlá.

The bailiff Kristian Taube sat on his shabby sofa, once covered with black leather, and stuck his reddening nose, adorned with ivory-framed spectacles, deep into some yellowing papers spread out in front of him.

He was a queer curmudgeon, this bailiff!

From a respectful distance the guard looked at him with a timid squint, over the grill of the old-fashioned desk. He stood at attention, his heels together, his arms dangling at the sides of his shabby coat.

He had been standing at attention for a considerable time, but the bailiff had not even tendered him a respectable rise of the head. At last he was pleased to snort, and then finally he spoke in a long, drawn-out, quite serious, even strict voice.

"You aren't going to put up with those gypsies here—understand?"

The guard did not even stir, and was silent.

"Are you some kind of Tartar? You aren't going to put up with any gypsies here, you're going to have them whipped off the estate. Got it?"

Again the guard did not move.

"I'll have you whipped off yourself!" thundered the bailiff, enraged by the guard's lack of movement.

"As you will, Your Excellency," the guard answered. "As you will, but the gypsies will remain at Dubiny."

"They'll remain, when I won't have it?" the bailiff now raged. "That'd be it!" Did he know whom he was addressing?

"The gypsies will remain at Dubiny," the guard repeated calmly, "because Her Excellency the Princess will herself act as godmother to the newborn gypsy infant. And so the gypsies will stay at Dubiny."

"You're crazy—got it!" wheezed the Bailiff.

"Not a bit—it's the will of Her Highness the Princess," the guard answered heroically.

"Do you think you can put me off with something like that? Me? You're quite mistaken! Understand!—I'll go right up to the manorhouse and speak to the princess. A fine thing that'd be! Her Highness godmother—to that riff-raff! Where did you hear that?

234

Why, I thought you were smarter than that, but I see you're just a block of wood with a hole in it!"

The block of wood with the hole in it stood calmly in its place. The bailiff could hardly contain his rage, but sought consolation in his snuffbox, banged on the desk, tossed about all the papers that were on the little writing table, and at last stood up and thundered at the frozen guard.

"I'll make sure, see? I'll make sure what's going on, and if it isn't the way you say, God be merciful! Hear me? And now clear out!"

* * *

In the cosy salon, furnished in Chinese style, the room with the finest view out onto the estate parks, a small company was seated on the gloomy November afternoon.

The princess played hostess. The prince sat at the window, smoked a strong cigar and apparently gave no heed to the conversation which went on at the table. It was a rather motley company: Tausch, manager of the estate, a small but muscular little man; the priest Roštlapil, a jovial countryman with a wide, everlastingly smiling face; Laštovička, the deeply humble choirmaster, who uninterruptedly bowed and apologized, without knowing why himself; the chief forester Fuchs, who was evidently terribly bored and would gladly have played a hand of his beloved tarok— but without higher initiative there was no chance of that.

The prince was obviously contemptuous of the whole society. Whistling loudly to himself above the conversation, he looked ostentatiously out onto the misty park.

The princess served tea herself.

The priest was speaking.

"You would not believe it, Your Highness, how those gypsies cling to the Lord God. After what happened yesterday I now have quite different views and opinions about them."

"What could have happened to you, Father?" the princess asked with a smile.

"It was All Saints Day,[1] and a gypsy came to me, and without a word he put down a gold piece on the table. 'What do you want?' I asked him a bit sharply. 'It's for a mass, your reverence, tomorrow's All Souls.' That touched me. Keep your gold piece,'

I told him, 'you need it more than I do, and I'll remember your dead tomorrow during the general prayer. God go with you.' 'Oh, no,' the gypsy objected, 'you wouldn't remember them, and I want you to say a mass; otherwise you won't say it.' And he left the gold piece lying on the table and shuffled off. You see, with the best will in the world I couldn't give him back his gold piece—I had to say the mass for him," the priest reported, sipping his tea.

"I don't believe either that they're bad people," said the teacher.

"But still they don't belong in our woods, and we hate to see them there," objected the chief forester, "wherever they turn up, you find their campfire sites and sometimes worse souvenirs."

"Please, what's got into you?" the estate manager Tausch objected. "You drive them away ten times and they come back again; it's better not to pay any attention to them: they're here and then they're gone again. What difference does it make?"

"The manager is right," the princess said as she rocked on the ottoman and sipped her tea with zest. "He's right; yes, I can say I feel real sympathy for those poor people, and I've even decided to stand as godmother for one of the babies. . . ."

"Bailiff Taube is here," a gallooned servant announced.

The bailiff entered, bowing low. No one paid any attention to him; he remained standing humbly by the door, and the princess went on:

"To stand as godmother for the baby born yesterday here at Dubiny."

"A noble act, Your Highness," said the priest, touched.

"At least there'll be some fun here," the chief forester emphasized ironically.

The prince drummed phlegmatically on the window.

The bailiff Taube stood stupefied.

"Ah, it's our bailiff," the princess echoed.

"Your Highness. . . ." Taube stammered.

"Please sit down—do you know, tomorrow we're celebrating—it's a gypsy christening; the reverend father will baptize the child, and I'll be the godmother—you don't know how I'm looking forward to it!"

"It's a curious idea, Your Highness, but please consider. . . ."

"The bailiff doesn't care much for gypsies," Father Roštlapil emphasized caustically.

"I'm in agreement with the bailiff," said the chief forester, "we take a more cautious view of those matters."

"Don't mind, Your Highness, don't mind," said the manager, "Sometimes our views may not all agree. . . ."

"Let's make them come together with a game of tarok, and see if I'm not right," the princess continued the conversation with a smile.

"Certainly, a fine idea, Your Highness," the chief forester rejoiced. "Gypsies are people too. . . ."

"Of course, but they don't play tarok," at the window the prince said ironically.

They played.

"And what is the happy father's name?" the estate manager asked after a while.

"They call him Míša," said the priest, "and the child will apparently be called Marie Eugenie, after Her Highness."

The rest of the conversation gave way to the bustle of the game.

*   *   *

"How is my godchild doing?" the princess asked of a swarthy man who stood under the balcony twisting his cap in his hand as he looked up at her with an expression of boundless respect.

"Thank you, Your Highness," said Míša. "She's well and why wouldn't she be, with such good fortune. . . ."

The princess stood on the balcony, leaning on the rail against the heraldic lions of her crest, as she smoked a cigarette. It was some five days since the christening. It had been celebrated in style—no one could remember anything like it. The gypsy infant was actually christened Marie Eugenie, the whole tribe had been given lavish gifts and the baby, it was said, had received thirty ducats for her dowry.

But let us be fair, Míša had not slipped in while authorities were not looking. It was by chance the princess had caught sight of him over by the fence to which clung vines of beans growing by the pheasant run, and had called him over. He stood there dumbfounded. He was really a handsome man, with a strong body, of erect stance and with a dark black beard.

The princess exhaled blue clouds of smoke from her cigarette and looked with pleasure now at Mĩša, now at the yellowing tops of the trees of the neighboring park.

"The mother's well too, Mĩša?"

"She is, she's well," the interrogated Mĩša answered reassuringly.

"Does she have everything she needs?"

"Everything, Your Highness."

"But Mĩša, there's something she doesn't have."

"No, Your Highness."

"Chicken soup with noodles," laughed the princess.

"No, she doesn't have that, where would she get it, poor woman."

"Well, take it to her yourself. Look, right there by the fence a hen is rooting, she's fat enough; catch her and cook some chicken soup with noodles for your wife."

Mĩša hesitated.

"Don't wait," laughed the princess. "I can give you a chicken, at least! How stupid you are! Catch it and run!"

With marvellous agility Mĩša stole up to the fence with its bean vines, and before you could count five the hen had vanished into his breast without a sound. The princess laughed loud.

"You're very good at that, Mĩša," she called after him, throwing away the butt of her cigarette.

Mĩša did not hear her, for he was already gone.

*   *   *

It was his misfortune.

If he wished to get away from the manorhouse to the woods, he had to pass the bailiff's dwelling. It was a one-storied house overgrown with vines. The villagers called it the "barracks." Mĩša had to pass the barracks, there was no escaping it.

But what of it, he would slip past somehow, and even if he didn't, the princess had given him the chicken, and in case of need she would certainly acknowledge it. So Mĩša walked on without fear. Bailiff Taube stood in his doorway smoking a long pipe.

"Where are you going, fellow!" he thundered at Mĩša.

"Home, sir, to my wife."

"And what have you got under your coat, you scoundrel?"

Before Míša could reply the hen betrayed him; apparently he had pressed it too lovingly to his breast.

"Haven't I said it?" cried the bailiff, "Wherever you have a gypsy, there you have a thief! Give that hen here."

"I got it from the princess," the gypsy sobbed timidly.

"Any thief could say that. Give it here!"

But to his misfortune Míša began to run and thus only confirmed the bailiff's suspicions.

"Thief! Catch the thief! Catch him! " the bailiff cried as loud as he could.

Míša ran.

"A gypsy caught a hen here—catch him, catch him!" cried the bailiff, waving the long stem of his pipe.

Míša ran.

The hired hands were returning from the field. Some of them stopped and looked after Míša; others, seeing that he was running, eagerly set out after him.

"Whoever brings him back gets a tolar!" shouted the bailiff.

At that even the most diffident gave chase.

And Míša ran.

A wild, desperate chase for a man began. The hired hands were strong and agile, they hoped to earn the tolar and the bailiff's favor, besides which they felt that innate antipathy country people feel for gypsies, together perhaps with envy at the princess' favor— all this had its effect and the hands ran as fast as they could.

And Míša ran.

At first it was easy. Why couldn't he make it? The child of the wilderness had wings on his heels. But, even though he had a good head start, the hands were rapidly catching up with him. They chased him into a field where not long ago they had harvested potatoes. The soil was full of holes and Míša kept tripping. He squeezed the hen to his breast in desperation and hardly paid heed to where he was running, he only ran and ran and ran.

He heard voices behind him. He did not even look back. He should have done so: he would have seen that he did not need to race so madly, that he could save his energy—they were still quite a way behind him. But he did not look back and there shouts confused him: he thought they were at his heels, and he redoubled his mad pace.

239

The best runners of the village were chasing him. To all that we have mentioned we can add an injured sense of village honor—they couldn't catch a gypsy! The whole countryside would have gossipped about it, they would have been an object of public ridicule. So! After him!

And Míša kept running.

The land stretched out flat toward the horizon, here marked with the waves of newly plowed furrows, there with holes where potatoes had grown, a treacherous, deceitful, slippery soil for a runner. He could hardly catch his breath, circles appeared before his eyes, there was a humming in his ears, his chest rose and fell wildly, a cold sweat sparkled on his temples, but he kept on running. He glanced at the sky. It was gray, as if someone had pushed over it the great, motionless lid of a gigantic coffin. It was growing dark, and here and there large, heavy drops of rain fell like tears onto the plowed field.

And Míša kept on running.

Now the whole world whirled around with him. The hands must already be right behind him, he could hear trampling and shouts. But keep on running: there on the horizon was the black of the forest, there was his home, his friends who would protect him . . . tomorrow everything would be cleared up and his wife would still have a good meal tonight.

He did not complete the thought. The circles about him were more deeply colored and they whirled more rapidly, something spasmodically constricted his throat like the blow of a fist, something snapped in his head, and Míša lay on the damp earth, clasping the hen underneath him.

But it was not the end. He sat up again, he might have run still more if he had followed the correct course of its earlier flight, but since his mind was gone, he rushed in just the opposite direction—into the arms of his persecutors.

At that the first stone struck him on the head.

It only flashed, and he did not even feel pain, only something hot gushing forth in a rich stream across his face. He did not even reach to feel the place, so he would not have to put the chicken down, but ran on.

A rain of sticks and stones followed. Míša fell to the ground, his face in the clay. In a wild triumph the hands hurled themselves on him, stamping on him and trampling him literally into the ground. He still drew breath, he still turned over; when he tried to look at the sky and utter the name of his wife and his child, a heavy clump of earth fell on his face and deadened everything.

They left him to lie there where he had fallen, only they tore the dead chicken out from under him and, as a trophy, carried it back to the bailiff.

* * *

Next day Bailiff Taube stood, crushed, in the Chinese salon. He stood by the door like a criminal, he did not say a word, he did not even dare raise his eyes.

At the window stood the priest Roštlapil, his kindly face a mass of wrinkles, and from time to time he sighed deeply.

The princess walked up and down the salon in nervous agitation. Yes, tears could be seen on her beautiful pale face.

All of a sudden she stopped short in front of the bailiff and addressed him in a sharp voice. It penetrated right to the bailiff's bones, for he trembled.

"Do you know you killed a man yesterday?"

The bailiff did not answer. He only bowed his head lower.

The priest nodded his head seriously and the princess continued, "Go away, just dare show yourself here again, I'm disgusted with you. I won't see you again—ever! Understand?"

* * *

In the corridor the prince met him. The bailiff tried to step aside as far as it was possible, but the prince laughed, stopped short and clapped him on the shoulder. He spoke kindly to him.

"You're a fine fellow, Taube, I'm glad to have you!"

NOTE

1. All Saints Day is November 1; All Souls Day is November 2.

241

JULIUS ZEYER

Zeyer was born in 1841 in Prague, the son of a well-to-do businessman who dealt in lumber and woodworking. His education was technical, pursued with the intention of taking over his father's business, but in 1862, on a trip through Central Europe, he resolved to devote himself to writing. In 1873 he travelled to Russia as a tutor employed by a noble family. His many succeeding trips about Europe and the Near East brought him into contact with many tongues and cultures.

Zeyer was a friend of the great poet Jaroslav Vrchlický, and like Vrchlický he worked to introduce new, exotic themes to Czech literature. A lesser talent then Vrchlický, he was weak in literary invention and preferred to adapt ready-made literary subjects, as in the case of the present tale, a strongly modified oral legend. His preference is often for the exotic, the romantic, for strong passions and absolute and ideal natures. His romanticism was ultimately reinforced by a mystic religious conversion he experienced after a spritual breakdown in 1887. Along with religion, a powerfully estheticist attitude infects his work, and even his religiosity is strongly tinged with estheticism.

Zeyer wrote both poetry and prose. The latter, in spite of his marked preference for romantic epithets and stylistic formulas and cliches, is probably stronger. It has a pronounced rhythm and this is presumably what Zeyer intended; sound effect is preferred by him to sense (a trait typical of Vrchlický's and Zeyer's poetry as well). Zeyer's masterpiece is probably his long novel, Jan Marija Plojhar *(1891), the symbolic account of the sickness and death of a Czech patriot in Italy. Full of an impassioned Czech patriotism, the novel won the favor of Zeyer's compatriots as perhaps no other ever has.*

The present story is taken from Zeyer's Three Legends of the Crucifix *(1895).*

SAMKO THE BIRD (A SLOVAK LEGEND)

The night was dark as the fate of the Slovak land, a storm rumbled in the distance like the savage rage of the Mongol horde, which down to today still oppresses that persecuted people. The darkness was so heavy the mountains could not be seen. The forests murmured, the torrent raced down among the rocks, surly,

243

cold, unfriendly. In one spot only was it full of a ruddy glow, as if someone had strewn a treasure of gold and rubies in its shallows. The color came from the light of the open doors of a nearby farmhouse. There a huge fire lashed in the stone fireplace of an immense kitchen; on it a whole ram was being roasted. Men with bright eyes and harsh faces were sitting close by on a wooden bench, drinking from clay mugs. The doors were wide open; it was hot by that merry crackling fire which shone out onto the river and the path leading along one of its banks. On this path now appeared the tall, lean figure of a young man. He wore a torn blouse and his feet were bare. His blond hair fell soft and long on his bony shoulders; his eyes were like a piece of the azure sky, shy and dreamy and gentle. His face was pale and ravaged by misery, deathly sad and marked with a bloody stripe which stretched from his right temple across his face to under his left ear. The poor man stopped a few paces from the door; he did not dare go farther. His lips trembled, and in the dark night and the heavy air there resounded, in place of words, a kind of bird twitter, soft, sweet and sad. The music reached the whitewashed kitchen, lit by the blaze, and the master came out onto the threshold. The bird sound in the dark night, with a storm coming on, had aroused his suspicions. He sought for a bird and found a man.

"Who's that?" he asked in a rough voice, as he shaded his eyes with his hand and peered out.

The pale wretch with the bloody lash on his face started with pain and looked around as if he wished to be certain he was standing in the place he had sought, and his eyes filled with tears. Yes, here his house had once stood, and here his field had lain! They had not lied to him in jest when they had told him: "All that was once yours now belongs to others. Foreigners came from Germany, and your lord and ours gave them what had been yous."

"Who's that?" the rough voice repeated in a foreign accent.

The pale man wiped away a tear in the dark night, and now a kind of smile of sacrifice shone from his eyes, he tried to speak, but instead of words again something similar to a sad, sweet, touching twitter of a thrush issued from his lips. He took a step forward and the light fell full on his wizened figure.

"A vagabond!" the German said sharply and mistrustfully. "Go away!"

244

Meanwhile another man had come up to the master and said, laughing, "You needn't be afraid of him. He's crazy. They call him the 'Bird.' He was one of the people who built the castle. Today they chased out all that riff-raff, now that they finally have the ramparts finished. They don't need these people any longer, and now they don't know what to do with them. You mustn't harm the 'Bird,' but I wouldn't let him into the house. He's most likely a thief."

He had a large piece of bread in his hand and though he called the beggar names, still he showed him a certain amount of patience. He tossed him the chunk from a distance, as to a dog. It fell at the beggar's feet and he, thinking it was a stone, drew back a step instead of leaning over to pick up the gift of charity. The man who had thrown the bread now grew angry at such ingratitude.

"He won't take bread!" he raged. "He'd like to sneak into the house!"

And now he picked up a stone and threw it at the beggar. It struck him on the shoulder. From the wretch's lips there issued something more like the scream of a wounded bird than a human cry. He drew slowly back into the dark. But the men in the kitchen, hearing their friend curse, had come out, and half drunk, some of them laughing, others in rage, now turned to look for clods and stones and, calling names, they hurled after the beggar, the now quickly fleeing Samko the Bird, a real rain of missiles. He ran alongside the river, as far as he could draw breath. Then he turned around and perceived that he was no longer followed. The night had concealed him from people's malice. Meanwhile the storm had broken and the rain poured from the skies in a deluge. To Samko the din was more agreeable than the abuse of the angry men. He knew where he was; he knew that nearby there was a shallow cave in the cliff. He recognized it, remembered that there was soft moss there, and went in. There he was completely secure from the rain and wind. He sat silently down on the ground, leaned his head against the rock, and his hands drooped to his lap. For a long time he breathed hard, thinking of nothing in a state of semi-torpor, then, when his blood ceased to din in his ears and his heart to beat against his ribs, said sadly to himself, "Where can I go?" But no reply to this question resounded in his soul. His whole conception of existence and happiness, of life and the

245

world, was this forest wilderness in which he had been born, like his father, and like the father of his father, this wilderness by the river where on the steep hillsides thousand-year-old trees full of birds' nests stood lost in meditation and murmured and rocked, trees full of music and perfume, trees whose great shadows fell on the soft grass strewn with the stars of white and yellow flowers. This was Samko's whole earth. Its borders were the steeply jutting peaks of the Tatras, above which clouds swam on, their unyielding foreheads lashed by the mighty pinions of the whirlwind, from the depths of which sprang silver springs. Beyond the Tatras there was nothing, perhaps, but no matter how broad the world might be, Samko loved only this beautiful nook in which he had first caught sight of the sunlight and the faces of his parents. This nook was like a nest to him.

On the riverbank stood a white hut, and behind it undulated two small fields, cut in two by a brook and a row of alders. One, in which flax was blooming, was blue; the other, which bore rye, was yellow. His great-grandmother would sit all summer long by the door of the hut and spin. In spring Samko would tend carefully to the fields, he would hitch himself to the plow, like his father before him, while his great-grandmother, laying aside her distaff, would plow. Her long hair, white as milk, would fly in the wind like a mane, and her full, still strong, resonant voice would bless the brown earth, breathing its fresh perfume and giving promise of bread. Great-grandmother was wise and holy. She understood the speech of the forest birds, and she learned great secrets from them. Samko too was beginning to understand them and he learned to answer them; he could sing like a thrush, warble like a nightingale, whistle like a blackbird. He could even scream like an eagle, for he had climbed as far as their nests on the peaks of the Tatras, and when at times he hung, at the risk of his life, over the precipices on the bottom of which the waters murmured, and among the clouds, his apprehension led him to utter the same noises eagles make, beating their wings, in fear for their fledglings, which Samko would pet in the nests.

But they need not have feared, for Samko had never harmed a living creature, not even a beatle, not even a fly or a bird, and the dark forest and the sunny meadow knew him and loved him. The birds were his friends, and none of them was alarmed when Samko would approach; on the contrary, they would fly to him

246

whenever he appeared. If he came at twilight, the finches and thrushes would accompany him; if he sat on the threshold of his house eating, the blackbirds would fly up for the feast and eat with him from the same dish; if he pulled the plow through the field, the lark would fly beside him along the furrow and sing to him. Samko loved the lark most of all his feathered friends, for of all the birds the lark was the most able to feel love for Our Lord, whose life Samko knew in detail from the tales of his great-grandmother. When Christ rose from the dead, the birds exulted with joy: the whole time he had lain in the grave they had been silent, and now they asked the Savior that they should remain with him forever. When the Lord told them that he would ascend into Heaven, the birds insisted on following him. They flew and flew, but slowly they grew faint, while Christ continued to ascend, so dizzily high did he climb to his heavenly glory. One by one they fell back to earth till only the lark was left, and he went on flying, even after the eagle could go no farther. The tender creature had such a powerful yearning for the Son of Man that he surpassed the eagle in his zeal and was victorious over him. But when he flew toward the sun, the infinite heat of the sky scorched his feathers so cruelly that he fell, at last cut down, back to earth to the grass, from where he continued to send his song after the Lord, a song pure as silver, penetrating the blue of the skies like a beam of light. Whenever the lark would sit on Samko's arm, touched, he would kiss those scorched wings, and the twitter with which Samko spoke to the bird of his feelings in truth had the sweetness, piety and the soaring flight of the lark's song. For the dove too Samko had a special affection, for with this bird the infant Christ had played in his cradle. Once the Virgin Mary has fastened an opal band around its little neck to keep it from flying away from the divine babe, and thus the stripe remained around the bird's neck as a token, and therefore the dove laughs so beautifully, so joyously, for it remembers the time when with its tiny pink beak it was permitted to touch the still pinker body of the little King of This World, that body which later was given to be crucified for us.

All this Samko knew from his great-grandmother, who understood the speech of the forest birds, from whom she had learned the secret of eternal life. That secret, which she did not wish to use herself, she intended to entrust to Samko's father, but too long she considered whether eternal life on earth is a happiness or a burden, she kept pondering it until one evening wild riders appeared in the forest wilderness at the hut and killed the master, Samko's father. His wife went mad with horror when his hot blood spattered her face; from that time like a frightened deer she ran over the mountains and valleys, and her wail pierced the heavens. She wailed so long her heart broke.

Samko was then a tender child and remained with the great-grandmother as the survivor of the whole family. With the birds and the trees he grew up far away from people, whom he caught sight of only now and then, like quickly passing phantoms. His great-grandmother taught him many things, but she did not reveal the secret of eternal life, for her mournful soul felt too strongly the weight of earthly existence, and she knew too evidently that for each of us that black day of fate comes whose heavy shadow falls across the weak light of our life, and that it never yet has disappeared, and that it cannot be a blessing to drag after one into the infinite the gloom of one's sad memories.

The black day of fate! As for each of us, it came too for poor Samko. He was then about fifteen. One evening unexpectedly in the forest wilderness by the river wild riders suddenly appeared, and they told Samko that not only he, but also this forest of God's and this sweet, golden field, this white house and all which the eye could reach belonged, so they said, to some lord. That lord now had need of Samko's person, and Samko was to come with them. As they spoke other riders came up, driving before them like cattle a crowd of people bound to one another with ropes, over whose heads whips lashed. One of the riders jumped down and approached Samko with a fetter. Samko, astonished, gave out a scream like an eagle and seized an axe to defend himself, but laughing cruelly they easily overpowered him, and when his great-grandmother cursed the brigands and rushed at them, crazed with despair, they set fire to the hut, threw the old woman into the flames where she perished, and together with her all the swallows which had nested on the hut's wooden cornice, and all the doves which had laughed in the entry. Bound, Samko watched this terrible sight frozen with horror.

And the next day began with cutting the forest on the slopes, and Samko and those wretches bound to each other had to fell the trunks of those old ashtrees and pines, firs and oaks, those columns of that green sanctuary where he had grown up. Frightened from their shady home, which crumbled into dust, the birds fled, but their companion, less fortunate, must help drag the trees to the steep slopes from where they could be rolled far down to the valley below. He heard those primeval giants of the deep forest groan, he heard their twigs crack and break, he heard them rumble and thunder down below where, coming to rest, they lay like corpses. His heart broke. He looked after the birds fleeing to the tall peaks, to the sunny side of the blue mountains, he looked at the ashes of his house, where the skeleton of his great-grandmother lay shining, he looked at the trampled fields where those savage ruffians' horses pastured, and in his head darkness reigned. Why had God punished him so? Or was the land where he had been born cursed perhaps for all time? And did each of its sons bear a part of that curse? It seemed so.

But the ravagers did not give him much time for reflection. They drove him like the other flocks of people, cracking whips before them. He soon learned for what the lord to whom he belonged needed him. He wished to build a huge, strong, firm castle, from which terror was to extend over the broad land. His fortress was to stand on a high cliff so that the people of that land fallen into slavery should know to whom they should pay homage. Samko and the other unfortunates had been dragged here to build. They were perishing from weariness and toil that they might weave a whip for themselves. For five years Samko groaned in that misery, at the construction of the ramparts and the breaking of rocks in the quarries. All that time he was a beast of burden. His youthful strength, the springtime of his life, the joy of earthly being he buried in those quarries, in those walls and ramparts.

Samko worked harder than all the others, for he did not know how to resist, and his companions used him as badly as they were used by their masters, adding from their own work to his. Besides all that, Samko was an eternal object of ridicule. He could not speak fluently, for he had spent more time in the company of birds than of people, and each of his sighs turned into the sad, soft twitter of a thrush, which found more of a response from the dumb cliffs in the quarry than in the hearts of men, hardened by misfortunes and injustices. In contempt they called him Samko the Bird, and he took the name gladly, for in his everlasting dream of past happiness he constantly and faithfully remembered the feathered companions of his childhood in the deep forest, and the recollection gave him strength to endure the misery of his present life. They, those songsters of sunnily clear vision, they were still free and happy! And who knew: would they not come back to him some time? How touchingly he made twittering sounds in his sleep when he dreamed he had wings and was flying toward the blue peaks of the Tatras, jutting into the heavens, toward the sun, to those peaks where the eagles nested and whence those silvery springs poured from which the blackbirds and forest doves drank! When he was then wakened with rough words and driven out to hard toil, his nickname "Bird" came as something like a sweet consolation, like a promise mingling with the current of rough, unfeeling sounds.

So passed a long five years, full of suffering for him, and the castle was finished. What to do now with the people who had built it? There was nothing to do but send them away. Let them find remote places in which to die of hunger. So fierce mercenaries with long whips rode on their wild horses into the crowd collected beneath the castle to await the orders of its lord. The horses crushed people under their hooves and the lashes of the whips struck those who were running. One cruel lash caught Samko on the face and there etched, as a souvenir, a mark of slavery with its bloody stripe.

"Why does that man whip me?" Samko wondered, writhing with pain and wiping away the blood and tears. He raised his head to the dumb sky, but then he recollected Christ and his beloved wounds, and was silent. And then he felt something akin to joy. They had driven him out! He could go wherever he wished? He would return to that wilderness where he had been born. People had told him, of course, that another house stood there, that everything which had been his had been given by his lord to others. But how could that be? Surely they only wished to torment him with such talk, to make fun of his concern. So he had dragged himself to the spot where the white hut had once stood, where his great-grandmother had sat and spun, as she listened to the talk of the forest birds. He had dragged himself there and found a farm, from the gates of which they had chased him away with stones! And now he lay here in his cave refuge and asked, "Where can I go?" And there was no answer to that question! In his head there was mist only, and only as in a flash he dimly beheld the steep peaks of the Tatras, around which the eagles circled and from which the silvery waters flowed.

250

"There!" he said with a weak smile. The din of the rain lulled him with its monotonous music, and Samko fell quietly asleep. The word "there" turned on his lips into the short, weak, sweet whistle of a sick bird.

The first rosy rays of the sun came to wake Samko in his cave grown up with moss. He got up and washed in the river. He found a few ripe bilberries and wild strawberries, and thus partly appeased his hunger. Then he set out where his feet carried him. He walked along the stream in the direction leading away from the farm where he had been stoned the day before. He walked all day long, spent the night under a blossoming bush, and the next day, when the sun was already high in the heavens, caught sight of a town in which there towered aloft a mighty church with tall handsome towers, made of columns forming upper storeys in the air; the higher they went the thinner the columns became, supporting their arches, and the highest arches, beneath the roof itself, formed a kind of huge cage in which hung the bells, just then ringing festively and pouring their mighty ring out into the pure golden air. Samko would certainly have avoided the town, for he knew that wherever there were people he could expect nothing but mockery, violence and undeserved, blind hatred, but these sounds, quivering in the blue of the skies, called to him. For Samko a bell was something akin to a huge metal eagle with an angelic voice; a bell, in truth, was for him a bird settled high above human hatred, the neighbor of the clouds, the companion of the winds, and it was an unhappy bird, for it was imprisoned, tied to a rope, and its song, deep and sad, was a great lament. Samko headed toward the town where the ringing called him. He would go to church. There he would see the image of Christ robed in white against a sparkling gold background, Christ with his great, dark eyes, looking down from his height at him below in the gloom, without mockery, with kindness, without contempt, without harshness. The lips of those images smiled on everyone, and Samko could not remember that anyone had ever smiled at him since his great-grandmother had been killed! And in Christ's hands raised in blessing there would be no whip!

The look full of love, full of sympathy! How Samko's heart glowed at the mere thought. He hastened toward the town.

The streets were full of people in festive garments, the houses were hung with garlands, and on the high roofs there flew long banners. No one paid any attention to Samko and, without insult, without abuse or rough words the poor fellow, amazed at such unaccustomed kindness, reached the great town square where stood the beautiful church he had seen from a distance. But the press there was terrible; in a little while Samko was in such a dense crowd that he could not take a step and could hardly breathe. From the talk about him he comprehended what was going on.

The Byzantine Emperor and the ten kings of the East were returning from a visit made to the German Emperor, and their journey took them toward the River Danube, on which they would sail on gilded boats with purple sails, embroidered with pearls and silver. In an hour they were to reach the town; from the tower the dust could already be seen which the horses of their escort raised to the sky. The King of Hungary rode before them with his suite. In the church a solemn mass would be celebrated for them and great thanks would be given God that the steps of the mighty of the earth had led them past this small town. The honor of the visit would be engraved in golden letters on a stone tablet in the church. So the people told and rejoiced.

But their rejoicing soon turned into anxious lamentation.

Savage Magyars on frantic horses suddenly flooded the square and pulled the people to the ground. Thus their king wished to ready a living carpet of his slaves for himself and his guests, so that their horses should not touch the dust and mud of the city. The annointed of the Lord and their suites could thus reach the portal of the church on a paving of human spines. Frightful blows of flat swords and long whips with iron points fell on the heads and shoulders of those who resisted the attempt to make of their bodies a pavement for these lofty personages who were to do God the honor of their visit to his house. The doleful weeping of the women and the loud curses of the men mixed with the bells' deep pealing, full of mournfulness and sublimity. The escort was already riding from the gate on their proud horses. First the guard of the Hungarian king, full of dirt and gold: the Asiatic, half-savage faces of the nobles were poorly washed, though their beards were twined with pearls and from the folds of their silken garments these vainly Christianized beasts strewed previous stones and vermin. Behind them rode the King of Hungary with a great sceptre in his hand, then, on horses white as milk, came the knights of the Byzantine Emperor, a glorious and beautiful sight akin to a chorus of angels dressed in silver armor; finally the Byzantine Emperor himself appeared, surrounded by the ten kings in purple. He was clad in brocade intertwined with pearls and wore a tiara on his head which gleamed with diamonds and emeralds. Samko, lying on the ground in the dust, saw all this flash by above him like a flying comet, beautiful and ill-omened. He beheld it as in a dream, for soon faintness seized him under the swift feet of the horses. He woke up in delicious coolness, in the gloom, to the scent of incense. All around shone starry light: it was the flames of golden lamps and countless candles, tall as columns.

Samko was in the church. He did not know how he had come there, the human wave had cast him there somehow, as the waves of the ocean throw shells on the beach. He lay among the beggars and cripples by the high bronze portals. Far away, near the altar itself on which the mass was celebrated he again caught sight of the Byzantine Emperor with the sparkling tiara on his head and surrounded by the ten kings of the East; they sat on a tribune covered with cloth of gold. In the majestic singing of the choir, in the roar of the silver organ the weeping of the beggars and cripples wounded by the horses' hooves was lost. Samko too felt pain in his ribs and on his shoulders, but he put up with it in silence, for he was accustomed to bear pain. He gazed at the altar. His eyes thirstily sought the image of Christ, that sweet consolement for every suffering. But he did not find it. That holy sight was veiled by a heavy crimson curtain, red as blood, on which there shone the crests, embroidered with silver and gold, of the kings who were there. In front of that curtain there stood, in a real forest of lights, a monstrance gleaming like the sun from the blaze of whose gold and diamond rays a pale moon shone forth, the white sacred host, ineffably exalted in this snowy simplicity amid all that human, loud, intrusive pomp. Samko fixed his gaze on it and hastily knelt and bowed his head. A ray of sweet feeling had penetrated his great grief. He raised his head and looked again at the monstrance. Frozen, he saw it suddenly grow and turn into a kind of building constructed of the glow of the moon, with crystal gates which opened silently, and from within that starlight tent the white host floated out like a vision. And lo! It was Christ himself! He was dressed in cloth which was coarse but white as snow, his face was pale, his eyes dark and full of mercy, his smile sunny and full of love. Samko supposed that he would take a seat at the side of the Byzantine Emperor, but he walked past the tribune without a glance, slowly through the church he floated in a cloud of incense and candlesmoke, heading towards the gloom where the crippled and the beggars wailed, and there he took his seat among them. At that moment Samko could no longer see him, but he felt the evident comfort of his presence, his soul was penetrated by a gleam of light. And on the faces of all those sufferers around him bliss was suddenly apparent. No one any longer felt the pain of his wounds, light poured from his eyes and each felt as if he had grown wings. Samko was stupefied in his happiness. He raised his eyes in thanks towards heaven. At that moment an old, simple priest appeared in the pulpit. He had a cross in his hand, and first he blessed the emperor and the kings and then the people. His task was to address the crowned guests. But he stood dumb, he could not find words, and fear came over him, he knew not why. Then there resounded through the quiet church something like the sweet twitter of a thrush. It was Samko's involuntary thanks, full of sweet bliss and like unto a prayer. Amazed the priest looked in the direction from which the bird's greeting had sounded, a greeting which, it seemed to him, was intended to give him courage, and he was yet more amazed when he saw all the beggars and cripples illuminated by some supernatural light. Sudden grief appeared on his face as he remembered their poverty, and sudden ecstasy followed that grief, for he understood that God loved them. It was as if the Master were compelling him to bow before the majesty of human suffering and pay homage to it. He bowed his head to those who, he knew, had a little while before been trampled by the horses, and in a voice full of tears as he fixed his gaze on Samko's eyes which shone like the stars that shone then when the angels sang, "Peace on earth to men of good will." The priest said softly, "Blessed be he who walketh on a thorny path, for he shall achieve paradise!"

Samko laughed as when the sun rises. There was no longer any darkness in his head, no longer did that question, "Where can I go?" have for him vague horror, that crushing burden! The mystery of his whole life was solved! Samko fell on his face and for a long time thanked God.

Samko did not stir until the church was emptied. Then he walked in silence to the sacristy, for he wished to see the old priest

254

and to thank him for his good advice. He found him still in the sacristy in the company of several people with whom he was speaking. Samko walked straight up to him.

"What do you wish?" the priest asked kindly; he had recognized Samko.

In his simplicity Samko did not know how to thank him and what actually he should say, but finally he pronounced softly, "I will go to Heaven."

There resounded the suppressed laughter of the people present, and one of them asked him, "And how will you get there, fool?"

"On the thorny way," Samko answered simply. The laughter was no longer suppressed, and Samko's eyes showed surprise that here too, in this holy place and in the presence of this kind priest, he should meet with jeers. Great sorrow appeared in his face, but then he turned to the priest and his eyes were so dreamy and contemplative that through them the priest could see to the bottom of his soul. He placed his hand on his head and said, touched, "Truly you shall go to Heaven! God loves you. Remember me in your prayers."

Now laughter could be heard no more.

"I will do that," Samko said simply, kissed the priest's vestment and went out quietly through the open door onto the square full of sunlight and bustle.

Outside the town it was not hard to find a path grown with thorns and thistles, for the poor Slovak land was only slowly emerging from darkness to light, that poor Slovak land, trampled by the Asiatic plunderers under whose yoke it still groans today. Only recently had people come back from their refuges in the cliffs to the deserted fields, grown up with tares, and Aryans again took over their work, the fruits of which belonged and still unjustly belong to Central Asians.[1]

So it was not difficult for Samko to find a path where thorns and thistles ran wild. They pierced his bare feet, and that path of martyrdom he walked many days and nights, he suffered hunger and thirst and on the parched rocks he left a bloody trail behind him. He lived on roots and blackberries; only here and there in the wilderness at some ruined dwelling hidden in the dark of the forest or built on the side of some naked mountain slope did he find a piece of black bread. The people who lived there, poor and

255

miserable like him, were glad to give him alms—though they always laughed at him when he replied to their questions about the goal of his long, dismal journey. But Samko paid no heed, he did not get angry and he did not become confused. His faith was firm and he did not lack for consolation: he now had that which he had longed for so fervently for years—freedom! He had the rustle of the proud trees, he felt the breeze of the winds' mighty wings and to his heart's content he heard the sweet, dreamy, friendly song of the birds, those faithful companions of his childhood! How many times on his way had the thrushes accompanied him to the edge of a wood! How many times had the larks greeted him, fluttering like a flock of sparks high above the very clouds, with their exultant songs! How many times the doves nesting in the rocks had comforted his forlorn soul with their joyful, sweet laughter! What was that slight clutching of the heart when people laughed at him compared with that great opening up of the soul at the noise of the trees, the whistle of the winds and the song of creatures floating in the air and bathed in golden light, those plumed vessels of joy, overflowing with their sweet, ebullient, yearning, dream-bearing sounds! True, blood streamed from his feet, sweat poured from his brow, but within him he already knew that foregleam of the paradise he sought and in whose attainment he firmly believed.

But one evening he was so exhausted that he had scarcely strength to drag himself along. He stopped on a steep hillside, at the end of fresh young birch wood. Below he could see in the gathering mist something like a white castle, but without ramparts or bastions; around it old trees stood thick and rocked their tops, lit up by the sunlight, with dignity. The mist was tinged with violet and great stripes of rosy light penetrated it, and the white walls of the buildings were splashed with the light of the setting sun as with gold. Samko held fast to a bush and in curiosity bent over the valley which lay far beneath him; then the earth gave way under him, the twig he was holding broke, and Samko rolled without power or control, like a felled tree on the hillside, far, far down, with giddy speed, so that his mind was dark and in his eyes were sparks. Finally he landed somewhere and lay there unconscious. He had almost killed himself. When he awoke, it was already quite dark. Before him a high wall projected in which, a few paces away, a great door yawned open wide. Behind him was the high slope on which, in the enchanting dark of the stars, birches with silver trunks quivered. A stream babbled by his head, as if it were whispering to him. Samko drank a little water and got to his feet. They shook, but they carried him. All his limbs ached, but none was broken. He leaned against the wall, dragged himself along to the gate and went in. Now he found himself in an enchanted garden with perfume and flowers, sleeping, but exhaling their balsam into the silent night! And white waters gushed straight up like sparks, as if they sought to fly to the stars, and fell back again into the borders of a basin of bright, gleaming stone. Nightingales warbled in the thickets. Samko walked about a little and said to himself: "Have I come to my goal? Oh, truly, this is Paradise!" And his heart pounded, for he expected that on one of the paths he would meet the Lord God, Christ, or the Virgin Mary.

But the garden was quite empty and Samko came to a great building, the same he had seen from the slope. From its huge windows on one side light poured as if from the moon. Samko looked in. He saw an enormous hall: white columns bore a vaulting covered with gold stars, silver lamps rocked there on long chains and glowed like morning stars; steps of white stone, broad as a highway, at the sides of which, on an equally white stone railing, stood the statues of angels as if made of snow, with golden wings. The steps led up to another hall, still larger, gray as a forest but lit here and there with iridescent lights, and from that mysterious space there flowed organ music. At the far end of that hall, against a background of gold, a great statue of the Mother of God sat on a throne of ivory, wearing a white garment with an azure cape, a star on one shoulder, a star in the crown, with great, dark eyes, with hands raised in blessing. And on the steps there walked many elders and youths and men; their forms were also arrayed in white garments, their feet were fastened in black sandals, their hands were clasped and their eyes bowed in prayer.

"They are the blessed ones," Samko whispered to himself.

But he could not think more. Weakness overcame him so that he felt he would stagger and fall. Involuntarily he caught at a strap hanging beside him by the door, one which till then he had not noticed, and falling on the ground, he heard the heavy ring of a bell. As if in a dream he saw that the door opened and that one of the white-clad figures bent over him. Exhausted, overcome with hunger and thirst, he was lost in a deep faint.

Samko did not know that he had sunk down on the threshold of a wealthy cloister, and did not feel that, touched by his poverty, they had carried him inside.

Samko came to himself the next morning. He saw that he was lying on a bed of sweet-smelling hay, covered with a rough but snow-white canvas, in a simple, clean chamber with the sky smiling at him through the open window and the trees rustling. Scent and the chatter of the birds reached into the room from the garden. By his bed stood one of those blessed ones he had seen on the stairs the evening before. He gazed at the sick man with kindness and sympathy. When Samko smiled at him, he smiled too, took a cup of maple wood full of wine, and bent down to the sick man's lips. The wine ran through Samko's body like a ray of sunshine. Then the monk gave him some food and Samko ate and felt his strength grow. The monk then began to question him: who was he, where did he come from and where did his journey take him? Samko told him briefly, told him how he had suffered and how finally he had set out to search for Paradise, according to the old priest's counsel.

"And so," he said at last, "I've found Paradise. I won't be driven out of it, will I?"

The monk looked at him in surprise, then a smile played around his lips, but a kind smile.

"You will not be driven out," he said at last. He went off and left the happy Samko to a refreshing sleep. He told his comrades who had just gathered in the refectory all that he had learned about Samko, and with smiles they all agreed that Samko should not be driven out of his Paradise. It was decided that Samko would be assigned to work in the garden and, in view of his exhausted state, that the work there should be light. And so Samko remained in Paradise. There was no more happy creature than he. He could stroll about the cloister as he pleased, he could take walks in the garden and in the woods, and his light work he performed as he was able. He did not remain idle. Besides the garden, he occupied himself in the woods, brought wood from there and made the fire in the kitchen as well as one in the refectory for evenings when it was cold or rainy. He loved to hear the roar of the fire; those lashing flames seemed to him to resemble a huge bird with golden red wings which beat till sparks flew out of them. After the monks' dinner he would walk around the table with a dish and collect food, which he would then share with the birds in the garden and the woods. How happy Samko was! He no longer knew what misery was, and in the eyes of those monks robed in white he never saw an evil look, on their lips he never saw malicious laughter, he never heard offensive words from them. How should he not believe that he was among the blessed? That his simplicity sometimes became an object of merriment for them he did not suspect, for they never permitted him to feel this. They regarded him as a half-crazy creature for whom they felt compassion, whom they would never have tormented but whom they could not quite regard as possessed of an immortal soul or as a creature who was their equal. They were too convinced of the fact that they stood far, far above him in the power of their reason. But that they should comprehend and esteem that simplicity of mind which saw Paradise in mere love—for this their hearts were too proud, too full of the world, even though high walls and deep solitude separated them from its vanities.

Thus Samko had no friends among them, he was their toy, tolerated among them like some kind of dumb creature on whom they heaped kindness and alms, but whom it would never have occurred to them in their dreams to love. But Samko's soul did not remain forlorn, and though condemned by people, it found a friend whose existence none of those men ever suspected!

It happened that Samko once entered a certain cell where many discarded objects were lying; there, in the lumber and trash, an old, half-rotten cross stuck out. Samko began to dig it out and saw it was a wood crucifix. It was very old, of crude workmanship. Samko felt sorry for this discarded image of the Lord. He set it against the wall, washed and cleaned it and then cleaned out the entire cell. Later he brought green branches there and wove garlands which he hung about the walls, and covered the pavement thickly with field flowers, and so the cell resembled a kind of forest sanctuary. He opened the window so that light could pour in, and at once the birds sat in curiosity on the sill and chirped sweetly, as if they wished to entertain Christ, at which Samko laughed in delight. He knelt and gazed ardently at the statue. Its face was pallid, sad, tormented, the eyes extinguished, on the forehead were great drops of blood, the body was wizened, every rib could be seen, and blood streamed from the knees. The face was deeply expressive: there was infinitely much fervor and simplicity in the conception and execution of that crucifix, but the new times comprehended the high inner significance and value of that art just as little as the monks were able to esteem Samko's simple heart. But its great simplicity was quite within Samko's reach, and it spoke powerfully to his deeply feeling and worldly innocent soul. He wept over the crucifixion and also for the fact that it had been cast away there in the trash and dust and left in neglect. For Samko the statue, which looked down and seemed to suffer, had a soul. He could think of nothing else than this living image of God, even though he would go to the forest for wood, or to the garden to work. After the monks' dinner he would bring his dish there and sit on the threshold. But didn't Christ on his cross appear pale with hunger? Samko was silent with pain. He got up and walked across the dim cell as if in a dream. He raised his eyes timidly to the Crucified, eyes filling up with tears, and his lips whispered timidly, "Poor Lord, they have forgotten you! Don't you suffer hunger? You are pale, so pale!" And almost blinded with tears, he raised his dish to the Savior and said, "Dear guest, will you not eat?"

Then the wooden Christ inclined his tortured head, suddenly lit with an ineffably beautiful smile; his lips touched the dish and the Lord ate.

Samko was ecstatic. From that day he knew what full, great, unbounded happiness was. His heart glowed like a perfumed rose, his soul grew like the infinity of heaven and, like it, was full of stars! Day after day he knelt beneath the cross and poured out the riches of his feelings, unknown to men, at the Savior's feet, like priceless balsam from the East. Words such as he had never heard came to his lips, songs more beautiful than any nightingale's warble sounded in his breast and he found human expression for them; a more mighty exultation than the plumed flight of eagles or whirlwinds raised him aloft to azure heights, and the whole boundless depth of the skies found their places amid the inner spirit of that man whose friend was Christ! And Christ, who grasps all worlds in his palm, for whose greatness there is no human conception, was there every day, the guest of the simple-hearted Samko, and every day ate from his plate with a smile. Now in truth it was no wonder that Samko supposed he was in Paradise,

260

and everywhere—in the garden, in the woods, in the corridors of the cloister—he repeated without ceasing and in ecstasy, "My way was thorny, but I arrived, on it I reached Paradise!"

Some people heard this and laughed at him. And more and more of them learned of it, though he did not suspect. Then one day they welcomed three foreign bishops at the monastery, where they entertained them royally. Daily there were great feasts, and once cheered by wine, the monks talked at the table about Samko and how he thought he was in Paradise and how he supposed that they were blessed souls. There was great laughter, and one of the bishops asked to see the simple-minded Samko. They got up from the table and went out to the garden in search of shade beneath the rustling trees and the cool of the gushing waters. They passed the cell in which Samko was just then talking with Christ and sharing his food with him.

One of the monks heard and recognized Samko's voice, and he gave a sign that they should all be quiet, and the whole company approached the door of the cell, which a draft had opened, with suppressed laughter. Samko, his face turned to the crucifix, did not see the door and did not know what was going on. But the bishops and monks, prepared to laugh, fell on their faces in terror, for they saw Christ on the old cross, with the whitest radiance coming from him and with his head bent down to Samko, just at the moment he was saying to him, "I have been your guest long enough now, in your Paradise, Samko. Now you shall be my guest, in my Paradise, where you shall remain forever with me."

Samko smiled and, hearing the noise made by the monks and bishops who were falling to their knees, looked around. Then all of them observed how beautiful Samko was: his eyes were like stars, his hair like rays of the sun, and his face made sublime with that boundless goodness, that paleness which is the result of great abnegation all one's life and of long suffering. All had tears in their eyes, and the monks were amazed at how blind they had been! The veils dropped from their eyes and they at once realized how far above them the simple, believing, ardently and simply loving Samko was, and they came into the cell and bowed to him and fell on their faces before the miraculous crucifix. But Samko did not understand them, his eyes wandered, his soul was already preparing for the departure to that other Paradise to which Christ, our beloved Lord, had called him. The Bishops supported Samko's sinking head and the prior of the monastery said solemnly, "You are dying and we no longer have an opportunity to pay you the honor we owe! How happy we should have been to carry you on our hands! May your soul intercede with God for us! Your body will remain here, and I promise that we will erect a gravestone of marble, and there we will bury you, wrapped in cloth of gold."

But the dying Samko shook his head.

"Bury me on a crossroad," he said softly, "without a cross or an inscription, without a tablet or a tomb. That is my last will."

Then he fell silent. From his lips a soft bird whistle stirred the air. That was his final breath. He no longer stirred. But the wall behind him vanished and the monks saw there the sky so dark azure in its depths, almost black, and a thick rain of miraculously beautiful stars fell there and in the twinkling of their lights there could be seen in the far, far distance a vision of the Savior; there was something there akin to a bright impression of a saintly smile and the vision beckoning them on, and amid the falling stars, along a path no longer strewn with thorns but with lilies, Samko's spirit rose aloft, pleasing as a ray of light, airy as a bird!

The whole night the monks passed in prayer. The next morning they arrayed the body of him whose soul was with Christ in a white garment and buried it on a crossroads, as Samko had wished. They recalled the heavenly pure smile, sad and touching, with which he had pronounced that final wish, and in vain they asked one another why it had been that this man, so loved of God, wished to remain unknown to the world. They could not divine the answer. They could not divine that he himself wished it so, because at the final moment of his earthly existence he had comprehended, in a flash, the whole of his life and its significance. He wanted people to trample on his heart after his death as they had trampled on it all his life. All those trampling feet kindled sparks in his heart with their steps of ingratitude, sparks of love to kindle a light within him, shining through the night of suffering onto that thorny path that had brought him to Paradise!

NOTE

1. Aryans, formerly a usual term for speakers of the Indo-European languages; here the reference is to the Slovaks. The Hungarians or Magyars, who ruled the Slovaks

until the formation of an independent Czechoslovak Republic at the end of World War I, speak a Finno-Ugric, i.e., a non-Indo-European language.

The term "Aryan" was also frequently applied to supposed differences in culture and even race, which were associated with linguistic differences, and good deal of unjustified prejudice against so-called "non-Aryan" peoples was implied by the term. The later use by the Nazis of the term is an extreme case in point.

Zeyer's strong anti-Magyar sentiment as expressed in this story requires some comment. His dislike of the Magyars is clearly the obverse of his strong love for the Slavs, to whom the Slovaks belonged. The coming of the Magyars to Europe at the end of the tenth century did in fact disrupt Slavic unity, since the Magyars conquered and occupied what until then had been a Slavic, and in part a Slovak, land.

ALOIS JIRÁSEK

*More than any other writer, Jirásek made Old Czech history come alive
for modern readers, and gave them a sense of a national past. He was born in
1851 in Hronov in Northeastern Bohemia, near the Silesian border, the son
of a baker. He attended a German high school in Broumov, then Czech high
school in Hradec Králové, and later he studied history in the Faculty of
Philosophy at Prague University. He taught history first in the high school in
Litomyšl, and subsequently in Prague. His writings made him a celebrated
national figure, and he was named a senator after the formation of the independent Czechoslovak state.*

*Jirásek's type of historical novel grows out of the work of Sir Walter
Scott. Like Scott, he mixes real personages and events with fictional personages and fictional plots, and like Scott he fills his novels with colorful
historical details. He had an excellent knowledge of these, and a good sense
for broad historical and popular currents. Thus he could make history come
alive in his novels and tales, and these have considerable energy, though their
ideology is often oversimplified. Following the Czech historian Palacký,
Jirásek regarded the Hussite Period as the high point in Czech history, a time
of struggle for both national and individual freedom. The following period—
the era depicted in the present story—leading up to the disastrous defeat at
White Hill (1620), he saw as a time of national decline. The era of Austrian
rule following 1620 he viewed as a "dark time," a name which was widely
taken up and used in Czech historical ideology.*

*Jirásek is more noted for his many, multi-volume novels than for his
stories, but he did write a number of books of shorter narratives, in particular
the volume* Old Czech Legends *(1894). The present story was first published
in 1917.*

THE LAST OF THE ROŽMBERKS

In a dim, silent moment in solitude I once glimpsed a vision
from the distant past, one that did not vanish like a timid shadow,
of a "son of Adam in Eden, a man subject to many declines and
downfalls of the soul," a pleasure-lover, later a penitent, the last
of the Rožmberks.[1]

265

I see him in the high-vaulted chamber of Třeboň Castle,[2] a room adorned with the precious Gobelin tapestries, on the wide oaken bed under its canopy—an old man, afflicted with illness. By his bed a night table, on the table bottles and little boxes with medicines, above the table on a bracket—a death's head.

And a living, youthful head, pensive, supported against the back of the easy chair with its blue cloth upholstery standing in the corner opposite the bed, the young, curly head of Jiřík Otík Bradský z Labouně, one of two pages who served the lord in his illness. By the bed on the carpet lay a great white bitch, the off-spring of the Netherlands breed sent here years ago by Lord Petr from Brussels to Bohemia, from the time when he had tarried there with William of Orange,[3] when, as a young man, he was making his peregrinations about the Empire, the Netherlands and England, and when Queen Elizabeth had received him in London with suitable Christian affability, had dismissed him with favor and years later had called him to mind when she read the letter of intercession he had sent to her on behalf of its bearer, Lord Slavata z Košumberka.

The autumn day was drawing to a close; in its last light there shone white the healthy teeth of the bare skull. There light still shone, but under the canopy on the bed there was only a mournful twilight in the shadow of that which was here without cease, from dawn till late at night, the heavy shadow of death. How many weeks Lord Petr Vok had lain here now, often in torment, worn out with suffering, decrepit; his once reddish beard and blond hair now gray, almost pure white. The once sturdy man of graceful figure, lively, waggish, the lover of all the arts and crafts, the bold hunter feared by beasts, the hero in battle. But now—

Who was this man, who had once served as field commander and general of the Czech army of four thousand cavalry and sixteen thousand foot soldiers, an army he led into Hungary to fight against the Turks, and for which he himself, from his own estates, had outfitted some two thousand men?

On a tall, beautiful bay horse he rode out, in a feathered hat and a coat made of elkskin, from his castle of Krumlov[4] he rode out with his large and resplendent train. In front of him twelve retainers in red tunics; behind them on a white horse a drummer striking an Italian drum hung about the horse's neck; behind the drummer trumpeteers riding in a single file.

All these went before Lord Petr; alongside him rode Lord Petr Prostiborský z Vrtby, his lieutenant, Lord Radoslav Vchynský, the chief quartermaster, and Lord Adam z Lobkovic, the commander of cavalry. Lord Prostiborský carried the great banner of the Kingdom of Bohemia, the red standard with the white lion; on Lord Prostiborský's right rode Albrecht Slavata and on his left Lord Adam Předenice, all three on dappled white steeds with long tails. Behind the lords came a host of courtiers, among them the lord's five pages, all on horseback. Behind them a long train of wagons for both people and baggage; with them some forty horses as well as post horses; in all the horses of the Lord High General and his courtiers numbered more than two hundred.

Gloriously they rode out and gloriously they returned, having relieved Komárno.[5]

But what was left of that glory—the handsome bay which had borne Lord Petr into battle and back from it and which now stood in the vaulted chamber of Třeboň Castle—stuffed. So Lord Petr had preserved him as a memorial when the horse had died from old age. And Lord Petr himself—lo, exhausted and tortured with illness, lying on his bed in the shadow of death.

That shadow had first been recognized by Dr. Matiáš Timin, the court physician, and it was also observed by Anastasius Hök and Severin Schato, physicians brought in for consultation. They observed it and agreed that they could not frighten it away, that it would not disappear, that there was nothing to be done. And still they stood at the lord's bedside, they consulted one another and they wrote out long prescriptions.

In this time of late afternoon again came, as usual, first Matiáš Timin, bareheaded, and after him Severin Schato, with a yellowed face, long and spare, both clad in dark costumes and short capes. After them there came the fat Dr. Anastasius Hök, late, out of breath and in a hurry. A new arrival at court, dressed in a dark Sunday costume, black stockings, a white collar, and a sprig of rosemary with a ribbon on his breast. He had forgotten this sign of merriment and had left it on as he came here from the great feast, from the wedding festivities, so to speak, his mouth still greasy, his face still flushed and his eyes watery and dimmed by drink.

His brother, Lord Petr's German secretary, had married Lady Anežka z Kolchrejtu. Lord Petr had arranged the wedding, as he always did for his courtiers and officials, as he had already done at Bechyně[6] for Gabriel de Blonde, his painter, and later here at Třeboň for the painter Tomáš Třebochovský, when he married the little Anička.

The secretary's wedding was celebrated in style; for two days they had been at it and now it was the third day of celebration for courtiers and honored guests: Lord Jiří z Švamberka, Count ze Serinu, Lord Petr ze Švamberka, Lord Mrakeš z Ličova, along with no small number of other men of knightly rank with their ladies and their daughters. They feasted and drank by half glasses and bottoms up, but mostly the latter, and they had already dispatched over thirty kegs of wine. They had quenched their thirst full well, and day and night they had been at their pleasures and varied entertainments. And upstairs in solitude the solitary old man lay, in pain and torment.

Into the mournful autumn twilight came the physicians, at their head Dr. Timin. He stood by the bed and bent his bare head under the green canopy. The emaciated, yellow head of the sick man did not stir. His closed eyelids did not open or even blink when the physician's stifled "Your Grace—" stirred the air.

The sick man was not asleep; he heard, for he asked weakly: "Is that you, Timin. . . ?"

"It is I, Your Grace. Have the pains eased. . . ?"

"No."

The doctor took his faded hand, testing his pulse.

"Well, then, we'll give you a sleeping draught for the night—"

"I don't want it." The voice was weak, but it sounded certain. For a while the doctor waited in silence, considering, but then, when he was on the point of making the offer again to convince his lord, the sick man opened his eyes, fixed them on the canopy of his bed and humbly and devotedly sighed.

"Ah, My God, how strangely you comfort me." And he gazed fixedly there; he did not notice, even forgot that the doctor was standing over him. Only when the doctor asked if the lord might not want something, he closed his lids again and sighed.

"No, leave me."

Timin withdrew and gave the two other doctors a sign. Near the tall doors the black-robed collocation looked around at the white dog, for she was whining. Across the threshold, Dr. Schato

268

remarked drily in the antechamber, "That dog shares her master's suffering."

Dr. Timin agreed that she certainly did, but Hök, as if he had not heard him, did not even nod, nor did he stop as his colleagues had; he was in a great hurry to get back to the wedding feast, to the merry bustle and hubbub, to the full glasses. Timin, facing Schato, told him that Lord Petr had refused his medicine but told him also of his pious speech.

"What he says now has the smell of true faith and devotion and undoubting hope," he added. "Now he is acting according to his motto."

"Yes, of course. In silentio et spe."[7]

"He is silent, patiently he bears God's punishment and he hopes, he hopes for eternal life. Only of that does he think now. Only a week ago he was thinking about a quite different sort of life. Then I heard him say as he sighed, 'O unhappy Czech land, how will you fare?' He said it again and even for the third time. Then he was thinking of the cares of politics, of religion, of the disorders.[8] But not now."

They went out and slowly descended the wide staircase.

"At least he no longer has strange fantasies," Dr. Schato recalled. "He no longer calls for Old Barbarka the dwarf and he no longer gives orders such as, 'Švejnoch, untie your whiskers!' "

The doctor was referring to an old courtier whom Lord Petr had inherited from the late lord, his brother Vilém. That same Švejnoch no longer did anything, he only shot sparrows and wore his beard tied up in a ball beneath his chin; he would unbind it and let it dangle (it stretched almost to his knees), and he would comb it only when Lord Petr received honored guests.

The doctors proceeded down the stairs.

The white dog whined in the chamber by the bed and was silent. But she got up—she was quite tall—slowly placed her throat and head on the bed and gently, as if caressing it, licked the sick man's dried up hand, which lay on the cover, with her long narrow tongue. The page, young Bradský, did not notice. He was gazing after the doctors, gazing toward the doors, and when they went out his mind ran ahead with Dr. Hök down to the great corner room where the table was set and where there was merrymaking and laughter, where the poet Šimon Lomnický[9] was entertaining the company with his verses and where—this idea held the youth's fancy—there would be dancing, dancing, beautiful ladies and young women and Kristinka Boubínská, Kristinka, the amiable Kristinka Boubínská z Újezda. Suddenly he tore himself away from the picture he had drawn. His master had apparently called. And once again—

"Otík," sounded softly under the canopy. The page was at once at his side.

"Your Grace—"

"Are there singers there?" Lord Petr asked in a weak voice. "Call them here and have them sing—that may be medicine for me—" he sighed softly. But young Bradský was already leaping away, he had heard the command. He rushed to fulfill the will of his lord.

Lord Petr was a lover of song, of song and music, even from his youth. In foreign lands on his travels he had always looked to find it and after many years he still had a special recollection of London and the music he had heard there, especially the occasion when Queen Elizabeth had entered the church with a magnificent procession, when many lords and courtiers walked before her, when they carried a sword before her in a sheath bound in red velvet, a gold cross and two silver gilded sceptres glittering with precious stones, when behind the queen came more than forty ladies and young women in cloth of gold, in white, high collars, when the queen sat down under a canopy and the cathedral resounded with songs of praise, and when later in the church they held a concert.

Music was Lord Petr's love and consolation later as well when he had lived at Bechyně; there he kept his own orchestra and his own conductor, provided with the best and most expensive instruments, trombones, Italian horns and so forth and so forth. They played at table in the grand chamber, or when he supped with guests in the garden under a marquee, and his trumpeteers trumpeted fine pieces after the bell had called the guests to table, or when they arrived and when they departed, at Bechyně and at Krumlov and now here at Třeboň. In those castles, in their gardens and parks beautiful French and Italian "mutets" resounded during the humid evenings, the compositions of Orlando Lasso, Oracio Vecchi, Agostino Agazzari, the lovely motets and graceful cantilenas of Lord Petr's own choir.

270

Then everything gave Petr Vok pleasure, music, song, venturesome hunting expeditions, and building: he built magnificent edifices and kept his own painters, and he cherished eighteen prettily painted figures, extremely poetic ones, of Venus, a gift from the Lord of Hradec. And he himself, Lord Petr, owned twelve living Venuses, fair chambermaids who served at his table as well as at his bath and in his quiet bedchamber, Venuses from the various ends of the earth, including a Spaniard, a French and a Turkish girl. He was especially taken with Elishka Fedorovna from Moscow, a naughty but charming wench, and with the young Zuzanka, a Czech. For when he had caught sight of the latter in Soběslav and returned to Bechyně, inflamed with passion, he sent the citizens of Soběslav a letter in which he directed them to dispatch Zuzka, daughter of Zikmund the miller, to him at once on a cart "without delay or fail."

Bechyně was a paradise, Krumlov was a paradise. He lived in pleasure, he lived for the world and for its sake forgot about the life of the soul. In his youth, to be sure, he had sought for God's truth and had read the books of the Gospels, and in his mature years he had inclined, the last of his family, a family which for centuries had always served the German Emperor faithfully in each of its generations, to the Unity of Czech Brethern. Finally indeed he partook openly of the communion in two kinds from the hands of a priest of the Brethern.[10] He went on living in pleasure, however, and for the world. But the years went on, his Venuses faded, Elishka Fedorovna was married, Zuzanka aged and turned fat, and his own hair grew white. His frivolous thoughts vanished, and reflection and bitterness and illness came to take their place. This happened at Třeboň. And gradually he ceased to live for pleasure and he began to admit that there was no more difficult art than life itself. He began to meditate on temporal and eternal life.

It was then he had put up the skull in his bedchamber and had commanded Sylvestr, his expert goldsmith, to chisel him another one, a tiny skull of pure gold and to carve on its front the motto "Momento mori!" and on the back "Cogita aeternitatem."[11] And this mournful ornament he wore on a golden chain on his breast—

And then the one of whom he thought so often now and of whose existence he constantly reminded himself—death—came

271

near him. Illness struck him—how many illnesses. He took to his bed and did not get up. For weeks now he had been lying in pain, often in torment, and now he thought fixedly only of that time when he would be separated from his body and would be with Christ.

And that evening he did not want either medicine or his physician. He longed for another remedy; he longed to hear a pleasing harmony of sound which might give him relief. He waited, waited impatiently for it. He called Otík back again. The youth came only after some time had gone by; he announced that he had collected the singers but did not admit that while doing so he had stopped by below at the doors of the great corner room and that through them he had taken a good look at the noisy wedding company in order to catch a glimpse of Kristinka, that he had spied out her loving head and had attracted her look, the look of her fair eyes, a sweet, amatory look. He could still see it and think about it, even when he settled back again into the armchair to finish that service which today seemed so hard, so long, so endless.

In the antechamber suddenly the noise of muffled steps and then suddenly silence again. And from that silence there began slowly to flow, into the silence of the chamber, a subdued fountain of sweet sounds, the song of men's voices which were deep together with those which were softer and higher, all in a sweet harmony. The singers could not be seen. They sang with low voices. Their song flowed through the open doors in a muffled, soft sound, neither amatory nor flirtatious. A canticle from the Brothers' hymnal, serious, low and ardent with faith in God, was wafted towards the sick man's bed; like welcome moisture it bubbled and seethed and gladdened the parched soil.

The thirsty soul of the sick man drank it greedily, and attended the pious words of heartfelt resignation and contrite petition for eternal mercy. The soul drank in the sounds, and the body forgot, the pain abated. Lord Petr listened as if in a transport.

As the singing had begun, so it ended. Like a dying fountain it sounded softer and softer until it was blown away. And again the soft sound of muffled steps in the antechamber, then silence. The rapid breathing of the sick man became calm and his eyes closed. He did not hear the servant come in and bring a light, two wax candles in a silver candlestick. The servant entered silently and silently he disappeared.

272

In his armchair young Bradský tore himself from his dream of Kristinka, arose, listened in the direction of the bed, then came closer and looked under the canopy. Lord Petr did not stir, he lay like dead. He had fallen asleep; he was sleeping. Over him young, exuberant life with its hot blood—and downstairs the merry music sounded, calling, luring, inviting. Dancing there and merriment. An amorous head nods, and fair, smiling eyes entice. The youth quickly turned away and was already at the door. There he stopped under the canopy; Lord Petr was fast asleep.

The youth disappeared.

In the chamber was calm and silence. The white dog dozed a bit, curled up by the bed. Gloom in the corners, gloom under the coffered ceiling; even the skull on the bracket over the table was in shadow. The light of the candles trembled along the wall; in it came to life the delicate colors of the precious Gobelin, showing a landscape with an antique temple, with ardent nymphs in a sacred grove.

Moment ran by chasing moment.

Lord Petr opened his eyes and his first thought was of the singing. Had he heard it, or was it a dream—he had heard it, he had listened to it and his pain had turned numb and had vanished. This was the medicine for soul and body. And how well he had fallen asleep and slept so calmly and for so long. He could not even remember such a sleep. He felt well, he was stronger and he felt no pain.

Sounds fell on the deep, peaceful silence, the dark echo of music; downstairs the voices of violins and flutes resounded playfully, calling to the dance—

Lord Petr did not turn away; for him this was no vanity, and he listened intently. The merry voices, the life in them, and the voice of life. So it had been, so he had been comforted. He listened, moved. The dying spark was kindled again and burned, love for life, the wistful longing for it.

He stirred on the bed, then slowly lowered his wasted, dried up legs on the carpet. The dog leaped up and pressed against him, lashing her tail as she whined with joy and gazed into his eyes impatiently—

*   *   *

Downstairs there was noise and merriment. The musicians played on a podium in the corner of the great room, lit by a chandelier full of white wax candles. By the walls and at the windows were groups of older people, lords and ladies, in brocade, in silk, in white lace collars, with gold chains on their necks and over their breasts. The young people were dancing. They bowed to each other in a courtly manner, they took each other by the fingers of their raised hands, they turned about, they came forward and again went back with a resilent, graceful step and again faced each other with a bow.

So too did young Bradský, so too Kristinka Boubínská z Újezda. They looked into one another's eyes, eyes glowing with youth and happiness; in his bliss Otík forgot his lord, his night's service by the sick man's bed, the whole world.

In the next room Bacchus ruled. Tables full of glasses, goblets, tankards; about them crowded the thirsty guests, merry, at the end table Abraham z Mecerodu, Lord Petr's court ornament dedicated to the literary arts, who always composed good wishes for the New Year for Lord Petr and who wrote *carmine sapphico,*[12] was arguing with Šimon Lomnický about some matter of versification. Both were struggling rudely with heavy tongue, both were red, both looked like roosters. Beside them a cluster of noblemen were guffawing as Firbič the jester was nettling the old Frenchman, the lord's footman, and saying what trouble he had with him, and as the Frenchman defended himself merrily in his colorful Czech.

By the gigantic green stove with mouldings stood old Švejnoch in a long brown tunic of an older fashion, but he could hardly see it since he had unbound the knot of his beard and his beard, the white beard, streamed in long strands down over his chest, down over his stomach, to his knees, and beyond his knees in a thick flood. Like Moses he stood with his majestic look, but far from majestic was his banter and teasing of old Mug, once a miller's wife, now in service in the women's quarters of the castle, so that she could readily pinch a tankard of beer at wedding festivities or at christenings. And the more she drank, the more she puckered her lips, so that they nicknamed her The Mug. Years before she would run through the town on April First, a green wooden kit on her back, for Lord Petr had sent her, sometimes with rocks and glasses, through the town and on beyond, to Veselí, to Lomnice.[13]

She liked to drink, and she liked to get drunk, and old Švejnoch with his majestic air also liked to drink; he and The Mug were birds of a feather. And now they were at it again. He guffawed at the tipsy woman and with a serious air stroked his unending beard and with his fingers combed its silvery strands. Until suddenly he stopped and stiffened; for no apparent reason The Mug squealed and stood frozen in fright, her rolling eyes fixed on the open doors leading to the staircase.

They all turned in that direction. Noise, cries of terror and fright.

They got up, they stretched their necks.

In a long white nightshirt of cambric a tall, wizened figure was descending, its face like wax, and beside it, at its feet, a great white bitch. The old man like a skeleton—it was frightful to look at him—it seemed as if death had shuffled in amidst all this exuberant life—it was His Grace! Lord Petr! Yes, it was he—

Feeble and uncertain was his step, as if his trembling feet could not support him; it was a wonder the dog, which pressed close to him, did not knock him over. The lord—the lord! His face a yellowish pallor, his eyes sunk deep, murky, with brownish circles under them—

The whole chamber was on its feet, and they pushed out of the dancehall. But the musicians could not see, and went on playing. Joyous music accompanying fright and confusion. The sick man stopped on the bottom stair; his feet trembled under him and sank, he grabbed with his hand, seeking support, and at that moment he tottered, sank and fell on the faithful dog.

Old Švejnoch was the first to reach his lord; he bent over him and covered him with the long veil of his beard. In sudden fright young Otík tore away from Kristinka and rushed up to the bedchamber for Dr. Timin; the youth heard someone calling for a physician and forgot that Dr. Hök was there among the guests. But the latter was so drunk he surely would not have recognized Lord Petr.

The music stopped. They carried Lord Petr back upstairs, the dog at their heels and their feet, and laid him down on the bed under the canopy. And again the shadow of death fell there. It would not release the lord, release him to the life he loved so well—

275

In the bedchamber all was silent again. But downstairs it was lively, and the music struck up again. They had only had a fright but, drunk with wine and with pleasure, they had not sobered up; the rough demands of enjoyment and of life again resounded. And young Otík, Lord Petr's page, curled up in the armchair, listened to the far-away sounds of the violins, flutes and cornets, recollecting how lovely that had been before and how affable Kristinka had been, and morose and out of sorts he gazed at the sick man's bed.

In his black fur Dr. Timin sat by the bed and inclined his bare head under the canopy. Lord Petr lay with tight closed eyelids, sighing hard and exhorting them in his delirium, yet insistently.

"Let us go now—let us make the journey. Now! Let us go in the name of the one God, blessed for all ages. Amen, amen. Lord Jesus Christ—amen."

NOTES

1. The Rožmberks were an old South Bohemian noble family which, in the fifteenth century, became the wealthiest among the great Czech lords. Lord Petr Vok, the last of the family, died without children in 1611; his great wealth then passed to the Švamberk family.

2. Třeboň, a town and castle in Southern Bohemia near České Budějovice.

3. William of Orange, or William the Silent (1533-1584), Stadtholder of Holland, leader of the Dutch resistance to the Spanish occupation of the Netherlands.

4. Krumlov (today Český Krumlov), town and castle in Southern Bohemia, not far from Třeboň.

5. Komárno, a town then in Hungary, today in South Central Slovakia. The battle in question was conducted against the invading Turks in 1594.

6. Bechyně, a town in Southern Bohemia, near Tábor.

7. In silence and hope (Latin).

8. A reference to the unrest in the land occasioned by religious strife among the Catholics, Utraquists and Protestants, as well as to the weakness of the Emperor, Rudolf II, finally driven from the throne in 1611.

9. Šimon Lomnický (1552-1622), a well-known Southern Czech poet and hymn writer.

10. The Czech Brethern, or Unity of Czech Brethern, a Czech Protestant group founded in the fifteenth century and deriving many of its teachings from the writings of Petr Chelčický. They followed the Czech Utraquists in receiving the Communion "in two kinds," i.e., the laity took both the consecrated bread and the wine. The Moravian Church in the United States takes its origin from this church.

The statement that Lord Petr's family "had always served the German Emperor faithfully" implies that it had previously been Catholic in religion.

11. "Remember death!" and "Think of eternal things" (Latin).

12. Sapphic song, a classic Greek lyric poem in a particular metre and stanzaic form, popular in its revival during the Renaissance, especially for love poetry.

13. The reference here is to an April Fools' Day prank: on the First of April people were sometimes sent on "fool's errands" or otherwise tricked.

276

JOSEF K. ŠLEJHAR

Josef K. Šlejhar (1864-1914) was a leading representative of the Czech naturalist writers. Born in a village in Eastern Bohemia, Šlejhar studied chemistry in Prague, but never completed his studies, becoming a farmer and later a teacher in commercial school. His best work consists of his early stories and sketches of the countryside which, in contrast to the idyllic pictures created by the Czech romantics and early realists, he portrayed as grim, harsh, indifferent to human suffering. His writing illustrates his philosophy of determinism and cruel struggle for survival, inspired in part by his philosophical grounding in positivism and Darwinian evolution, but fed by his own life circumstances and antisocial character. Šlejhar pushed his determinist conception of the interrelation of man and Nature to an almost mystical extreme, drawing elaborate parallels between them, as in his novella, The Melancholy Chicken *(1889), which portrayed the growth of a deformed little chicken along with the slow death of an unwanted child.*

Though much of his work is spoiled by strained and exaggerated effects, Šlejhar's early work is almost unquestionably the high point of Czech naturalism. He is a writer still insufficiently appreciated by his countrymen, and he has scarcely penetrated to readers abroad. The present story is taken from his early collection, Impressions from Life and Society (Dojmy z přírody a *společnosti, 1894).*

IN THE STRAWSTACK

It was late winter afternoon. The gray sky grew dim above the snowy plain, and the fragment of mournful landscape resembled a mind turned rigid: speechless and vacuously contemplative.

At the back of a farm which had roamed far beyond the village into the jumble of white fields, behind a stable pushed still deeper out into the snowy whirl, a stack of threshed straw loomed from the snowdrifts. Left without place in the stable, it had been banished here and abandoned to the mercies of the wild tangle of frosts and booming winds.

Like some hesitant, swaying shadow a horribly poor man, wrapped in rags, dragged himself here in the winter twilight, and as the shadows of oncoming night rushed on one could recognize a tramp, a person without goal or shelter, one could make out his face, a grinning manifestation of despair at the fierce cold and of horror at his own tenacious hunger. It is hard to express that look in words, and the fact that he was dragging a child's body which lacked all strength or control, by the hand, makes the picture even more pitiful.

The night wanderer stopped at the stack, releasing the hand of the child, who collapsed on the frozen snow. Himself skirting the edges of the blurred pile with its piercing frozen stalks and its snowy plaster which burned like ice, he drove one foot into it, groped with one hand and at last succeeded in making a narrow opening which led to the heart of the stack, on its northern side. He dragged the child here and, wriggling his body vigorously he worked his way into the stack; then, grasping the child, who hardly cared what happened, he disappeared with it inside. . . .

All was silent and deserted as before. It was dark on the earth and dark in the heavens; only on the horizon a vague stripe reflecting the snow gleamed white, and all was clasped firm in the icy breath of frost.

Some time after ten o'clock the back door of the farmhouse squeaked and a dried-up, lanky man emerged to let a dog out into the night; at once he turned back, shaken by the cold, and closed the door tight, locking it.

The dog rushed out into the dark: like a gigantic black spot it whirled about the farm, jumping with a heavy leap over the fence and hurling itself toward the stable, where it stopped.

It was a powerful animal; in the dark one could make out only its glowing eyes, restless, wandering and malevolent, with their greenish gleam which clung to the darkness like two treacherous will-o'the-wisps. The dog listened. Then it whined, gave a long hoarse rattling sound and its muzzle, snapping in the dark, broke into a bark, a sound more like a savage cry of despair torn from it at discontinuous intervals, a sound which is only called barking. The air quivered and the darkness trembled at the nighttime roar of the released dog; the roar covered the village and reached out to the empty fields, even forcing its way into the stack. The half-asleep night wanderer trembled and the crouching child beside him shook through all its limbs.

The dog snapped in all directions, scenting something suspicious. For this reason it did not crawl into its kennel but barked more and more furiously. Again it rushed out into the dark and ran about the farm, chasing a tell-tale scent hanging in the air, and did not make for its kennel; a few steps from the threshing-floor it veered away and hurled itself straight at the strawstack, panting and fuming.

The tramp could hear the dog's thundering paces. He could sense its nearness and all of a sudden he felt a sharp jolt like a heavy fall.

Again he quivered and the child whimpered in fright, pushing toward the tramp's feet. The dog backed off from the stack, ran wildly around it and, aiming straight at the covered opening, pushed inside. A fist, armed with sharp bits of straw, struck its snout; it howled, jumped back from the hole and began barking with all the fury of a brute beast. Again it took the offensive, but again it encountered a frozen clump of straw. It had wounded its eye, and the spurting blood at once froze in the cold on the animal's snout.

At the same time the sound of a child's crying came from the stack, but so muffled, mournful and fearful it was more like the frozen quivering of the snowy plains. Another, deeper voice silenced the child with a whisper and hoarsely cursed the oncoming beast.

The dog did not slacken in its efforts. Obviously it was a well-trained, cunning animal. Repeating its first attack on the hole, again without success, it began to paw at the straw at the base of the stack. Woe to the tramp should it succeed in its efforts. A mad rush which shattered the frozen snowcrust broke through and raked the frozen sheaves of straw; there resounded an empassioned howling, a tormented barking with which the dog's whole inner being seemed to turn into one frightful cry, the body, jerking with fury, and the eyes, which now flared not in points, but in two flaming emerald-green torrents a witness to the maddened beast's strength and the consequences of its bloodthirstiness. The dog did not care that it was tearing its claws from which blood flowed, trickling in thin streams and seeping into the snow as if the snow itself were dripping blood; it scented living flesh and blood and a snarling savage wildness woke within it which knew neither deliberation nor mercy. Such dogs are kept on isolated farms.

The tramp clenched his teeth. The grin on his terrified face expressed his desperate determination, and his goggling eyes flitted wildly in manifest fear and served equally to proclaim vengeance on the tale-teller should it succeed in reaching him. The clenched fist of one hand was held to seize its muzzle, to crush the animal or kill it, while the other hand clasped the twitching child, nearly lifeless in its anxious swoon. . . .

Midnight approached. The cold was extraordinary. Its penetrating stream, till now silent, resounded like a treacherous spectre as a harsh wind arose which, passing over the stiff earth, rang out and fluttered hoarsely. And it reached into the tramp's lair and there took effect like a breath of plague. . . .

The dog went on with its attacks and the tramp defended himself.

Voices resounded from in front of the stable. The dog's fearful barking had aroused the farmer, and with the groom and the farm hand he had come out to ascertain what was going on. The terror of night made the men anxious, and the dog's clamor was truly frightening. Huddled together they made their way, fearful of attack. The mournful light made by their lantern tossing in the wind reflected on the now reddened snow and illuminated the scene, telling them what must have occurred. The groom, a tall angular fellow with a club in his hand, spoke roughly.

"It's some tramp . . . some thief . . . we've got him trapped."

The farmer shouted at the dog which, completely absorbed in its own task, paid him no attention. When it failed to heed him he roared and kicked at it with all his strength. The beast hurled its fiery glance in the farmer's direction, but recollecting itself, its eyes dimmed and dropped; the dog whined, tottered toward its master's feet and fawned over him. The farmer bent over the opening and cried, "Whoever you are, come out of there!"

Silence, not even a whisper.

"You'll come out, all right, you villain," the farmer roared and urged the dog on at the stack. The dog hurled itself at the opening, again struck the armed fist, yelped and pushed itself in deeper with spasmodic leaps. And, urged on repeatedly by the farmer, the groom and the hand, it penetrated into the stack by sheer force, tearing and snapping in all directions.

Now the stack spoke up, and how it spoke. With a moan, a prayer, a curse.

"Let up. . . . For God's sake, let up—I'm coming out. . . ."

They called off the dog and dragged it back. The tramp crawled out. Misery gaped on his countenance. His right arm was bitten and hung down limp, and his sleeve was soaked in blood. His face was a thicket of horrors.

"Murderers!" he moaned. The men guffawed and the farmer struck him.

"None of your lip," he bawled. "Clear out, or the dog will finish the lesson, you loafer. . . ."

The tramp's face contorted, his voice rattled hoarsely and he would gladly have throttled the farmer. But in the nick of time he caught sight of the dog's malevolent eyes, their pupils both one blaze, its body trembling with fury, like a snake trailing at the farmer's feet, seeking to tear and kill him. And he thought of the child . . . and wavered. Once more the groom held the club over his back and the dog barked. He considered that the child would be better off in the stack, and then he could return for it under cover of deep night; somehow he would manage to trick the dog.

He set out from the stack at an angle, accompanied by the abuse of the men and the dog's barking. He was about to disappear in the darkness, staggering with exhaustion, when again the dog's bark sounded as furiously as before when it was attacking, belching the same venom from its furious jaws. The tramp heard the rustle of the straw as the dog leaped at the stack and penetrated the opening, and he heard the voice say in malice:

"Ah, another one, so climb on out, you rascal!"

This time he did not hesitate. Back he turned with a leap and from a distance he groaned for his child; his cry was a dry rattle which could hardly tear forth from his throat. Again the dog was called off and the three men cursed more furiously than before; the dog trembled all over with eagerness.

Casting his eyes on those who stood around and who now were like spectres in the reddish light, with foam on his lips and with a wildly contorted face, the tramp pulled the child forth with his left hand. But he pulled out a motionless body. He set it on its feet, but the feet gave way and the little body collapsed in the snow. The tramp wailed, took it in his left arm, pressed his own ugly face against its face and again disappeared in the darkness. "Good night," he said to the men, and thus he blurted out his sole, grisly curse on them. His wounded arm fell limp. Bit by bit he disappeared, and now even his shadow was only darkness. The men from the farm followed him, relieved to have expelled an alien menace. And the dog's bark too accompanied him on his miserable journey. . . . Such dogs serve well on isolated farms.

The cold raged, the cold burned, and the groaning night was empty.

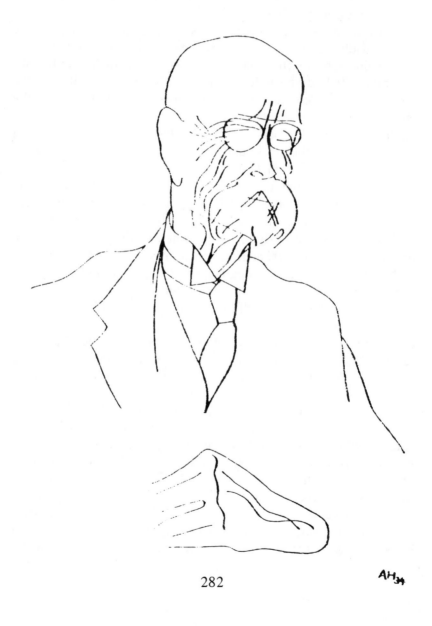

TOMÁŠ GARRIGUE MASARYK

A great statesman and thinker, no doubt the outstanding Czech figure of modern times, Masaryk was born in 1850 in Eastern Moravia, the son of an estate worker. Against great odds he succeeded in acquiring an education, attending German gymnasium in Brno and then studying at the University of Vienna, which he completed in 1876. He travelled extensively in Central Europe and in Russia, where he acquired a deep familiarity with Russian literature and thought. Subsequently he was also attracted to the Anglo-Saxon world; his wife, Charlotte Garrigue (whose family name he adopted as his own middle name) came from the United States, a country which he later visited in 1902 and 1907, developing a keen interest in American realist literature. His doctoral dissertation, on suicide, employed the statistical and analytic techniques of the new science of sociology, which he ardently championed. He was appointed associate professor at the Czech University in Prague in 1882, and full professor in 1896.

Masaryk's extremely broad, diverse intellectual activity, can only be suggested here. In philosophy he was a follower of Comte and the English empiricists, and his important work, The Foundations of Concrete Logic *(1885), continued Comte's work in classifying the sciences and defining their proper subject matter. He reacted against extreme positivism by arguing for the importance of teleological values in science, and for the importance of both religion and morality as bases for human life.*

As a leader and statesman, Masaryk sought to strengthen the ideological basis for Czech nationalism. He accepted Palacký's views on Czech history as a struggle between German physical power and the ideal of Czech spiritual freedom, an ideal which, like Palacký, he found exemplified in the Hussite Revolution and the Czech Reformation.

Masaryk was also a keen literary and social critic. As the leader of the Czech realist party, his criticism emphasized the need for literature and social thought to focus on contemporary life and its problems, and he discouraged empty patriotism which concentrated on dreams of a great Czech past. His opposition to "Titanism" in literature–to romantic absolutes and romantic "supermen"–found a sympathetic echo in much of Czech literature of the 1920's and 1930's, particularly in the work of Karel Čapek.

During World War II Masaryk visited both Russia and the United States, actively working for the foundation of an independent Czechoslovak Republic. He succeeded in convincing the Allies of the justice of this cause, and he himself was chosen president of the new Czechoslovak Republic by acclamation. His thought helped to provide a basis for the democracy and liberalism of the new state, and he was subsequently venerated by his countrymen as a supremely great national leader. Though it can be argued that he was not sufficiently a realist to take into account the larger European and world problems which after his death in 1937 were to engulf the new republic, it is also apparent that his thought, properly interpreted and followed, could well provide a firmer foundation for the conduct of national and international affairs.

The selections below are excerpts from Masaryk's study of Czech history, Jan Hus: Our Rebirth and Our Reformation *(1896). The American reader who is surprised at Masaryk's distaste for liberalism should perhaps be told that in Europe there is a strong historical tendency to identify the concept of liberalism with secularism and non-Christian humanism; Masaryk is insisting here that the Czech national tradition maintain a strong basis in religious and ethical values.*

From JAN HUS

> *Seek the truth, hear the truth,*
> *learn the truth, love the truth,*
> *speak the truth, hold to the*
> *truth, defend the truth till death.*
> *Jan Hus*

Our national rebirth, to achieve which we have been making conscious efforts almost one hundred years, was at its very beginnings a spiritual struggle against the pressures of the Counter-Reformation, a continuation of the efforts and ideas of the Reformation for which Hus underwent martyrdom.

Our term "rebirth" is related to the French *renaissance,* and by employing it we signify the initiation of a new era in our land in much the same sense as the French word has been used to denote that new era in science and in art which opposed the medieval world view Catholicism had formulated.[1] In the domain of religion and the Church the terms "reform" and "Reformation" are used. All these and similar conceptions we understand in the light of the fact that we hold the abandonment of the medieval view of the world and the corresponding social order, an abandonment more or less thorough and radical, to be progress, development, advance in that it brought perfection, correction, setting things to rights. This conception, as well as the word itself, we understand to be new and modern.

Our own "renaissance," our rebirth (awakening, resurrection, etc.) was set against the same medieval view, and set against it for the second time in that in the course of history our first attempt at rebirth and reformation was slowed and then stopped by the concerted effort of the Counter-Reformation. It is quite natural, then, that our new efforts to achieve a rebirth have linked themselves historically to our religious Reformation: it is a second effort following on a first one.

That our rebirth was indeed an attempt to continue Hus's work we see from the personalities of our so-called "awakeners" and their efforts: Dobrovský, Kollár, Šafařík, Palacký, Havlíček, five leaders who consciously continue in the path set by Hus.

Our first awakeners were clergymen (Dobrovský, Kollár), and we should note how harmoniously our Catholic and Protestant clergymen work together for their people against the stagnation of the Counter-Reformation. . . .[2]

Descendants of the Czech Brethern, who followed Hus and who were Protestants by confession (Kollár, Šafařík, Palacký) formulated our national program for rebirth. In particular Palacký, the father of his people, expounded for us the meaning of our history and our Reformation and gave us the fundamental conception of Czech history: the *religious ideal of brotherhood*—and he proclaimed that ideal to be at the same time his own ideal and the ideal of the Czech national effort at revival.[3]

Finally it was Havlíček who, if we may say so, wrote the (Kutná Hora) epistles for that gospel of rebirth—from Dobrovský to Palacký and Havlíček there runs a continuous and conscious effort to link their efforts with the spiritual legacy of the first reformers and to continue in their spirit.[4]

Not only the personalities of our awakeners, whose status and challenge show them historically to have been the followers of the religious reformers, but their teaching also links them and us to our forefathers. The *ideal of humanity,* the basic and pivotal idea which directs all of the effort of national awakening and rebirth, is the idea of our Reformation: humanity is only another word for Brotherhood and on this idea Palacký, in particular, based our national program.

We are Hus's people, and we like to call ourselves so—but are we then really Hus's people?

We are not. Not yet.

In our national effort there is a great lack of inner, spiritual life; awareness that our revival program must be a continuation of our reform traditions is weak. Surprising symptoms of this lack are the fact that our historical scholarship has scarcely advanced beyond Palacký, that no history has so far been written of our Church and its development, even of the movement of the Counter-Reformation, the fact that in Hus's own land his writings have never been published, that it is foreigners, rather, who study Hus and his life work. And how the negotiations over a proposed monument to Hus drag on—all this casts a strange light indeed on Hus's own people. . . .

Into our program of rebirth *liberalism* has penetrated, and our revival efforts to achieve enlightenment and education have in many respects bogged down in a more or less eclectic imitation of a variety of European models, while we have no conscious, systematic, organic continuation of our revival and reform ideas. Those ideas we have on paper—but in reality we do not act according to them.

Liberalism is in its essence philosophical rationalism, unilaterally negating the religious and ethical meaning of life and culture; in a social sense it is an aristocratic and plutocratic philosophy. Liberalism was formulated in the eighteenth century, in particular in France, and it brought to pass a great revolution as well as several smaller ones, especially the one of 1848. Successive political reactions were unable to cope with it: they themselves were essentially liberal, and sought only to return things to some previous political condition, from reasons of practical advantage. In this manner they actually reinforced liberalism. Liberal and revolutionary constitutionalism was thus accepted—and its philosophic base was also accepted, or at least tolerated. Thus liberalism became the usual philosophy of our age—in particular our journalism, following the liberal tradition of constitutionalism, has been and is liberal. Liberalism is a great contract of the age to maintain society any old way, on a defective revolutionary foundation, here and there to repair something in the structure, sometimes to touch up one or another of the support pillars, but only to touch them; no thorough-going revision or reform must be

286

permitted—that is the catch-word of all liberalism.

This liberalism is in fundamental disagreement with the basic idea of our rebirth, the idea of humanity, insofar as it welled up in our land from the Czech Brethern.[5] For our Brethern were something quite different from the *fraternité* of the French Revolution. Our Brethern were founded on feeling and a religious idea, while revolutionary brotherhood was the negation of religious feeling and had its source in classical humanism and in a one-sided rationalism. Though he did not reject it, Komenský correctly and systematically subordinated classical humanism to religious and ethical teaching.[6]

Most persons will perhaps not be concerned for such fine distinctions, but they are not merely conceptual distinctions; they are at the same time existential and national distinctions. Our national, Czech ideal of humanity is not identical with revolutionary humanism; from lack of observance of the difference there comes our eclecticism and our inability to link up correctly with our past and to continue in a truly Czech spirit.

The Czech humanist ideal has its historical and factual foundation in our Reformation, and not in the French Revolution; liberal humanism is not identical with the idea of humanity found in our Reformation. Whoever wishes to think and to feel in a Czech spirit must be aware of the difference.

This foreign liberalism crept into our national program of revival which our awakeners took from our Reformation, and thus there arose a fateful discord in the basic ideas of our national program.

This liberalism did harm at once, both morally and socially. On one hand our nation had been awakened and revived, fed by reformation ideals which, in spite of all the effort of the Counter-Reformation, were not entirely forgotten. But at the same time many foreign ideas entered for which our nation was not yet prepared, ideas which in many respects went counter to our Reformation idea. Thus half-way measures and alienation from true national character became rooted in our nation, which had yielded to the Counter-Reformation pressure rather unenthusiastically. Liberalism supported the work of the enforced Counter-Reformation. Our decadence had been of the first order and it had been first and foremost a moral one, and we must therefore first of all be reborn morally—and for such a task liberalism was incapable. Politically it continued the work of the Counter-Reformation by forcing a foreign language on us, while it also harmed us spiritually by remaining contented with a philosophy of negation and with a patchwork character for ethics and society. . . .

Because the Reformation was essentially religious, it was not opposed to philosophy or science: religion and science, real religion and real science and philosophy do not exclude one another.

The Reformation began with the University—or at least was led by the University. Hus drew his philosophical preparation from Wyclif.[7] With him went the people: among philosophy, science, higher education, between the intellectuals and the people there were not differences. Following Hus the Brethern, while observing the religious reform, were also concerned for learning: Komenský became the teacher of the whole world.

Like Hus and Komenský, our awakeners reawakened us with enlightenment and bent their efforts towards creating culture. Dobrovský founded the scientific study of Slavistics . . . , Kollár based his national program on the philosophy of history; following Kollár, and like him, they all (Šafařík, Palacký, Havlíček) were grounded in Herder, Kant, Bolzano, later in Hegel and others.[8] As for the leaders of our Reformation, for our awakeners culture was both the goal and the chief technique of reform. There is no awakening, there is no reform without culture and progress, there is no moral reform without constant toil to achieve enlightenment. All cultural progress must serve the reform of morals and of life. Hus stood for ethical rebirth and a total change in man's way of life. The Reformation had an ethical goal. Toward this goal Hus's followers, the Czech Brethern, tended and just so their humanitarian ideal of rebirth had, besides its cultural component, a component and a goal that were moral and religious. . . .

Hus's reform had, finally, its natural consequence in achieving nationalism. Since it freed the individual conscience and liberated man from the external authority of the Church and State, and since it sought to spread culture and morality at the same time, the native language therefore became the natural medium for the replacement of the older Latin language.

Of course Hus was not a nationalist in the customary sense in which we employ the word today. "I love a good German more than a bad Czech," he wrote, and also, "The worst enemies are the ones at home." He was referring to the foes of his work. But in spite of the fact—even because of it—that the Reformation had no nationalist goal, it favored the development of the national language and national consciousness. It is of help to a language's development when a people feels and thinks powerfully: language spreads and becomes ennobled when people have something to tell their brethern, something to say to the world. And our reformers had something new and important to say to their own people and to the world. Hence the Czech Brethern, educating their people, also cultivated their own language. The *Bible of Kralice* is truly a national work, not a mere translation such as any learned professor might make, but the Scripture embodied with the point of view and with the feelings of Czechs, and hence it is the Czech Gospel.

Thus Hus's reform and the reform of his followers led to the foundation of a Czech Church, a national Church, the liturgical language of which was necessarily Czech. . . .

NOTES

1. Masaryk is here applying the French word *renaissance* to the Czech national "rebirth" or "revival" *(obrozenî)* of the late eighteenth and nineteenth centuries. This should not be confused with the general European Renaissance, which began in the fourteenth century and which, of course, also reached the Czech lands.

2. Josef Dobrovský (1753-1829) was famous as the "father" of Slavic studies. He was a Catholic priest, a member of the Jesuit Order until its dissolution in 1773. Ján Kollár (1793-1852), a patriotic Slovak poet, was a Lutheran clergyman.

3. Pavel Josef Šafařík (1795-1861) continued Dobrovský's study of Slavic antiquities. František Palacký (1798-1876) was the first modern historian of Bohemian and Moravian history. Palacký stood for autonomy for the non-Germanic peoples of the Hapsburg Empire; because of his political activities he is sometimes called "the father of his country."

4. Karel Havlíček (1821-1856) was a Czech poet and journalist who began the tradition of Czech political journalism. A liberal, he worked for the autonomy of the Czech nation. His *Kutná Hora Epistles,* referred to here by Masaryk, were an attack on the Catholic Church hierarchy in Austria and are actually parodies; Masaryk's reference to them is partly humorous.

5. The Czech Brethern were a Protestant sect founded by the followers of Petr Chelčický during the second half of the fifteenth century. They played a great role in working for the development of schools, raising the level of education of the clergy, and finally in producing a Protestant Bible in Czech (see Note 9).

6. Jan Amos Komenský (1592-1670), or as he named himself in Latin, Comenius, was the last Bishop of the Church of Czech Brethern.

7. Johann Gottfried von Herder (1744-1803) was a German romantic philosopher who was concerned for the preservation and spread of national ethnic culture and folklore. Herder foresaw a brilliant cultural future for the Slavs. Bernard Bolzano (1781-1848) was a Czech philosopher who taught at the University of Prague; his work on methodology of science and on logic influenced Masaryk.

8. John Wyclif (c. 1328-1384) was an English theologian and Church reformer; his writings were well known in Bohemia at the end of the fourteenth century and influenced Jan Hus.

9. *The Bible of Kralice* was a collective translation of the complete Bible carried out by the Unity of Czech Brethern (see Note 5) and published in 1596. In spite of the fact that the Catholic Counter-Reformation tended to limit the spread and influence of the Protestant Bible, it remained the standard Bible of Protestant Slovaks as well as Czechs in emigration, and after the Patent of Toleration was promulgated by the Emperor Joseph II in 1781, it again became the Bible of Czech Protestants at home. More than any other Czech Bible, it has played the role of a beloved literary text familiar to the people and influential on modern literary style and expression—in other words, a role not dissimilar to that played in German by the Bible of Martin Luther, or in the English-speaking world by the King James Bible.

ANTONÍN SOVA

Sova was born in 1864 in Pacov in Southern Bohemia, the son of a town schoolteacher and choirmaster. He studied in the Faculty of Law at Prague University, and entered the Prague civil service in 1887 as a clerk. In 1898 he was made director of the Prague City Library. He suffered for many years from a painful and debilitating spinal ailment, of which finally he died in 1928.

Sova is one of the greatest of the Czech symbolist poets. His poetry, which is both highly musical and highly imagistic, projects the poet's subjective spiritual states into the world of Nature about him. Not a poet of ideas, he nonetheless rejects the contemporary social order and dreams ecstatically of a better and juster world illuminated with faith and love. Besides intimate lyrics, he was a master of the ballad genre, and the author of some of the finest Czech ballads after Erben and Neruda.

Sova's prose is in many ways an extension of his poetry, infused with the same intense lyric qualities. The present story is taken from an early collection of stories published in 1898 as Prósa, *filled with the* fin-de-siècle *mood of futility and resignation. Though he excelled in subjective expression of mood and feeling, Sova sought to create a more objective novel, but largely failed in this. His novel* On Dalliance, Love and Betrayal *(1909) chronicles his own bitter marital experiences, while* Tóma Bojar *(1910) is weighted down with detailed characterizations of Southern Bohemian agrarian problems. More successful is a short novel,* Pankrác Budecius, Teacher *(1916), with its concise structure and rich archaic atmosphere.*

THE STIRRINGS OF SOLITARY STRINGS

The pale white Stáňa soon became commonplace there. Her fat, sunburned aunt and her uncle, a square-shouldered farmer, were no longer worried about her as they had been during the first days. Only Norbert, the scrubby, sickly son of the farmer's sister, that unfortunate woman who had come to her end by suicide a few years before, went on regarding Stáňa as a saint. He had obstinate whims which aroused pain in those who loved him and which nullified their efforts. His withered being had grown cross.

291

Everything betrayed his coming death. They had brought his cousin Stáňa from Prague only because he had remembered her and wanted her. And that was the only realistic one of all his notions.

He was a living outcry left after the farmer's poor sister, about whom they never spoke. She had given birth to him and poisoned herself. That was all. A sickly creature was born with a twisted spine. His legs were incapable of walking, wilted and wrinkled legs that dangled powerlessly from the chair, strange, singed legs, strange withered legs. But he was quiet and patient, intelligent and quick, silently observing everything from his chair, which creaked on its wheels.

On each afternoon of that warm summer Stáňa fondled Norbert, whom the farmhand wheeled out to the arbor stuck on the high wall of the granary. At first Norbert didn't want anyone else around. She smiled gratefully. She stroked his bare, waxen neck with her short, round fingers, and rumpling the curly hairs on it with particular pleasure she would exhale, sensually opening her great eyes as if there were some fairy-tale secret between them. Then she put her head on the pillow covering his ailing legs, inclined her face toward his chest and whispered, "Norbert, you are mine, mine, aren't you?"

And again she clasped his head, that wise, intelligent head, a bit too large, shapeless and arousing sympathy, lightly from behind with both hands, silently and softly. She drew it back toward herself, raising herself up a bit, and pressed her hot, burning lips under the waxen yellow of his chin, lips so passionate, so convulsively closed and twitching with inexpressable pain. She smiled with tears in her eyes.

The surly, morose lad frowned in alarm, hiccupping with the impressiveness of a nine-year-old child, since he could not comprehend what was happening to Stáňa and thought that she was saying goodbye to him. He broke out crying in fright: "Oh, Stáňa, are you going away again? You're leaving me again?" "Don't be afraid. Why would I go away?—I'm so happy here!" She straightened up, doubled her buxom body back and pushed her tousled hair from her forehead and eyes with a single movement with which she tucked their strands behind her rosy ears.

So they would sit here. . . . The green lacework of fox grapes hung over the arbor and covered it. It pushed at them. Its tendrils tickled her pale pink, half-bare arms which had grown out of last year's clothing. A fly flew past and a bee buzzed close by. Then a damselfly from the nearby stream twisted about the row of apple-trees above the flower beds . . . on over the fences to the meadow, the broad meadow. An unpainted, broken water-can, set on its side on the stone of the water baisin, reflected the afternoon sun towards them. The sweltering, humid days carried the scent of hay-making to them, the sound of voices disappearing beyond the garden wall, bright, rumbling sounds of whetted scythes and of a long, languid song. . . .

It was as if they were getting to know each other again after a long time. He was taciturn, and in his eyes Stáňa was a princess who saw and knew the great world, the world about which he only dreamed. At first she was afraid to talk, for fear she would anger him with some nonsense. So they sat for whole days. He so longed to visit the green forests and the towns of which Stáňa told him, the belltowers which reached into the clouds, the high ramparts with their holes for thundering cannons. She would talk of such things to the aged boy until he fell asleep. The handyman, who took off his enormous shoes with their wooden heels so carefully, would wheel him home lightly in his terrible life-long prison.

To the great broad orchard, where they wheeled Norbert into the sun and fresh air, there came only the school teacher, and then, after a few days, an old friend of his from student days, his guest, a literary man, apathetic, closed in, apparently indifferent to small blessings. He wore yellow trousers, an eccentric hat with a broad rim, and soft, silent shoes. He took walks with the teacher through the woods and idled in nature's sweet monotony. The teacher, who lived not far from the farm, was a slender man of perhaps thirty, with curly blond hair sunburned a dark yellow, wearing a perpetual woebegone expression on his timid face. Lost in thought as if he were listening to music singing somewhere in the heavens, in ecstasy over something which cannot be compre-hended, he resembled a man continually brooding about things which would rarely occur to the brain of a normal man. His lack of eloquence and his broken sentences attracted attention through their strange inner conflict of abstract and material concepts. He exuded a somewhat emotional intelligence of an untalented and half-educated person, a person who admired sublime things with-out really understanding them.

He and the literary man loved to gaze out onto the broad plains at views which awoke melancholy in them. They could sit for whole days on the grass by the stream. The writer was evidently devoured by some life event, so that he was looking for his spent life to wither away, for the grief of sultry, untrammeled days, evoking sentimental ecstasy, for the fever of hot rocks breathing from the solitary hillocks. They sat together to the crazy buzzing of the flies and the whirling and flashing of the damselflies, the weary dropping of golden circles as if someone were sifting the cement of time through the dense foliage of birches, hazels, alders and beeches. And with it all that swelling, damp scent of moss which puffed itself out in the darkening labyrinths of the forest setting! They sat in nooks on the edge of the woods, looking over the field boundaries beyond which lay the flat, flat plain, the potato fields without shrubs, with only the distant smoke above the blackened mounds of roofs of some villages, set low. . . .

*   *   *

When the writer first saw Norbert he at once grew excited. And so from a love of something special and perverse, in his company he would become a confiding, yielding child; his fancy was seized by this aged boy who wanted to learn so many things before he died.

And he loved him besides for the fact that, by some indirect influence, when he only saw the spindly legs dangle powerlessly and the large head nod, he would recall with disgust the words of a lady, a fluted, extraordinary dreamy soul whom he once had loved. Without having experienced passionate love, she married. With her husband she lived an egoistic life, selfish, full of excuses and rules. She feared to have the sort of normal children there are in cities.

Often when he thought of her, sitting close by Norbert, her remarks which by chance had stuck fast in his memory would stab and exasperate him. Both of them, husband and wife, with an uncertain smile as if they had reached the bottom of some profound truth without realizing how much base sexual fastidiousness there was in it, would proclaim it all around: "We do not want to have children. We would have no pleasure in life. Our youth would disappear. And then it's so ordinary. . . ."

And the writer always listened and opened his eyes; it seemed to him that marriage too was ordinary—and he pondered, "What is pleasure in life?"

Ah, Norbert, Norbert should never have been conceived.

*   *   *

Three people came to see him. They sat by him like nurses, and all three were at first drawn there by the giant power of a conviction: to ease his way on the eve of death. The gloomy teacher soon began to realize that it wasn't like that. . . . How ineffably, ineffably he had fallen in love with Stáňa when she appeared. . . . Suddenly he was astonished to realize that his role was thus pitifully undercut. She seemed to be preoccupied with her mission. There was no time for the books he offered her. In vain he said, "Something easy, then, like Donizetti, for four hands. Don't you think so? Ah, what melodies those are!" Or he reminded her again, "Then there's a concert piece for violin and piano—I've just received 'Memories of Granada'—the upper register's difficult, and I've transposed it down an octave."

As if he wished first to call it to her attention and lure her, often at evening time with the window open, he would several times tease the strings of his tuned viola. But he didn't bring it off. He had never played so miserably.

Fascinated all of a sudden by the newly arrived and blossoming Stáňa, who for him was a beauty, a triumph of light, a waft of scent, he could no longer calm the consuming trembling of his nerves.

He only sat and as in an hallucination listened from his place in front of Norbert's wheelchair on the piece of meadow which sloped down toward the brook and was turning more and more yellow with an ever increasing number of marsh-marigold blossoms.

He looked on jealously when Stáňa, laughing vaguely and with serpent-like movements, sewed something or other, or got Norbert's supper ready. She listened to the (assuredly phony) writer with such particular attentiveness. . . . A bit sophisticated, unrestrained, lacking the empty affectation of the young people

295

of Prague society, he brought to the village something of the unseen elegance of a swell. His face withered in the furrowed threads of veins strained with nervousness; his tousled short mane of stiff black hair, turning a dark gray, hung bizarrely over his black eyebrows. . . .

How annoyed and exasperated the teacher was: there no longer passed a day when he did not sit with Norbert and Stáňa in the garden, to the sound of their strange conversation in which he could not even take part. The friend talked eloquently and engagingly of things from his travels (ah, how it struck the teacher that it all was a tissue of lies!). He told of the steep fall and thundering storm of the Varrone waterfall . . . of August nights in Trieste . . . of bare-headed women on the corso fanning themselves when the air was like a furnace, to the music of a band, air that carried the scent of fish, and from the harbor . . . along a long mole were outlined between the lights long rows of fishermen's barks with rust-brown sails. . . . He prattled continually in his soft bass voice, "Gondola! Ayeey!" as if he were still listening to music on the Piazza San Marco. And he almost made Stáňa break into tears when he described to her the tomb of Romeo and Juliet in Verona, about which he himself, after the right effect had been aroused in her, began to have doubts.

*   *   *

One evening when the village was already asleep and the teacher was coming back from a stroll in his beloved beechwoods, which lay at the end of a damp piece of meadowland not far from the farm, he heard, close by, the sound of light, muffled footsteps. He made out Stáňa walking timidly in the dusk of gray haze, in the dark of the thick trees through which a few stars twinkled here and there. In the dark blue distance over the ripples of the mountains there flashed a continual lightning. Everything was streaked with a white and silver glow of the night's subdued light. The light struggled through the thickened outlines of hanging twigs and allowed the stream in the grass to shine through, so that it resembled a half-circular inlet covered by trees on all sides. It was a hot night. One that had become silent, stifled by the humidity of everything, a humidity which had covered the earth with dew early in its sleep.

296

The teacher sat down in the underbrush expectantly, as if riveted there, breathless, putting the stump of his cigar down on the grass involuntarily. He could not avoid making a rustle, and suspected that Stáňa had stopped to listen if anyone was there. But he was concealed by the thick trunks of the old beeches, the undergrowth of the alders, and the dark, the dark which oozed from the woods.

In awe he waited and turned pale with strange longing when he saw that Stáňa was slowly, with a lazy elegance, unbuttoning her light summer dress; he could hear the almost inaudible ring of the buckles, the rustle of the folds of her dress falling from her hips, vaguely outlined in the dusk. He saw how the bluish shadow of the moon touched them, changing with a swelling movement of the leaves, how it ensnared them, those delicate and tender hips of a woman maturing, turned to him in profile. In the misty dusk her raised arms, round and firm, which sought for her hairpins and unloosed the strands of her hair, not long but thick and curly, made more bearable the strange, pleasurable sense of shame with which he was overwhelmed, with his eyes fixed on the peaceful, hardly yet born wave of her rising breast, which in the subdued dusk light of the moon was not white, but rather a kind of fairy-tale blue, like her whole naked, slender body.

And so quietly, so as not to raise a noise and shock nature around her, she sat down, slowly submerging in the water her strong, well-formed legs with strong lines, trembling a bit and spasmodically clutching at some tree roots. The water reached up above her waist and its gleam shone on her back, her dark hair and her breast, which now appeared somehow enlarged and silvery white. . . .

There, in the direction from where Stáňa had come, on the other side of the stream, were the white walls of the farm shining through the dark. Dumb walls, without illumination or signs of life. . . .

Then suddenly it all went out. A gray-yellow cloud stretched over the moon and, in the complete absence of a breeze, did not wish to yield. The poor teacher, dumbfounded by the charm and the proximity of a woman's body, awed by its forms, could now hear only the drawn-out murmur of the stream, the breaking of the waves and Stáňa's languid breathing as she bathed. The twigs only cracked, the silence only coalasced, made ghastly by that gray-yellow cloud.

He saw Stáňa as she went away with uncombed hair, in the same tight clothes she had worn to come, and he was sad that he had seen her so, sad as if he had harmed her, debased her in his dreams, and he was consumed by his secret. . . .

The next day he appeared in the orchard pale and cast down. He experienced dizzy spells when, as on other days, he sat down in front of Norbert and Stáňa. In the whole of his naive life no event had so agitated him as had last evening's; he could not even look at Stáňa lest his heart beat with pleasure, pain and shame. On top of it all, her eyes were so clear and green that day that he felt the melancholy of the whole episode of yesterday, which had so bewitched and depressed him. But not only the melancholy. That great pain of an insignificant person in whom Stáňa, as he had come recently to realize, could not take the kind of interest he would have wished.

Impatience and envy welled up in him when Stáňa would at times smile at his friend's jokes as their conversations became freer and more intimate.

With painful expectation he observed the gleam in her eyes when the writer finally walked up with his lazy, quiet step, with his fresh look, and flirting, offered her a nosegay of roses from his buttonhole.

He thought . . . , "Now at last we are neglecting Norbert. . . ."

They went off together for a moment to pick some flowers on the meadow, Stáňa with her quick short steps which made her long dress rustle, he overcoming his apathy, with a seriousness as if it were matter of God knew what.

The teacher, condemned to sit by Norbert, to correct the drawings which some time before he used to praise so, began to hate his friend and guest from the bottom of his soul. He was more taciturn and sulky.

"Are you fond of Stáňa?" he asked him, his voice faltering, that same evening, as they were left alone in the orchard at dusk. They were smoking, lying on their backs, and listening to the music of the crickets from behind the granary wall.

"Insofar as one can love such children. Young and foolish ones."

"Oh, that's frightful. I'm terribly fond of her," the teacher stammered in a transport. "Don't take her away from me," he

298

entreated like a child about to cry. And with great vehemence he started to rave about Stáňa.

"She must be bored here . . . something's stirring in her . . . ," the writer muttered, and lit a cigar in the dark. "But she's nothing more . . . than . . . a piece of flesh. . . ."

"I mean it seriously," sighed the teacher, when they were turning off to pass by her windows. "Ah, what's happened to your tact?"

"What difficulties then. . . . Oh, you'll land her easily enough." The writer stopped short, gazed into the dark and muttered, "Well, she would tempt me . . . and maybe. . . ."

"Don't talk that way, I say. . . ."

"It's only the female in her that tempts me . . . and then as an experiment . . . for study. . . ."

"I'll break your head if you talk like that," the teacher groaned resolutely and passionately. They had both stopped and were looking at one another, the teacher ardently, his eyes bloodshot, his friend with mocking surprise, full of dry sarcasm.

"Oh, that's funny! Good man!"

"That's contemptible of you!"

"Contemptible? What do you mean?"

"I. . . . You don't care about her . . . and you give her the opportunity. . . . She'll fall in love. . . ."

"And what of that?" Women poison us too, they really do. The animals. They only want to get married. I can still feel their claws in my heart."

"You're corrupting a child."

"I felt a desire to speak my heart out. Nothing more. Can you help it if you overreach yourself? That you drive crazy a somewhat more simply shaped female soul? That it wasn't really meant seriously, except that it showed up your melancholy, your sentimentality from a long summer day? And then it all came out so pointless, believe me . . . phooey . . . you dolt. . . ."

"It's still contemptible. I want you to leave her alone," the morose teacher cried resolutely, in a shaking voice, quivering with rage.

"I would like to inspire her—to make her feel love even for you," the writer continued drily and demonically. "That stirs you up! But I'm only your guest," he added in a serious, altered tone. "I don't care about her. I'll never speak to her. Good night."

* * *

For a long time the writer could not make up his mind to leave. For several days now he did not appear in the orchard. Then too, the sun began to cool at the end of August, and there came shorter, cooler afternoons lit with yellow. The easily chilled Norbert, who at the outset of autumn grew more morose and, if possible, even drier, no longer wanted to sit in the orchard, especially when the writer, who could amuse him, was not there.

"Where could that gentleman have gone?" he often asked.

"We don't need you," he said to the teacher, who in silence followed Stáňa with his look, blushing all over. She would quietly reproach the boy, and it took her a long time to soothe him.

Then the real cold set in and they no longer went to the orchard. The teacher, the circumscribed dreamer, pure, his voice resounding in hymns, and the writer, masked, wrapped up in the rough, cynical phrases of a man who discredits everything in advance, embitters it with sarcasm, cuts down his own flight—they became disgusted at having to live together thus. It was on a cold, raw morning that the writer went to the farm to take his leave. But how surprised he was at the strange event which had occurred the night before. Poor Norbert had died that night, as if the wind had blown him out. Stáňa and the farmer had gone off to town to provide what was needed for the funeral. There was almost no one at home.

Ah, how that touched him all of a sudden. In front of the creaking gates a crowd of village women had collected. Something like the odor of burnt peacock feathers was wafted to him from the paving, and someone's weeping, loud, drawn-out and disconsolate weeping, seemed to float through the windows. He was frightened at Norbert's death and at the emptiness all around. He saw the deserted orchard still in the mist, the place where Norbert's wheelchair had stood, in front of the same bench on which they had sat. He crossed the orchard in haste, wrapping himself up carefully in his greatcoat against the cold, and could not make up his mind whether he should wait for Stáňa so he could say a few words to her and take his leave. Tears involuntarily came into his eyes. . . . He thought of the dead boy, so tiny. . . . It was his heart, his weak heart! . . . it had ticked out—all had been extinguished—the way it happens. His death had freed people from the memory of his mother, who had borne him out of wedlock.

He turned back in agitation and banged closed the orchard gate. It squeaked so timidly. The whistling youngster who was carrying his small bag was slowly disappearing behind him in the illuminated mist of morning, which rolled in on the tops of the black spruce trees and the fields laid out in squares. . . . The roosters crowed from the farms, the dogs gave their prolonged barks. The autumn day grew bright.

*   *   *

They ended the funeral hymn and the people went off. The procession had passed.

"Requiescat in pace!" droned to its end through the building. The scent of incense had saturated the whole house, and even reached out into the orchard, and Stáňa's head ached from the black cloth, the flowers, hymns and speeches of the women, from the coffin in which Norbert lay and which they fastened shut before her eyes. At last they carried him away and thus disappeared the reason for which Stáňa had come here. He had died and she was no longer needed. Everything here reminded her of Norbert. She had become used to him and she loved him. They did not know what they could give her to do now. She sat in her black dress by the window where his chair had formerly stood, the chair which the very day after his death they had moved up to the attic. At last her pleas persuaded them. They decided to take her home.

They set out while it was still night so that they would have less trouble arriving in time. With her they sent the seventy-year-old, her grandfather, white-haired, clean-shaven, whose soft shirt collar scattered whiteness through the dark of morning. The teacher, pale, without sleep, trembling with grief and the questions he had never asked, as if he had left everything for the last day, only asked that he be given a ride part way, to some conference he was attending, as he claimed.

The old man took his seat beside her, stretched several times, crossed his legs once more and squeezed her against the wall of the wall of the dusty, rickety coach. The teacher sat across from them.

The night was a cold one, freezing, the sky was full of broken, black clouds. The coach rattled along languidly; the measured rumble of the horse's hooves made Stáňa sleepy. The village vanished, its outlines were lost in the dark, the lights in individual houses went out. A gentle nostalgia seemed to sing in her soul, and with fixed eyes she gazed into the shapeless darkness.

Everything was under that diffused, steely darkness, everything save for a few brighter, ruffled little clouds, airy and tinged yellow, light as feathers, constantly changing. Mysteriously low, rustling, sobbing voices were born for an imminent dying. Stáňa's eyes looked sadly out from her hood, which her soft hand had arranged from a plaid thrown over her shoulders by her anxious grandfather. Did she seem, half awake, to be listening to that which rumbled from the depths of the night, that which glimmered and flashed in the conjectured distance? From the stony fields the voice of the crickets no longer sounded, under the alders the voices of the frogs no longer stirred; it was dreary, frozen. Their ride, at a noiseless, sluggish tempo, went continually up hill; from the damp meadows they were entering the black forest. It revealed through the underbrush the green-tinged coins of the first gleam of dawn. With it the dark gray highway acquired sharp outlines in relief as it dragged up hill across little stone bridges, and with it the timid aspens, tempted out to dark grassy spots, acquired a provocative grief.

The small bay stopped, perhaps tired or something. . . . She stretched her neck and whinnied amid the deaf silence of the forest. Her voice undulated the air and intermingled with the light of dawning, it splashed several times against the walls of the slopes and as a soulless, light murmur was lost in the hills a mile away.

The old man woke up; he stretched his long, meagre, withered legs and began to babble something sleepily, in the whispery faltering voice of a phonograph. Then he fell asleep again.

A brook hidden by the black walls of the pines purled melodically closeby and mingled with the voices which swirled out of the night's depths. "Look, it's just down that hill now," the teacher spoke up timidly. "Then you'll be in town and then . . . you'll take the train. Look, there are the Glades, there is the Cone and . . . and. . . ."[1]

Going down the hill the coach again began to rumble and the old brakes creaked with cracking moans.

"Prague is beautiful, ah, Prague!" sighed the teacher, leaning over toward Stáňa, with the expression of those people who regard Prague as if it were a salvation. "But here too it's lovely, and the main thing is it's healthy, really healthy! Come back again, you'll see . . . the morning in the dew, ah . . . the scent of resin . . . you walk out to the places you know . . . the blackbirds singing. . . . If you come back. . . ."

Stáňa smiled faintly and her eyes sparkled. "I don't have anyone to see and I wouldn't care for it. When Norbert died . . . and then there'll be so much other work now!"

Till now her only idea of Prague came from school, from waking up in the morning till evening prayers, the corridors of the institute, the shuffling gait of the janitor, blackboards covered with numbers and examples, browned maps, plaster busts of the emperor, the lectures and habits of teachers vain and jealous of their reputations, abilities and conscientiousness. Oh, how she looked forward to it all now!

"It's too bad about poor Norbert!" sighed the teacher. "And he had talent! I've still got his sketches. . . ."

"Couldn't you send me some of them?" asked Stáňa in a tone of ardent eagerness. She felt fright and wept a bit now at the thought of Norbert.

"You'll feel sad there. I know. Stay with us," the teacher dared propose when he saw the church cross in the hollow flit past and when they were crossing the railroad track, black as if strewn with coal.

Over the jumble of gray houses, sleepy, lined with yellowed bushes and trees, in the confused colors of the aquarelle-tinged morning the sun, as if dead, stiffly filled its ball with a reddish gold fire. It was cold, but it poured its light onto the lashing frost, which seemed to yield a bit.

The teacher felt somewhat relieved. "What about my friend, will he think of us? You liked him, didn't you?"

"Oh, no," said Stáňa, blushing all over. "It was Norbert . . . and the autumn killed him! Why isn't it summer still?"

He was exultant in spirit. He thought he should tell her everything. "If I can assure you. . . ."

"So?"

303

"I've been so uncommonly fond of you . . . and I've adored you so, so much!"

Her great eyes lit up with surprise. She did not understand it all, but it flattered her. The teacher was perhaps indifferent to her like anybody else. But from thankfulness she smiled silently, confused somewhat by the first confession of a grown man. . . .

"And if you should ever require my services. . . ." But Stáňa did not require any services and did not comprehend his assurance. She only felt somehow sorry for him as they rode onto the gray streets of the town. She felt sorry for him at the station when he shook her hand and when she did not know what she could say to him . . . for Norbert . . . or for herself. . . .

The teacher was still standing on the platform, with a sad smile, full of hope and emotion. The train gave a prolonged whistle, the cars moved, the couplings stretched spasmodically with a rattling noise, the smoke stifled its choking breath. It dusted the yellowed trees and the green ivy . . . and vanished circling on the plain. . . .

In the teacher the summer idyll had not yet come to its end. A kind of joyful hymn, carried aloft, filled his soul. She would return, she must return! Oh, he hadn't been able to say it to her, he hadn't! He lacked eloquence. He would write a letter, a fiery hymn, fantastically beautiful, ah, and his hope remained for him! A saint. . . .

VIKTOR DYK

Born in 1877 near Mělník in north-central Bohemia, Viktor Dyk was the son of an estate manager. He attended high school in Prague, where he was a student of the historical novelist Alois Jirásek, and later the Faculty of Law of Prague University. On completion of his studies he turned to literature and journalism. He entered politics, supporting the Radical Progressive Party, but failed to win election to the Austrian Parliament. During World War I he was imprisoned for some months for a novel on a Russian theme which was actually a satire of Austria. After the foundation of the Czechoslovak Republic he served in the National Assembly as a senator. He died of heart failure in 1931 when he was swimming on the Adriatic Coast.

As a poet and writer of fiction Dyk specialized in depicting end-of-the-century decadence and spiritual weakness and disillusionment, especially of the middle classes from which he came. His attitude toward life was sceptical and ironic, and his lyric poems and stories tried to catch the mood of irony and vanity of human existence. Yet he had a powerful belief in the Czech nationalist cause, which provided almost the only ray of hope in his world.

Dyk lacked the formal power necessary for longer works, and his political novels, though interesting as portrayals of society, are largely failures. He is more successful in smaller forms where his irony and sarcasm pay off better. His play, How Don Quixote Found Wisdom *(1913), ironically reflects the eternal gap between romantic dream and realistic disillusionment; the same theme nostalgically pervades his long story,* The Rat-Catcher *(1915), drawn from the legend of the pied piper of Hamlin. Another play on a fairy-tale theme,* Ondřej and the Dragon *(1921), debunks romanticism by showing that its dreams are founded in illusion.*

The present story, typical of Dyk's shorter fiction, is taken from the collection entitled The Song of the Willow, *published in 1908.*

THE LOCKET

It was the end. His body was growing cold. The beat of his restless heart had stopped, as if a clock had run down.

She shivered lightly.

305

She was afraid of his bluish lips which could no longer speak. She was afraid of the silence by the bed where he had lain so many days suffering from halucinations.

Heavily, almost tottering, she got to the open window. She bent over to look out. Below the city roared; its whole uproar penetrated the room. . . . It was a lovely spring day; the cold old men would surely be warming themselves in the parks, and the youthful heart would feel unaccustomed tenderness. . . .

The contrast touched her with penetrating grief: she felt for a moment as if the depths were dragging her down, and clutched at a chair. It was light vertigo. She was quite exhausted and the spring air had benumbed her senses.

A stubborn, fierce battle for life had been waged here. It took many days of high fever to destroy that strong man who was now a corpse. He had resisted tenaciously. Piece by piece death had entered him as if he were a captured fortress. And now it was the end. He had succumbed. And almost all those around him.

They had expected it. For a long time they had expected it. After two weeks Dr. Řehák, wrinkling his forehead, began to say, "Be ready for everything." But the expected catastrophe backed off. "Some strange capacity of the organism to resist," the doctor twisted his head.

Recollection mingled with the sense of the present. A noise could be heard . . . the murmur of voices, violent barking. A visit? She felt so weak that she was no longer even capable of feeling pain. The reaction came. She fell into a kind of faint. . . .

*   *   *

When she came to her senses, the silence amazed her. She sat up. She remembered everything. And all at once, without her being able to say how, it came to her: the locket.

The dead man lay in the next room. Unquestionably he was still there. Would she have strength enough to go there? She experienced an incomprehensible, painful desire. At last she could do no injury to the dead man. He would no longer defend his treasure. And shamed to the depths of her soul, with bent, furtive eyes she opened the door—

The noise resounded in the silence and shook her. She was there. . . . The dead man was lying on the bed. . . . A few steps and the deed would be done.

She approached the dead man. His face terrified her, and she turned her glance away. But she could not master her desire—

At last she held the object of so many arguments. It was a desire satisfied too late. And at a high price— Now that she had it her hands trembled uncertainly. No one came to take away her booty. The dead man was really dead. But the prize burned in her hand. She recollected all that had gone before.

*   *   *

She was a widow when he met her. In the bloom of her life. Her first husband had died after only three years of marriage. It had been a sensible marriage. She did not love her husband too much. He was not repulsive to her. They tolerated one another like two people who have no reason to quarrel; they made an accommodation out of a desire for comfort rather than from virtue. When her husband died, she put on mourning and wore it for a suitable period. The dead man would have done the same, without question, and with as calm a heart as she possessed.

Then her second husband came along. They were in love. Were they really in love? He often struck her as cold. Why was he so withdrawn? She had the feeling he was hiding something. A part of his inner being was shut away from her as if behind seven locks. Jealousy came. Why? She knew nothing definite. But all that was hostile, mysterious, foreign was made incarnate in one idea: the locket. He hid it from her. She was not permitted ever to open it. It was a secret. Without question Karel loved her, and had nothing to hide. But why then was she never permitted to see its inside? And why could her husband never part from it? Her hatred became a superstition. The locket was the cause of all evil which came to her. It was the enemy, it set something mysterious and treacherous between them. How many times had she battled for it! In vain. Who is it, she asked. He smiled without answering. A woman? Yes. She asked him to show her the inside of the locket. In vain. And it was difficult for him to refuse her anything. But this he refused. He smiled when she asked; he smiled when she threatened. All her weapons broke against his calm and his firmness. She carried on a desperate struggle with all the sophistication of a jealous wife. But in the end she had to admit that she had given in. It was in vain. The locket remained a secret. Her

307

husband's resistance toughened from the struggle. She saw that she would have to go to the limit, and this she feared to do: she loved Karel too much to be capable of cruelty toward him. And so she was silent. They no longer talked of the locket. Only a wound was left, a feeling of submission to a mysterious enemy whom she could not conquer and who ever defended her place in her beloved husband's heart. How fortunate her rival was! She was dead. And yet still so alive. She had perhaps never loved Karel (she had made up a whole story about it, fabricating some romantic involvement), and he was still hers. She had disgarded him and let her have him. As a favor.

How many times that shadow had come back, how many times she had encountered the victorious glance of that unknown adventuress! She no longer exists, Karel had said then seriously. Well then, she would object during those days when she still did not recognize the futility of her effort, why keep it a secret—she's dead. . . . It's childish, she would repeat. And wasn't it equally childish on his part? But he loved her, though; he told her he was in love with her.

He stopped her mouth with one energetic hand while embracing her with the other. "Child," he told her with smiling eyes which rendered her powerless, "Child, you know very well you need not be afraid of anything!" And bending over her and suddenly growing serious, he said softly, "You wouldn't want it, you know. Think that it's a secret amulet. It wouldn't be a good thing. . . . Believe me, it wouldn't be good."

*   *   *

Now she held the locket in her hands. She could learn the features of that woman for whom over the years he had kept a discrete tenderness and whom he had so jealously guarded from anyone's gaze.

A false triumph! It was too late already to celebrate. He had guarded her till his last breath. They were not permitted to take it from him. From time to time his hand had anxiously reached for the locket. When her husband was running a fever she had associated all his words of tenderness and love—how much that withdrawn, silent man could love!—with the unknown woman whom she so envied. He raved deliriously of her; truly it was the feeling of a young man who loves for the first time. She felt herself excluded. Never had he loved her like that; for her he had only a smile or harshness. Each of his words wounded her. Oh, she would have known how to strangle that demon, had he lived! Her hands clasped spasmodically at the thought. Oh, to satisfy all her longing for vengeance and her bitterness.

She made up her mind.

Her hand still trembled, but in spite of that she opened the gate to the inviolable secret. The keenness of her hatred conquered her respect for the dead. She would see the one who had robbed her of so much love. She would see!

She opened the locket.

*   *   *

It was quiet. Only the clock went on ticking, and her heart pounding.

She stood there paralyzed.

All the blood ran from her face. Her hand spasmodically caught at the bedframe. . . .

How weak she felt. . . .

The locket fell to the floor.

The jingling noise aroused her from her fainting spell. She trembled. A sob broke in her throat. Was it grief of heart or a woman's offended pride? She stretched out her arms as if she were trying to catch at something. A chilly feeling crushed her. From her eyes parched with so much weeping a few tears burst forth.

—It was her own photograph, a photograph of her at the age of eighteen, when he had not known her—

Jaroslav Hašek

DIE

ABENTEUER

DES BRAVEN

SOLDATEN

SCHWEJK

KIEPENHEUER & WITSCH

KUNNON SOTAMIES
SVEJK
I OSA JAROSLAV HAŠEK
kansankulttuuri 9

JAROSLAV HAŠEK

dobrý vojak
SVEJK

JAROSLAV HAŠEK

DIE ABENTEUER
DES BRAVEN SOLDATEN
Schwejk

Jacoslav Hašek

Den tappre
SOLDATEN SVEJK
"man kiknar av skratt"

THE GOOD SOLDIER
SCHWEIK
JAROSLAV HASEK

ILLUSTRATED BY JOSEPH LADA

PENGUIN BOOKS

愚直兵士
シュベイクの奇行
（前線へ）

ヤロスラフ ハシェク著
辻 恒彦 訳

三一書房

譯 文

一九五四年
八月號

JAROSLAV HAŠEK

Born in 1883, Hašek was the son of a high-school teacher in Prague. He studied in a business high school and, after a brief interval in which he tried his hand at various jobs, he became a writer. He contributed journalistic articles and humorous sketches and tales to different newspapers and magazines, and often demonstrated an eclecticism of political views and a sense for practical joking that were quite untraditional: at times he would even polemicize with his own political articles by writing under pseudonyms in other newspapers!

From 1912 Hašek began to publish collections of his humorous tales; in the same year he brought out the tale which contained the first portrait of his celebrated comic hero, the Good Soldier Švejk. Hašek served in the Austrian Army during World War I, but promptly deserted, like many Czechs, to the Russian side and subsequently joined the Czech Legion which was being recruited from among Czech prisoners in Russia. After the October Revolution of 1917, he joined the Bolshevik Party and served in the Red Army as a political commissar, writing propaganda articles and speeches. Anticipating the breakout of revolution in his homeland, he returned to Prague in 1920, but subsequently confined his activity to literature, especially to the completion of his famous novel, The Adventures of the Good Soldier Švejk in the World War, *which appeared serially in 1921-22, but which was interrupted by Hašek's death and later completed by another writer. A heavy drinker, Hašek's health was undermined by alcoholism, and he died in 1923.*

Hašek's Good Soldier Švejk *has become a world classic, though it was frequently disowned by Czech literary critics and national leaders who viewed it as disrespectful of authority and even subversive. Still, its hero Švejk has become emblematic as a comic hero whose apparent idiocy protects him from the tyranny of self-important, autocratic authority; he is a kind of Sancho Panza without Don Quixote. The novel has been translated into many languages of the world and has had an enormous popular following and literary influence. It is also rightly celebrated for its sense of absurd humor and frequent parody of the rules of formal logic.*

Hašek's stories possess many of the same virtues as his novel, though they are extremely uneven and repetitive in their themes (as is, indeed, the novel). The best of them excell in their spirit of comic absurdity and grotesque (sometimes "black") humor. They lack literary polish, but it is

311

obvious that their author did not place much stock in literary tradition and was seeking systematically to break away from it. Unfortunately, he did not always succeed, and his comic invention sometimes lagged behind his sense of grotesque, nonconformist purpose.

CLASS DISTINCTIONS

Bailiff Nykles and Administrator Paser, both of whom served on a great estate, were close friends. Every day they sat drinking together at a table in the spacious village tavern. They were famous as such an inseparable pair that it was obvious it was the two of them who perpetrated all the tricks which so often roused the village. Bailiff Nykles was extremely fond of Administrator Paser, but still something so frightening lay between them that at times it would bring to Nykles' countenance an expression of deep gloom. And the thing was so extraordinary it would arouse him to the greatest agitation of which his gentle soul was capable. Whenever the two of them would drink together at the tavern and follow it up with one of their merry tricks, one which generally consisted in catching the night policeman on duty and tossing him into the millrace, then throughout the entire village one would hear only the single comment that "yesterday Bailiff Nykles was soused like a pig, and Mr. Paser, the administrator, was just a bit lively."

So we cannot be surprised if Bailiff Nykles longed fervently to change matters, once he had realized how things were and what was being talked of in the village. He took up sobriety and, when Administrator Paser would have three glasses to drink, he had only one, so that in the end it came out that the administrator had had 30 and he only 10. So then they were in the precise proportion of 1:3 and that day they perpetrated nothing. Silent and wrapped in his thoughts Nykles propped up the administrator, who made an uproar throughout the entire village and called the tavernkeeper Tiska names, while Nykles behaved most properly. But the next day he only learned what Tiska had replied to the question of why they had detained him so long the other night. "Well, you know, Bailiff Nykles was soused like a pig, and Mr. Paser was just a bit lively."

Nykles comprehended that this was the result of great class contradictions, that a great social conflict was operating here, and it was his desire that he, Nykles, could be equal to the administrator and that people would say of him:

"Sure, the bailiff was a bit lively, and Paser was soused like a pig."

But his longing was never fulfilled. As people were accustomed to say, they went on saying from respect for the administrator, and no matter how little the bailiff drank, when he was out with the administrator and they were coming back to the manor at half-past twelve at night, Nykles would finally hear the administrator utter that cruel word which always made him so despondent: "Why, I'm just a bit lively again today."

So in the end Bailiff Nykles swam with the current, realizing that even if both of them should get equally tight, he would always be soused like a pig and the administrator just a bit lively.

The latter gentleman could hardly stay on his feet and the bailiff was walking at his side, without a waver. But the administrator was a "bit lively" and he, as usual, was "soused."

One day it happened that both of them, the administrator and Nykles, were in the same state—as they put in the speech of that region, both were getting "bowled over." The bailiff drank in the full consciousness that nothing would be of any avail, while the administrator drank with complete freedom from concern, aware of his good reputation. Then they came out of the tavern and, quite giddy, they found someone in uniform on the village square whom they pushed into the local pond. This was one of their usual tricks, for which the administrator would pay off the village policeman by treating him to a mug of beer and a cigar in the evening. The proverb has it that no one can escape his fate, and they didn't escape it. It wasn't the village policeman, but a state trooper. A state patrolman making his rounds is under the protection of paragraph 81 of the code, which speaks freely of the assault and battery that is committed when anyone raises his hand against an official personage.

This meant arrest and trial for both of them, and for such matters there is the district court in Jičín. Both of them pled intoxication and brought the tavern-keeper as a witness, together with the village elder and three other peasants, all of whom had been present that fatal evening when the two of them had drunk their thirty mugs of beer.

313

The first witness was the tavern-keeper Tiska. "Tell us, witness," the president of the court said, "how it was with Mr. Nykles. In what condition was he when he left your restaurant?"

"If it please you, Your Honor," Tiska said, deliberating, "Nykles here was drunk, Your Honor, as God is above me—he was soused like a pig."

"And how about Administrator Paser, Mr. Tiska?"

Tavern-keeper Tiska looked at the administrator with respect and said with fervor, "Your Honor, Mr. Paser was just a bit lively."

They noted it all down.

Then came the other witnesses, and they answered the same thing: "The Bailiff, he was soused like a pig, but the administrator was just a bit lively."

So the matter was quite clear and the verdict came accordingly. The administrator, since he was only "lively," was sentenced to a month in jail, while the "soused pig" Nykles was let go. since he had not been conscious of his actions. And Bailiff Nykles experienced one more satisfaction, for after the verdict was announced the administrator called out despairingly, "My God, gentlemen, why I was soused like a pig too."

But that didn't change matters.

THE PERSECUTION OF THE FIRST CHRISTIANS
IN VINOHRADY

Mr. Kopejtko often came to our establishment. He was an extremely righteous gentleman who showed all too well how heartily he despised us. We had not spoken in a precisely pious way of the dear Lord, and he considered it his sacred duty, when he had reached the tenth glass, to defend God. And so we called him "the first Christian in Královské Vinohrady."[1] Wrapped up in his overcoat, he would come in lost in thought, silent—just so the First Christians would come to the Old Roman hostelries, packed with Roman mercenaries. And when, in this blasphemous atmosphere, he would raise his glass of beer, he did so with a sanctified exaltedness, as if it were the days of St. Peter in the catacombs and he were raising a ciborium. The ultimate mark of his malicious contempt was the fact that, when leaving, he would call over to our table, "Well, God be with you!"

We tried many times to take his God away from him, but he would always shake his head with dumb resignation and say, "That's all in vain, say what you will. In the faith in which I have been born—in that Faith I shall die." Sometimes he would vary it: "In the faith in which I was nurtured. . . ."

He was an undertaker by profession and it may be just that which worked on his pious mind, though otherwise he didn't bother to express himself concerning the last rites with a proper dose of piety, saying, "I had a lot of trouble with that old hag today till I got her crammed into her coffin." Nor did his piety prevent him from being a passionate card player.

So it happened that one day on Saturday, when we were playing twenty-one, he asked us to let him join in. At first he had luck, because he would cross himself at the beginning of each hand. But then the cards failed him and he lost every kreutzer of his weekly pay. In a vague awareness that if he could only play on, he might win it all back again, he asked us to lend him five crowns, so that he could go on playing. So our own five crowns would be staked against us.

"With the greatest pleasure, dear friend," we told him, "but put your watch up as a pledge and declare that you don't believe in God." The bank had exactly five crowns in it.

In Kopejtko's soul one of those great spiritual struggles was going on.

Similar facial expressions were certainly worn by those Christians of Nero's time, when, brought before the ruler, they were told to declare that they would give up their God.

"Never!" Kopejtko cried.

"Then we'll play without you!"

That meant as much as when, in Rome, the ruler cried, "Toss them to the wild beasts!"

Kopejtko's face obviously indicated his suffering, and the terrible, frightful struggle.

In place of the wild beasts of the Roman circus, the picture of his wife stood out in his soul.

"Sirs," he said all of a sudden, handing us his watch, "I don't belive in God."

He was given the five crowns and he cried, when he got his cards, "I do too believe in God, and I'm staking against the whole bank!"

He lost. Then he cried, "I don't believe in God!" and for his wedding ring borrowed ten crowns from the tavern-keeper and lost them at the cry: "And still there is a God in this world!"

Then he staked his great coat and lost it there. Finally his wife came for him.

The next Sunday he went off to the Holy Mountain to make atonement and brought the tavern-keeper back a rosary.

NOTE

1. Královské Vinohrady ("The Royal Vineyards"), once outside Prague, but in Hašek's day, a middle class residential district of the city.

KAREL ČAPEK

Karel Čapek, without question the best-known Czech writer of belles-lettres both in his own land and abroad, was born in 1890 in Northeastern Bohemia, a land which gave so many writers to the Czech people. He completed his gymnasium studies in Prague, where his parents moved in 1907, and then studied at the Faculty of Philosophy of the University. Soon after completion of his university studies in 1911 he began to write short, sometimes humorous pieces for the literary magazines, often together with his elder brother Josef, with whom he was later frequently to collaborate. His studies at the University strengthened his interest in philosophy, and his writing is characterized by its deeply philosophical character. He was influenced by Bergson and the American pragmatists, especially William James, and he published a treatise on pragmatism in 1918.

Poor health kept Čapek out of military service during World War I. Soon after the War his plays, R.U.R. (1920) and From the Life of Insects (1921, with Josef Čapek), achieved great popularity and made his reputation all over the world. R.U.R. introduced the term "robot" to the languages of the world and presented robots on the stage; Čapek was attempting in the play to point out the dangers of modern technological civilization for human life. A series of anti-Utopian plays and novels followed during the early 1920's. At the same time Čapek served as a regular contributor to the newspaper Lidové noviny; his frequent articles and feuilletons, written on an extremely broad variety of subjects, have great eloquence and fluency in the medium of a colloquialized, informal speech; influenced by Neruda, they are in fact popular essays. Čapek also wrote on his travels over Europe, on his hobbies, such as gardening, and on pet animals.

Late in the 1920's Čapek turned his attention to the popular form of the detective story, and produced two collections, Tales from One Pocket (1929) and Tales from the Other Pocket (1929). These were followed by a trilogy of philosophical novels devoted to the nature of individual freedom and the individual's relation to society: Hordubal (1933), Meteor (1934) and An Ordinary Life (1934). The trilogy is probably Čapek's masterpiece and the masterpiece of Czech philosophical fiction.

The rise of Hitler led Čapek to turn attention to the Nazi threat, and he produced a play, The White Plague (1937) in which he expressionistically depicted the threat of war and Nazi invasion. The Munich Settlement which divided up Czechoslovakia in 1938 broke Čapek's health, and he died at the end of the year, two months before Hitler's armies entered Prague.

317

Since the present volume terminates with 1918, we have chosen a previously untranslated story from the early collection Wayside Crosses *(1917). The volume is concerned with the possibility of miracle bringing salvation to individuals in their loneliness and alienation (a possibility the author denies); it is steeped with the gloomy atmosphere of the War and the anxiety of waiting. The present story, at the end of the volume. looks forward to the ultimate end of the War.*

HELP!

He noticed that he was on a broad slope covered with beautiful trees. It must be France, he suddenly conjectured, I must have gotten onto the wrong train. And it was an unusual train— full of strange faces which laughed at him as if he had been dressed badly, and running wildly on until the windows rattled.

Brož was frightened out of his sleep. Someone was knocking on the window.

"What is it?" Brož cried, his tongue stuck to his mouth.

"Please," a woman's voice, trembling, said from outside, "if you could only come at once and help us!"

"Go to Hell!" Brož answered and burrowed his head into the pillows. If he could only recapture the snapped filament of his dream! Revive sleep precisely at the point where it had been interrupted! A train, something about a train, Brož exerted himself, and suddenly it flashed through his mind with agonizing clarity: I should have asked what happened to them!

He jumped out of bed and ran to open the window. Cold and black the empty night rolled in from without. "Who's there?" he cried, but nothing replied. Then the cold gripped him, and he went back to lie down; once more he found his own dry warmth in the featherbeds and he took a greedy, unbounded pleasure in it; again his eyelids sank and his limbs relaxed into a coma. Oh, to sleep!

With wide open eyes Brož looked into the dark. Who could it have been? No one here in the village has any concern for me. Who would have sought help from me? It was a woman's voice. It was an incomprehensibly mournful voice. Perhaps it was a matter of life and death. But I'm not a doctor. But perhaps it was a matter of life and death.

Tormented, Brož turned to the window. It loomed like a cold blue oblong in the black, incommodious darkness. There was no fire anywhere. Silence, only the watch by his bedside was ticking away its staccato. What could have happened? Some accident? Perhaps it was nearby; someone was dying; somewhere someone was struggling helplessly with a difficult time. Anyway, I'm no doctor.

But the bed burned drily and wearily. Brož sat up in bed and from habit put on his glasses. How could I help them, anyway, he reflected. How could I come to their aid? Do I know anything that would give help? God, I can't even give advice or consolation: with mere words I would not know how to take any part of the load from anyone, nor could I give much sympathy. I want nothing, actually, except peace; nothing except to be rid of others. What could have happened?

At that point it occurred to him to light the lamp. They may notice that my house is lit up, he thought, and come back. It will shine like a lighthouse. If they do come, I can ask what's happened; at least I'll be sure then I couldn't actually give them any assistance. —Thus consoled in anticipation, Brož piled up pillows behind his back; tensely he waited for the gate to squeak and the same woman's voice to implore him from outside the window. But the ticking voice of the watch annoyed him. Vainly he tried to stop it. It was three o'clock. Suddenly in his chest he felt the ugly weight of anxiety and perturbance. No one was coming.

Reluctantly but hastily Brož started to dress. Surely, he thought, there will be a light there where it happened, and I can knock on the window. I'm not asleep anymore, anyway. I won't be any good to them, but— Perhaps they're helpless— Brož was confused in his hurry and quietly cursed the laces of his shoes; finally he succeeded in tying an unaccustomed knot and ran out in front of the house.

It was dark, completely dark. Brož went down the narrow street looking for the lighted window; never before had he seen the village so totally asleep, so alien to all that was stirring, so alien— Nowhere was there a lamp making its complaint, nowhere a strip of light from under the shutters. Alarmed he stopped in front of the chapel: in the windows a flame's dim light quivered and trembled. An eternal flame, he finally comprehended and went on, but nowhere was there a light; everywhere darkness,

319

except for a bit of pale glow filtering through the walls—

Silently Brož made his way back home, listening carefully in front of the mute houses. Did no moan resound from within, no quiet impotence tremble? Was no woman's voice weeping? Shivering, Brož probed the closed spaces of silence; nothing, not even heavy breathing, nothing— Could it be that no lacerating cry for help would come flying out of the broad night, out of the distance, from any side?

How alien was that sleeping world, which did not speak! Which did not cry out in pain! Which did not call for salvation! If only the slightest moan had arisen now, would he not have seized it so eagerly, would he not have leaned against it as if it were a pillar, would he not have turned to it as to a light kindled in the dark—

You want to help others, there sounded inside him derisively and clearly, and you cannot help yourself! But what, Brož thought in painful astonishment, what if it actually is like that? And, for that reason, ah, just for that reason, because you can't help yourself— One who can help will be able to help himself, but you, who cannot help. I wonder if it isn't just you who—

Brož stopped as if struck by lightning. You cannot help yourself! But what if it were actually so? That I need any sort of help . . . from myself or from anyone else? Is my lot then so bad? No, not at all! I keep to myself and I want nothing more. Only that I should live out my days for myself. I cannot help myself. In any way. Never had that occurred to me before. May it all stay the same as it has been: day after day, stretching out to infinity.

Day after day? Brož sat on a stone set to mark a corner and looked motionless out into the dark, as if clandestinely he were finishing an interrupted dream. Or as if he had dreamed it day after day, month and year, stretching on to infinity— Nothing would change any more; and what could change? Events flee and the years run by; but day comes back after day, as if nothing has happened. A day has passed by: what of it? Why, it was a day like the last; the same day would come again tomorrow. And if it too would only pass by!

And every day I can tell myself: I have lost nothing but a day. Nothing more than a day. Why then such anxiety? Brož rubbed his forehead hard. To rouse himself. I'm still sleepy. I've been stopped in my course, and the days have grown up around me like walls; day after day has been laid down, smooth and solid—

like bricks in a wall. Soon I will wake: but will it be a day composed of a thousand past ones—like walls? And again I will tell myself: this too is another day among the thousands piled up—like walls? Why did it come along? Yesterday there was only one less of them! Was it worth it —to wake for this one day?

All his sleepiness deserted him in an instant. Why, it was a prison, he comprehended suddenly in fright; how many years have I lived as if in prison! His eyes opened wide and it seemed to him as if all those years were shining forth like mournful candles: it was all strangely foreign to him, yet even more strangely familiar; everything, nothing, days without number. . . . Yes, a prison, Brož roused himself. And what if I will never wake up to a new day? Isn't that what I wait for each day (—yes, a prison!) and for which I have waited always, perhaps, he suddenly comprehended (—his past years shining forth like candles); have I not been stopped just so I can wait for a new day?

The past years shone out. Look, Lord, Brož whispered, gazing toward the heavens, I will no longer conceal it: I have been waiting for your help, for a miraculous liberation, for a great event to occur: a sudden light in the cracks, a loud voice and a hard knock on the door commanding: "Lazarus, rise!" How many years have I waited for the loud voice of the conqueror. It has not come, and I no longer count on it.

But if I am still waiting, then it is for help and liberation. For a voice summoning me to come forth from my prison. It may not be strong, but so weak that I must support it with my own voice. Perhaps it will not be a voice of command, but of entreaty: "Lazarus, rise, so that you can help us!"

You cannot help yourself: who then will help you? Who will come to free you, who cannot liberate yourself? Everything is asleep in an unknown world; grief squeals like a baby on the lips of the sleeper; a boyhood dream, something about a train, a fleeting dream is outlined on the walls of the prison. But suddenly to wake from your sleep. Will you recognize it and leap up, wide awake?

Perhaps you have been waiting for an earthquake: listen rather for a soft cry of entreaty. Perhaps the day you await will not come as a holiday, but as a workday, as life's Monday, as a new day.

Dawn was rising over the forest.